Love Lives

of the

Great Composers

from Gesualdo to Wagner

Basil Howitt

Sound And Vision

Contents

Dedication

To my wife Sue,
and to all musicians past and present who make life so
enjoyable.

Overture

In the only real pub left in the centre of Manchester UK, a poky, spartan, gem of a boozer without a juke box, gaming machine, pie-warmer, or even condoms in the gents, I was sitting alone with my fifth and final pint after my clarinettist friend Phil had left to catch his last bus home. Some friendly cyber-yuppies up from the south of England drew me into their conversation. They were in Manchester for a crash update course on something to do with bytes, bits and bugs, but right then they needed a good cheap nosh. Where could they go? And would I like another pint? Accepting with weak will, I pointed out that the world behind the pub was quite literally their soft, succulent oyster; they were already on the edge of China Town, with its £5 Special Chow Meins, whiffs of star-anise and garlic, clattering plates, and rhythmic cleaver chops muffled by swishing woks.

In response to their inevitable next question, what did I do for a living, I began my off-pat monologue about this book — which is certainly not yet a living, but has usually been good fun, which is some compensation. In no time, one of the young men broke in. The only time in his life he had ever been creative was when he had been apart from his fiancée for six months. The pain of separation, and the craving to be re-united with his beloved drew from him a flood of love letters to her which astonished no-one more than himself. Till then, poems and novels and all that stuff had been outside his orbit; and since he had married the lady, of course, he had written nothing.

Many composers have themselves written about how their love lives affected their creativity. Chopin in his early 20s was by far the most explicit on the theme in his soft-to-hard-porn correspondence with his beautiful and very liberated mistress, Countess Delphina Potocka, to whom he dedicated his F Minor Concerto and his "Minute" Waltz.

When they began their affair in 1832, Delphina, mother of five and separated from her rake of a husband, undoubtedly nursed Chopin, three years younger than herself, through his sexual noviceship into full priesthood. In the words of the romantic biographer G. F. Pourtalès (quoted in Ruth Jordan's *Nocturne: A Life of Chopin*) Delphina "offered him what he wanted long before he thought of asking for it". He was very soon addicted to the experience, like so many of the Countess's far more socially exalted previous and concurrent lovers. She had almost lost count of them; and no wonder, with her "dazzling white shoulders and generous breasts, dark blue eyes and golden hair worn in ringlets or piled into a bun". What's more, she was no bimbo, being well read, a pianist, composer and beautiful singer.

For the newly initiated Chopin, regular, rampant sex with Delphina was, he wrote to her in a letter of around 1833, disastrous for his creative urges:

> ... I have been thinking a great deal about inspiration and creativity and I have very slowly made an important discovery. Inspiration and ideas only come to me when I have not had a woman for a long time ...
> ... A creative person must keep women out of his life, the energy collecting in his system will not go from his cock and balls into the woman's womb but into his brain in the form of inspiration and will perhaps give birth to a great work of art. Think of it, the temptation which drives us men into a woman's arms can be transformed into inspiration! ...
> ... Think of it, my sweetest Phindela, how much of that precious fluid and energy I have wasted on you, ramming you to no purpose
> ... Ballads, polonaises, even a whole concerto may have been lost forever up your *des durka,* I can't tell how many. I have been so deeply engulfed in my love for you I have hardly created anything, everything creative went straight from my cock into your *des durka,* you are now carrying my music in your womb ...
> ... When the *diligence* [public stage coach] will at long last bring you back I'll cling so hard that for a whole week you won't be able to get me out of you. Bother all inspiration, ideas and works of art ...
> ... I kiss you all over your dear little body and inside.
> Your faithful Frycek, your most talented pupil who has mastered the art of love. [from Ruth Jordan's *Nocturne*]

The *des durka* reference would take time to explain, but its meaning is clear enough. The authenticity of some of Chopin's steamy letters to the Countess is very dubious, but the above one definitely seems to be part of what the *New Grove Dictionary of Music and Musicians* describes as "an authentic nucleus" of such correspondence.

Schumann was also very explicit, though without a trace of lewdness, on how privations in love stimulated creativity. He and Clara Wieck endured long and agonising separations imposed by Clara's tyrant of a father Friedrich Wieck, whose intransigence towards their marriage forced them to seek permission for it through the courts. In 1837 Schumann wrote to Clara of his discovery that "nothing sharpens the imagination as much as expecting and longing for something" with the result on this occasion being the 18 Characteristic Pieces entitled *Davidsbündlertänze* (Davidsbündler Dances). Again in 1838 he wrote: "I have been waiting for your letter and as a result have written books-ful of pieces — amazing, crazy, sober stuff. You'll stretch your eyes when you open it up ... You appear in the *Novelletten* [one of his longest and most demanding piano works in eight movements] in every possible circumstance, in every irresistible form ... They could only be written by one who knows such eyes as yours and has touched such lips as yours." And so it went on, with Schumann bursting forth in floods of heavenly song during the harrowing months of their legal battles with Wieck before they finally received permission from the court to marry in August 1840. "So utterly at the mercy of the ebb and flow of melody am I," he wrote to Clara, "that I feel almost swamped, oblivious to all the disgraceful goings on around me. I fear I shall not be able to bear this exhilaration for long."

The flow of great music from suffering in love has been endless. Aloisia Weber's rejection of Mozart in 1778 was clear-cut and very painful, yet drew from him a stunning and intensely moving series of seven concert arias for her between 1778 and 1788 (some six years after he had married her sister). The passionate heartache which Beethoven suffered on account of the great love of his life around the years 1804 to 1806, Josephine Deym, may well, suggests Ates Orga, be bound up with the lyrical ecstasy of the Fourth Symphony, the Fourth Piano Concerto, and the Violin concerto. (This was also the period of the *Eroica, Fidelio,* and the *Appassionata* piano sonata.) Josephine Deym certainly loved and revered Beethoven, but refused to satisfy the "sensual love" he craved from her.

Janácek at the age of 63 provides perhaps one of the most extreme cases of the creative fruitfulness of agonised, unrequited, fantasising love. "All my works, all my operas contain one painful love," he said, referring to his fixation with the young 26-year-old Kamilá Stösslová. The wife of an antiques dealer who was often away, Kamilá was uninterested in Janácek's works and only replied spasmodically to his hundreds of letters to her over a period of 11 years. In spite of its onesidedness, this affair was the creative force behind his late woman-orientated operas and directly inspired his string quartet of 1928 subtitled "Love Letters".

Happiness in love has also inspired wonderful music, of course. The supreme example is surely the most wonderful birthday present in the history of music from husband to wife, Wagner's *Siegfried Idyll* to Cosima on Christmas Day 1870, four months after she had at long, long last become his wife. No wonder Wagner and his 15 musicians played it three times on the staircase and the entire household at Tribschen was crying with happiness. Cosima also inspired the final love music in his opera *Siegfried* first produced at Bayreuth some six years later. "Everything is yours before I write it," he told her.

It's always very dangerous to read too much of a life into a work of art, of course, but many other works seemingly fired by happiness in love spring to mind. These include Haydn's joyful String Quartet in C major (No. 3 op. 33), written perhaps at the height of his rejuvenation, in his 50th-year, by the luscious young Italian singer Luigia Polzelli who had become his mistress at Esterháza under the nose of her aging, consumptive husband! "She (Polzelli) was quite clearly always in his mind in his music in the 1780s, and especially in Op. 33," suggests no less a scholarly figure than H.C. Robbins Landon in his mammoth and marvellous tome *Haydn at Esterháza*. Then there is Mendelssohn's glorious String Quartet in E minor (No. 2 op. 44), with its radiant slow movement, and his Second Piano Concerto in D minor (op. 40), both written between bouts of rumpy pumpy during his honeymoon with Cécile in 1837. His first Piano Concerto in G minor (op. 25), with its roller coaster outer movements and gorgeously romantic, cello dominated middle movement was also probably inspired by love — for the beautiful and very talented 16-year-old pianist Delphine von Schauroth on whom he had a crush and to whom he dedicated the work. After meeting her in Munich in 1830 at the start of his Grand Tour, he wrote to his sister Fanny that he was following Delphine around "like a pet lamb". "We flirted dreadfully," he added, "but there isn't any danger because I'm already in love with a Scotch girl whose name I don't know."

One could go on and on, but my cumulative impression — it's definitely no more than that at the moment — is that suffering and angst in love have produced more great art than has happiness. "They say in Vienna that Haydn's rather unhappy and childless marriage is the reason he composed so much," wrote Johan Frederik Berwald in his account of when, as a young touring *wunderkind,* he visited Haydn in 1799. That proves nothing, of course, but it fits in with my hunch.

*

The importance of muse figures in composers' lives cannot be exaggerated. As with Robert Graves and his succession of goddesses (who often lived *en famille* with the poet and his wife in Majorca), sexual activity has often been non-existent, or else a relatively insignificant aspect in the inspirational relationship. Haydn deeply valued the close and sympathetic interest of Maria von Genzinger, wife of the Esterházy physician, in all aspects of his creative life. So did Elgar in his relationship with Lady Alice Stuart-Wortley, his "Windflower" who was undoubtedly the "soul" of his Violin Concerto. "All stands still until you come and approve!", Elgar wrote to her in April 1910. He was indeed lucky that his dearly loved wife Caroline Alice could tolerate the deep mutual affection between Lady Alice and himself without feeling threatened by it.

Wagner's relationship with each of his two main muses Mathilde Wesendonck and Judith Gautier was certainly rather more tactile — plenty of kisses and embraces — but the likelihood is that he never got either of them into bed. Both women were essentially indulging and adoring groupies who became very caught up in serving his short-term creative and egocentric purposes — while he was composing *Tristan* and *Parsifal* respectively — before fading away, or, rather, being shown the door by the current irate Mrs Wagner.

Even Puccini, whose compositional style is said to "mimic sexuality" and consist of "endless foreplay leading up to intensely orgasmic but brief melodic climaxes" (Tom Sutcliffe, *The Guardian* 16th

April, 1994), had a muse relationship which was essentially non-sexual. True, Puccini did have at least two very passionate extra-marital affairs: one (much to the hysterical dismay of his publisher Ricordi) was with a young law student, Corinna, whom he met on a train, and another was with a German Baroness 17 years younger than himself, Josephine von Stängel, whom he met on the beach at Viareggio. But it was from Sybil Seligman, Italiophile wife of the very wealthy banker David Seligman, that Puccini drew creative sustenance and emotional support over many years. "It seems to me," he wrote to her, "that you are the person who has come closest to understanding my nature — and you are so far away from me ... I am sending you a little photograph to remember me by — a thousand affectionate thoughts for that exquisite and beautiful creature who is the best friend I have."

The ultimate disembodied, distant muse figure must be Tchaikovsky's Madame Nadezhda Filaretovna Frolovskaya von Meck, some ten years older than the composer. It suited both of them never to meet (except very briefly by accident), yet she swooned almost dementedly over his music, turned part of her house into a shrine to him, and sent him large sums of money (6,000 roubles a year plus many top-ups). She also showered expensive presents on him and provided him with blissful retreats in which to compose. "I doubt if you could ever realise how jealous I am of you," she wrote, "despite the lack of personal contact between us. Do you know that I am jealous in the most unforgivable way, as a woman is jealous of the man she loves? ... I don't want any change in our relationship. I simply want to be sure that nothing will change as my life draws to its close ... ".

She was almost certainly relieved he was a homosexual so that she neither had to "share" him with another woman, nor have to face the demands of a real relationship; a mother of 12 children, she once told Tchaikovsky that she wished they could be reproduced artificially. But for all their lack of direct contact — because of it? — Mme. von Meck was undoubtedly a powerful source of inspiration to him. "I think you are in such sympathy with my music," he wrote to her, "because I, too, yearn for the ideal. We share the same conflicts. Your doubts are as strong as mine; we swim in the soundless sea of scepticism, looking for a harbour that we never find. Isn't this the reason why my music means so much to you and is so close to your heart?"

Sadly, Mme. von Meck ended it all suddenly and enigmatically in October 1890. Apart from the loss of the money, Tchaikovsky was shattered and betrayed at the loss of such strong emotional and creative support.

*

Perhaps the most interesting question these yarns have thrown up is this: would women nowadays be willing to make the same kind of sacrifices for a great composer — assuming we were to have one — that intelligent women made in the 19th-century? If we ever had another Wagner, would there be a woman of the calibre of Cosima to endure the strains of living with a difficult egomaniacal genius? If there were another Elgar, would there be another Caroline Alice, of whom he wrote to a friend at her death: "You, who like some of my work, must thank *her* for all of it — not me."? Would there be another highly intelligent Princess Carolyne Sayn-Wittgenstein ("the blue-stocking of Woronice") to lay down her life for another Liszt who, she said, was "made to be cherished, adored and loved to death and madness"; and for whom, she told Marie d'Agoult, "there are devotions without limits"? Equally interestingly, apart from all the socio-musical factors, is one reason we *don't* have any Wagners and Liszts any more because there are no women around to make these kinds of sacrifices?

And, of course, one might ask the question in sexual reverse. Would we have more great female composers if men were prepared (and able) to look after them?

*

Perhaps the two most common meeting places for musical liaisons of every kind in this book are the piano stool and the opera rehearsal room. The number of beautiful young pianists who have fallen for their piano teachers, or singers for their maestros — and/or vice versa of course — is legion. You will read of countless such stories in this book, but the saddest by a long way is undoubtedly that of the dreamy young 17-year-old Franz Liszt and his beautiful pupil, the 16-year-old Countess Caroline de St Cricq. They fell deeply in love with each other. To Liszt she was forever "one of the purest earthly manifestations of God's blessing", yet marriage was out of the question. In spite of the pleas of Caroline's mother on her death bed to her husband, the Count would not countenance his daughter's marriage to a ruddy piano player, and palmed her off on some old fogey with piles of money. Sixteen years afterwards the sweethearts met again in Pau when Liszt, now with squillions of lovers under his belt as well as a harrowing major affair, was touring through the south west of France. They reminisced over their thwarted marriage and Liszt later sent Caroline a beautiful turquoise. He never forgot her and included a ring for her in his will of 1860, though sadly she died too young to know this. However, she was able to treasure the beautiful, Tristan-like farewell song he composed for her, *Ich möchte hingehn wie das Abendroth* (I want to pass away like the setting sun).

"I love you with all the power of my soul" she wrote to him in 1853, 25 years after their first meeting, "and wish for you the happiness that I myself shall no longer know ... Allow me ever to see in you the single shining star of my life."

The most bizarre tale in this book also involves Liszt and comes from Alan Walker's magnificent biography. Staying as the guest of the famous poet and statesman Lamartine and his English wife at his château at Monceau in 1845, Liszt set his cap at the poet's 24-year-old niece Countess Valentine de Cessiat and actually proposed to her.

Alas, Countess Valentine was far too attached to her middle-aged uncle to contemplate any other relationship, and seems to have been keeping him warm in bed. In the final tableaux of this strange tale we find Lamartine, widowed in 1863, successfully applying for permission from Pope Pius IX to marry his niece, and then dying in 1869. The Countess lived on for another 25 years.

***

"Thank you" lists can be boring and parochial, and must be brief. Thanks to my wife Sue for patiently reading through my drafts and voicing the indispensable reactions of an ordinary music lover with little musical knowledge; to David Barber, the book's editor, whose own experience as a writer on music for the general reader far exceeds mine and whose fresh, unstuffy style has, I hope, rubbed off on me at least a little; to John Reed for his priceless and infinitely patient correction in my Schubert chapter; to Henriette Harnisch for her help with one or two translations from German; and to John Whibley, manager of the orchestra in which I still play cello, the Manchester Camerata, for starting me off by commissioning many Pre-Concert Talks from me, and also my first book, *Life in a Penguin Suit.* And I must thank especially Hilary Ashwell, who actually got me this gig in circumstances it would take too long to explain.

I would also especially not like to thank Bloomsbury Press and Anna Pasternak's agent for not allowing me to quote, in my Wagner chapter, some drivel from *A Princess in Love:* the bit which describes Lady Diana's "seduction" of Captain James Hewitt. Diana, "starting to flail" because "her need was too much", walks across the room "with the ease of a dancer performing a well-worn routine", and slips on to James's lap "cupping her hands behind his neck". James is, natch, "both raging with desire and taken by surprise..." etc etc. It all struck me as being resonant with Wagner's first rather melodramatic extra-marital affair with the young frustrated English rose Jessie Laussot.

***

I have attempted to acknowledge all significant sources of information in the text or in the acknowledgements, apart from some newspaper clippings. My own experience of English journalists is that they are, when need be, rampant plagiarists almost to a man and woman, passing off their colleagues' scribblings as their own, often at second or third remove. There was even one occasion when a journalist for one of the broadsheets passed off reams of information she obtained from me, about the *mores* of composers and musicians, as her own. The lucky lady got her 500 quid whereas I didn't receive a penny.

***

Chapter 1

Don Carlo Gesualdo, Prince of Venosa, Count of Conza

Marvellous madrigalist, melancholiac, murderer and bi-sexual sado-masochist

Born: Unknown, 1560s
Died: Gesualdo, 8th September 1613

It is lust for which men debase themselves in order to submit the body and soul to the inconstant will and unbridled desire of an unbalanced and vain woman.
[Preamble, Corona manuscript of murder story]

*

We kick off with the most bizarre c.v. of any composer in this volume: a real-live prince who might have stepped straight out of the pages of *The Arabian Nights*, or into the pages of true-crime novelists Truman Capote or Ann Rule, if only they had been around in 1590.

Meet His Excellency Don Carlo Gesualdo, Prince of Venosa, Count of Conza, the highly progressive composer of some of the world's most beautiful, if austere, intense and esoteric madrigals. Although not well known, they are lauded by other great composers, especially Stravinsky. As a composer-prince, Gesualdo's stature is unique, though there have been several other rulers who turned out decent music — princes, Holy Roman Emperors and kings, especially the flute-playing Frederick the Great (121 flute sonatas, no less, plus four flute concertos, two overtures, three cantatas and several marches).

Gesualdo also has other claims to fame. After making precise and elaborate plans, he and three henchmen, well tooled-up with guns, swords, derks, daggers and halberds, shot and butchered his adulterous wife and her lover to death *in flagrante delicto* or, more prosaically, on the job. Actually, to be really precise, the adulterers were fast asleep "overcome by fatigue from such supreme pleasure". The faithless lady in question, Donna Maria d'Avalos (also Gesualdo's cousin) must have been quite a goer: she had already seen off two husbands by the age of 25, the first reportedly dying *forse per aver troppo reiterare con quella i congiugiamenti carnali* — in other words, from too much sex.

Gesualdo didn't write his madrigals doing time in a dungeon for his *crime passionel:* he lay low in his country castle at Gesualdo for a while to let things blow over and then married another high-ranking lady. The murder proved to be no more than a small blip in his career, such summary ways of dealing with infidelity being not unusual in those days. Indeed, when Gesualdo's second wife's cousin, Duke Alfonso d'Este, discovered that his notoriously libidinous sister was bedding a *cavaliere,* the obliging gentleman was quickly disposed of.

In a world of breathtaking double standards, Gesualdo had no problem in applying different rules of sexual conduct for himself. During his second marriage he had much more than a bit on the side with a succession of mistresses and concubines. To salve his conscience he was prone to beating his wife rotten (though I'm not sure how that would help), and to having himself flogged by a valet specially trained for the job. And when his wife managed to escape to her family for a break from her ordeals, Gesualdo consoled himself with a man in his bed, embracing him, so we're told, "in order to keep his back warm".

Gesualdo is a box-office bonanza waiting to happen in the "real lives" market. It is baffling that no Hollywood mogul or TV network has yet turned the composer's story into a mega-budget production. When will Steven Spielberg, NBC or Channel 4 descend on Naples, on the town Gesualdo (60 miles to the east) and on Ferrara with gaffers, gantries, clapperboards, costumed singers, lutenists, dancers of dosi-dos, a well-faked archicembalo and all the rest?

*

Before plunging into the murder, we had better briefly check out the protagonists in the script. Don Carlo Gesualdo, born either sometime during 1560-62, or very possibly in 1566, became a prince on the death of his 21-year-old elder brother Luigi in 1584. (The Gesualdo family had been elevated to princely status only two generations back when the composer's grandfather was made Prince of Venosa by King Philip of Spain. If you're interested in knowing more, it's very clearly explained in Professor Glenn Watkins's enthralling book *Gesualdo*.)

Marriage then, of course, was all to do with producing heirs and cementing political alliances, and the bride chosen for Gesualdo was his beautiful and charming cousin (his father's sister's daughter) Maria d'Avalos, already twice widowed. They married in 1586. The d'Avalos family and the Gesualdos were "first families of greatness and nobility in the city and kingdom of Naples". The third such family was the Carafas, one of whom, Frederigo, Marchese di San Lucido, had been Donna Maria's first husband (the one who had reportedly died from too much sex).

Donna Maria bore Gesualdo a son, Don Emmanuele, but there must have been some bug in the Carafa breed that made Donna Maria itch, because it was with another *cavaliere* in the Carafa family, Don Fabrizio, Duke of Andria, that she began a passionate affair within four years of her erstwhile happy marriage. Let the quaint-sounding, authenticated "Corona manuscript", in Professor Watkin's new translation of the version first unearthed by Angelo Borzelli, take up the story:

> ... The first messages of their desires were their glances which with the tongue of the heart of love betrayed the fire which burnt in each other's breast. From glances of love they proceeded to written messages, given to and received by faithful messengers, in which they invited each other to battle in the fields of love ...

To cut a long story short, Don Fabrizio and Donna Maria, with the help of accomplices and bribed servants, got down to business "many, many times for months on end". The whistle was blown by Don Fabrizio's uncle who, dirty old man, had himself importuned and lusted in vain after the heavenly Donna Maria. On discovering that she was "another's whore", the uncle blabbed to our hero who, though "more dead than alive" with shock at the news, resolved to catch them in action.

Meanwhile Don Fabrizio began to get very twitchy when he discovered that their secret was out, and was all for calling off the affair. But when the randy and now besotted Donna Maria taunted him with the charge of cowardice he declared his readiness to bear "the thrust of a sword" for her. Brushing aside Fabrizio's fears for her own safety, Donna Maria made it clear that she also would much rather suffer "the wound of cold steel" than his betrayal, so they agreed to die together for their love of each other. (Touching, isn't it?)

Gesualdo, rather like King Shahryar in the *Arabian Nights*, laid down bait for the adulterous couple by announcing his decision to go on an overnight hunting expedition (it was October 16th, 1590, just the right time of year for hunting) and by removing all the door locks of the palace "so that the princess should not suspect anything". Sure enough, the mice came out to play and carried on until they dropped. The prince returned with his henchmen (some handy relatives), silenced the petrified maid on guard and:

> ... breaking down the door of the bedroom with a blow of his foot, and entering therein ablaze with anger with his companions, found his wife lying naked in bed in the arms of the Duke.
> ... The Prince ... shaking himself from the stunned state which such a state had precipitated in him, slew the sleepy lovers with many dagger thrusts before they could catch their breath.

Having ordered the bodies to be dragged out of the room and left on the stairs, Gesualdo had a sign posted on the door of the palace explaining the reason for the slaughter. He promptly then went off to visit relatives in the state of Venosa.

Word quickly got around, as it usually does, and soon people from the city were running to the palace to gawk at the gory scene. Donna Maria's wounds, they would have noticed, were mostly in her belly, "and especially in those parts which most ought to be kept honest". The Duke had even more stab wounds than she did.

Reports also have it that while the bodies were lying on the stairs, a certain monk had sex with Donna Maria's body, even though she was dead. (It takes all kinds, I guess.)

The official investigation into the murder was carried out by the panoply of grandees of the Grand Court of the Vicaria. The main report, written by the Master of the Grand Court, Dominico Micene, is dated October 27th and is obviously the most sober and reliable account, though sober is hardly the word for some of the lurid detail. It doesn't differ significantly from the Corona manuscript though naturally it doesn't mention the necrophiliac monk nor does it hint at the intimate location of some of the lovers' wounds. (In view of Gesualdo's later widely reported cruelties to his second wife and himself, the sadistic genital mutilation is entirely plausible.) As to the corpse-abusing monk, given the proven perversions of minority elements of the clergy from time immemorial, this also could be genuine rather than tabloid touching-up.

What further news is there from the coroner's report? Well, it seems Don Fabrizio spiced up their energetic frolics by donning Donna Maria's nightie, doubtless for saucy games of hide and seek.

The main section finishes with an account of the arrangements made to dispose of the bodies, and an inventory of the weapons found in Gesualdo's own nearby room.

The second and third sections detail the evidence taken from Donna Maria's maid and Gesualdo's manservant. Although vivid and gripping as blow-by-blow verbatim accounts, neither adds much new information, except that the maid's evidence suggests that Gesualdo left Don Fabrizio to his henchmen while seeing off his wife himself. And from Gesualdo's servant Pietro Bardotti we glimpse another revealing streak in our composer-maniac. In spite of all his carefully laid plans and demented butchery, Gesualdo had a very hard job convincing himself that his mission had been accomplished:

> Then Don Carlos came out, his hands covered with blood, but he turned back and re-entered the room of the said Donna Maria, saying "I do not believe she is dead!"

Gesualdo's viciousness may have gone even further. It is at least possible that shortly before the murder Donna Maria had given birth to another child, whom Gesualdo believed to be by Carafa. If so, the gossipy-sounding reports of Gesualdo's sadistic murder of the child ring true enough. As relayed by the 19th-century writer Modestino, the traditional story goes that Gesualdo had the infant

> put in a cradle in the large hall of his castle, and suspended it with cords of silk hanging down from two nails which were hammered

into the arch. He then ordered that the crib be subjected to wild undulations, until through the violence of the motion, not being able to draw breath, the child rendered up its soul to God.

No wonder the novelist and critic Anatole France (1844-1924), in his short story *Le Puits de Sainte Claire,* called Gesualdo "a mastiff made up of fox and wolf and twice a stinking beast". Gesualdo was never called to account on any charge. Just as having the right connections today can get you off some criminal charges, so then, on the winks and nods of all the three eminent families involved, the murder was overlooked.

*

Reactions to the murder by Gesualdo's contemporaries seem to have weighed against the cuckolded killer in favour of the slain adulterers, and the leading Italian poet of the day, the beleaguered and intermittently insane Torquato Tasso, though careful not to offend his friend Gesualdo, expressed his grief over the death of the lovers eloquently:

> Whoever blames you for straying among the sad sighs [of love] let him accuse the sun which brought forth the day when the wandering stars so erred.

More redeeming reports of Gesualdo's subsequent actions also circulated and they make it impossible to fathom fully this complex musician-prince. He is supposed, Macbeth-like, to have razed the forest around his country castle to the ground as a kind of expiation of his sins. (Nowadays, of course, it would be necessary to do the exact opposite and plant saplings.) As further acts of atonement he built a Capuchin monastery with a chapel, Santa Maria Delle Grazie. He also commissioned a rather puzzling painting for the chapel. Even the experts don't quite know what to make of its elusive symbolism, but they generally agree it's meant to be redemptive.

Somehow or other, Gesualdo's horrifying and harrowing personal preoccupations did not prevent him from composing. Most of his important music flowed from his pen during the period 1586 to 1596, though he did not make his debut as a published composer in his own name until 1594. (His first book of madrigals had been published under a pseudonym some time before 1590.) As a prince, Gesualdo had to be very careful not to lower himself in the eyes of the world to the level of a professional musician, however talented!

*

Being a wife-murderer didn't stop Gesualdo from becoming an eligible widower, and another wife was soon found for him. Because of his papal connections (his uncle Alfonso being a cardinal) Gesualdo was mooted by the heirless Duke Alfonso II d'Este of Ferrara as a husband for his cousin Eleonora d'Este. Dispensing here with lengthy explanations, the duke hoped — in vain, as it turned out — that such a marriage might help prevent the Dukedom reverting to the papacy on his death.

On Gesualdo's side you might fairly say that he was keen to marry Leonora not for her herself or estate but for her cousin's music at the dazzling court of the House of Este at Ferrara. Its musical riches were abundant and renowned and leading practitioners in all branches of the arts gravitated there. (Duke Alfonso II was obviously as fanatical about music as Prince Nicolaus Esterházy was later to prove as Haydn's patron and employer.)

As was not then uncommon, Gesualdo had never met the lady before agreeing to marry her. Love or otherwise didn't really come into it, and, indeed, he was soon to be regarded as a bit of an oddball for showing a "Neapolitan" eagerness to meet his betrothed as soon as possible after his arrival in Ferrara!

He set off for Ferrara in 1594 with 300 pieces of luggage carried by 24 mules and 150 retainers, including two musicians from his *camerata*. Towards the end of the journey, Gesualdo's retinue was met at Argenta by the Duke's equerry, one Count Alfonso Fontanelli, a composer and *literato* who gives us a few more clues about our enigmatic composer in his letters to the Duke. Besides mentioning Gesualdo's quirky impatience to meet his future wife pronto on arrival, Fontanelli mentions the composer's reluctance to get up in the mornings, his expertise in hunting and sundry other matters. He also comments on Gesualdo's addiction to music and his esoteric compositions:

about music he spoke at such length that I have not heard so much in a whole year. ... It is obvious that his art is infinite, but it is full of attitudes and moves in an extraordinary way. However, everything is a matter of taste.

*

The wedding, which was followed by sumptuous and endless celebrations with jousting, music and dance, took place on February 21st, 1594. Celebratory odes, sonnets and madrigals flowed in profusion through the pens of inspired *literati*, including Tasso.

Between 1594 and 1596 Gesualdo immersed himself in composing and performing at the Ferranese court (he played lute, guitar and cembalo). Ferrara was awash with virtuoso singers and players only too pleased to tackle Gesualdo's new compositions (his first two books of five-part madrigals had been published in his own name in 1594), along with those of other court musicians. Prominent among these was the illustrious Luzzasco Luzzaschi, the Duke's *maestro di cappella* and one of Gesualdo's compositional models. The spread of talent also included the four famous sopranos — the Ladies of Ferrara — in the *concerto delle dame*, the assorted minstrels proficient on cornetti, tromboni, dolzaine, piffarotti, viole, ribecchini, lute, guitar, harp, clavicembalo, and even resident makers and repairers for these instruments. Also available was the amazing archicembalo, with its several keyboards and capacity for producing microtones.

The chronicler Girolamo Merenda describes what must have been paradise on earth for Gesualdo:

> as of this time in Italy, or perhaps even outside it, there is no concerto di donne better than this. And every day during summer-time, they began to sing after dinner at seven o'clock and continue until nine — the organist at the harpsichord, Signor Fiorino with the large lute, Signora Livia with a viola, Signora Guarina with a lute, and Signora Laura with the harp. And the Duke and Duchess are always present. They sing from part books together with a bass and two other voices, all singers of the Duke. In the winter time they begin at half past six and continue until after half past eight, and when princes come he takes them to the Duchess's quarters to listen to the concerto.

During these two years Gesualdo returned twice without his wife to his own country castle, but was back in Ferrara by the end of 1594 for further intensive bouts of music making, consolidating his reputation as a fully fledged front-ranking composer. He also enjoyed contact with musicians in neighbouring cities: Mantua, Venice, Padua and Florence and his third and fourth books of madrigals were published in 1595 and 1596.

Gesualdo did not, however, consolidate his reputation as a good husband, though whose charms (and punishments?) he enjoyed is anybody's guess. We hear through yet another Gesualdo commentator, Venceslao Santi, that "certain of his amorous adventures were so overt as to disgust Ferranese society". Word of the composer's cruelty to Donna Leonora also began to spread.

Sometime in 1596 he left Ferrara for good — once again without Donna Leonora, who by now had borne him a baby boy, Alfonsino, destined to live only a very short life. Gesualdo was intent on establishing his own *camerata* in his castle, and on withdrawing from the world as much as his princely position would allow.

Too ill and asthmatic to fetch his wife from Ferrara in person, Gesualdo made insistent requests to Duke Alfonso that Princess Leonora and Alfonsino be despatched to the marital home. Duke Alfonso died, however, on October 9th, 1597 — and with him also splendid the musical tradition at Ferrara. Finally, with the co-operation of her brother Don Cesare d'Este, and escorted by two of Gesualdo's emissaries, Princess Leonora and Alfonsino arrived at her new home in September 1597.

*

The abridged story from this point to the composer's death is one of deterioration in his personal behaviour and outlook, with a descent into morbid and reclusive melancholia, and into psychopathic and sado-masochistic deviance. Notwithstanding the possibility of gossipy embellishments, most of the following extracts from chronicles and letters paint a telling and consistent picture of what the tabloids would call a pervert:

> [Gesualdo] began to display bad treatment to his wife, arriving at
> the point of despising her, being very rude to her, beating her, and

making her give up all desire to live And all this to say nothing of her humiliation and other offences to her dignity, staying without any regard for her with two other women. [Santi]

... And for this reason he retired to Gesualdo, and never returned to Naples, attending to music, being extremely excellent in this regard. In the meantime he had a very beautiful concubine who attracted him in such a way that he had no eyes for the Princess Leonora. Yet when the Princess was far away, he would die of passion to see her, and then when she returned, he would not pay much attention to her. He could never sleep unless someone stayed with him, embracing him in order to keep his back warm. And for this purpose he had a certain Castelvietro of Modena, who was very dear to him, who continuously slept with him when the princess was away. [Spaccini]

... he was assailed and afflicted by a vast horde of demons which gave him no peace for many days on end unless ten or twelve young men, whom he kept specially for the purpose, were to beat him violently three times a day, during which operation he was wont to smile joyfully. [Don Ferrante della Marra, 1632]

... The Prince of Venosa, one of the best musicians of his age, was unable to go to the stool, without having been previously flogged by a valet kept expressly for the purpose.
[Campanella, medical treatise, 1635]

... a death hastened by a strange illness, which made it soothing for him to be given blows on the temples and other parts of the body by putting over those parts a small bundle of rags.
A strange recompense, indeed, that as the prince had elicited admiration and gladness from the listener with the melody and sweetness of his music and its sound, so he received relief and quietness in his internal pain from the heavy beatings.
[letter of Michele Giustiniani, 10th October, 1674]

Leonora's main consolation and support was her half-brother Cardinal Alessandro, who was certainly no celibate, having seduced a young girl who subsequently took refuge in a nunnery. Leonora is said to have formed "an unnaturally deep attachment" with her half-brother, though gossip at the time about incest has no firm basis.

(Two and a half centuries on, Mendelssohn could be said to have formed an unusually close relationship with his sister Fanny, though incest has never been alleged there.) Alessandro, together with Leonora's other brother Cesare, wanted to obtain a divorce for her, but she decided against it, "still having some affection for the prince". Leonora would not even allow her brothers to complain about her abuse to Gesualdo's uncle, Cardinal Alfonso.

Leonora's only respites from her marital hell (charted in a series of letters between 1604 and 1609) were her extended visits to Cesare in Modena. Gesualdo, predictably, opposed these visits, but was sometimes obliged to give way. There was, for example, the marriage of his own nephew in Modena in 1607, at which Leonora was deputed to attend.

In 1609 she once again retreated to Modena, this time for almost a year, in the hope of improving her now chronic illnesses. But in spite of a divorce having now been fixed with the Papal authorities, the Princess returned home to "console" her husband and to submit to more punishment. It is difficult to resist the conclusion that Leonora was to some extent addicted to maltreatment, to martyring herself to the beatings and to the infidelities — with both sexes, of course. She could undoubtedly have opted for freedom. Perhaps she relished the missionary thrill of being indispensable to a psychopath and emotional cripple — just as so many women have done so since then. It is amazing to learn today how convicted serial killers and rapists on both sides of the Atlantic have no shortage of death row groupies eager to bed, protect and redeem them: Ted Bundy and his acolytes, Peter Sutcliffe and his saucy offers, Charles Manson and the members of his "family", the Gainsville slasher, and many others.

Virtually nothing is known of the Gesualdos' lives from the time of Leonora's return in 1610 to the composer's death on September 8th, 1613. Referring to that event, "It cannot be doubted," comments Professor Watkins, "that [Leonora] must have felt a final sense of relief." That sounds like putting it very mildly; but maybe it isn't. It is even conceivable, sadly, that in being no longer able to turn her other cheek to an abusing husband Princess Leonora Gesualdo felt her life to have lost its central purpose.

After his death Leonora remained in the castle of Gesualdo for two years, attending as far as possible to the demanding requirements of her late husband's will. In 1615 she renounced her rights in the Gesualdo estate and returned for good to Modena. She was then compelled into another marriage (of which we know nothing), this time with the Pope's nephew Prince Nicolino Ludoviso of Bologna. Her last years were spent "in continuous prayers, alms, and holy works". She died at the age of 76.

*

To unjaded ears Gesualdo's music is startling — and electrifying — in its harmonic weirdness. As you listen your ear is constantly yanked into remote-sounding keys by startlingly abrupt chromatic shifts. Gesualdo seems, in his music, to inhabit an intensely private creative and harmonic world hardly less eccentric and disturbing than his personal life. One feels that he would been much happier as a non-officiating composer-priest (like Vivaldi), perhaps taking his pleasures when so inclined rather than wreaking and enduring havoc in very unsatisfactory permanent relationships.

***

CHAPTER 2

THE INCOMPARABLE M. DE LULLY
MOLIÈRE: L'AMOUR MÉDECIN (PREFACE) 1665

BORN: FLORENCE, 28TH NOVEMBER 1632
DIED: PARIS, 22ND MARCH 1687

... an extraordinary life of work and debauchery, using and abusing his energies. [Henri Prunières, Mercure de France, I-V-1916]

*

If the audience were told the truth, the concert halls where I most often play would be depleted in seconds. Some of our most loyal followers in my neck of the woods would be up and away if, before a performance of some of Lully's glittering and courtly dances, the conductor turned round and graphically recapped the very unsavoury facts of his personal life. And I certainly wouldn't spill the beans during my pre-concert talks on his overtures, minuets, gavottes, rigaudons, bourrées, passepieds and all the rest for risk of causing grave offence. If Lully were living today he would be locked away in the solitary wing of the slammer.

So if, like me, you are old enough and heterosexual enough to feel just a tad uneasy, though determinedly tolerant, when you see two young men holding hands in the street, or even smooching on the late buses after the gay clubs and pubs have disgorged their clientèle, you are hereby warned. What follows may temporarily moderate whatever pleasure you have so far gained or might have gained in the future from performances of potted versions of *Le Bourgeois Gentilhomme, Alceste* or *Armide et Renaud*. I say potted because we sadly rarely hear or see complete performances these days of Lully's ballets and operas.

To a lesser degree, the same warning applies to Schubert, though the evidence in his case is less ironclad. In both cases, neither composer's unsavoury private life affects one iota the quality of his works as independent creations.

In ancient Greece, of course, Lully's pursuit of young men wouldn't have raised an eyebrow. Older men's infatuations with younger ones were an accepted pattern in the social fabric, although cross-age male love affairs were subject to mockery. Spartan soldiers were even encouraged, it seems, to take their young male lovers with them into battle as a morale booster. Indeed, some Spartan brides were said to wear false beards on their wedding nights to wean their bridegrooms gently from homosexual habits. Lully may also have been in his element directing the fifes and drums under any number of rulers and military generals whose gaiety, demonstrably, or anecdotally, went well beyond their light-hearted moods: Alexander the Great, Julius Caesar, Frederick the Great, Richard the Lionheart and his notorious deputy William Longchamp, Lord Kitchener, Lawrence of Arabia, Earl Montgomery of Alamein, Earl Mountbatten of Burma, General Hector Macdonald of the Sudan campaign, and General John Nicholson of the Indian Raj, where homosexuality was rife among the Bengal lancers. However, if he had served in the Royal Navy, Lully would have needed to learn the meaning of the word patience — fat chance! — since legend has it that buggery was not permitted until after 90 days at sea.

*

It is a wonder that Lully found time to compose and direct any music at all, such was the breathtaking scale of his depravity in the slimepits of the Paris of Louis XIV — seemingly almost a reincarnation of the Sodom and Gomorrah of Bera and Birsha. Lully did undoubtedly have finer feelings for some of his catamites and lovers, and even for his wife and one or two other women, such as his principal singer Marthe Le Rochoix, for whom he penned some tender if not entirely serious verses. But most of his private life, after whooping it up with his pages, his young musicians and his aristocratic fellow sodomites in the Cabaret Bel-Air or elsewhere, was spent with his trousers down — in passionate sessions *à deux* with his young page boys, and in every conceivable grouping upwards with faces young and old, familiar and new. Actually, "private life" is hardly an applicable term for Lully, since he often flaunted his Ganymedes openly, even in front of his large family and one or two mistresses. These (a widow Maréchale de La Ferté, and a Madamoiselle Certain) he cultivated as a public concession to respectability, once even joking that he had "changed sides". His illness in 1678 was, indeed, widely lampooned as resulting from whore-mongering!

This book is supposed to be more about love than lust, though the volcanic frontiers, of course, are often completely invisible through dense clouds of steam and smoke. We certainly can't relate in detail all the sodomite antics of Lully and his circles from the time of his youthful infatuations, particularly with the rich and pretty Chausson, to his last binges with the aristo brothers Vendôme, and le Chevalier de Lorraine not long before his death at the age of 65. Chausson, who held regular orgies (attended by Lully) "from which women were meticulously excluded" at his home, was one of the comparatively few paederasts to be hung and burned at this time in the Place de Grève, after being caught in bed with a young page during a police raid.

Like his creative drive, Lully's libido rarely flagged until his last illness, and there are many vignettes and versified lampoons of him as a pot-bellied, incorrigible debaucher. Anyone really keen to broaden his or her education on homosexuality in Lully's circles can find a plethora of fascinating detail in R.H.F. Scott's biography *Jean-Baptiste Lully — The Founder of French Opera*, or better still, if reading French is not a problem, Henri Prunières' *La Vie Illustre et Libertine de Jean-Baptiste Lully*, on which the Scott book is based. There is also Prunières' short and pithy article quoted at the head of this chapter. Prunières, incidentally, who combines meticulous scholarship with imagination and human understanding, was no cloistered academic; as well as writing for *The New York Times* he was an active promoter of contemporary music in the 1920s.

Lully's lust for boys and young men seems to have been matched, as we shall see, by his lust for power, and his appetite for both seems to have fuelled, or been an indispensable concomitant to his manic creativity as a composer. We have no option but to take the Lully package as we find it. Neither did Lully's musically talented wife Madelaine (daughter of one of his colleagues Michel Lambert and much more loving than loved) and his three sons and three daughters; nor, for that matter, did even the king himself. Prunières' reading of the magnificent bronze bust of the composer sculpted by Coysevox seems to sum up the essence of the man: "intelligent vulgar face, flashing eyes, thick lips, clownish, sensual, fiery, all breathes out impudence".

*

One can easily understand the anxieties of parents of young musicians — English, German and Italian as well as French — trying to get a job in the king's *Grande Bande* (also called *Les Quatre Vingt Violons du Roi*) or, even better between 1656 and 1664, its renowned and highly disciplined élite offshoot, *La Petite Bande*. There was no finer playing job to be had in Europe; yet there was always a risk that Lully might develop a crush on their particular young lad, particularly if he had *castrat* or girlish features.

Prunières writes that Lully "very much prized the musicians under his control" and "would often buy them a few glasses of wine at the cabaret Bel-Air". If the glint in the master's eye was fixed firmly on you, that was presumably that: either get out or resign yourself to a sore backside for a few weeks. And at auditions, anyone not quite able to get round the tricky figurations of the trial piece — in later years it was the *Entrée des songes funestes* from *Atys* — would be very easy meat when invited to visit the master for a little extra tuition! One widely circulating quatrain sums it all up:

> One day Love said to his mother.
> ‧ Why am I not dressed?
> If Baptiste sees me naked
> My backside is done for.

All this of course has its modern heterosexual parallels in the *droits de seigneurs* exercised by conductors, leaders and fixers over nubile young ladies in the ever tighter freelance job markets. And even Oxford dons, according to the researches of Dr Gerald McCrum of Hertford College, show a demonstrable bias towards "fluffy blue-eyed girls" against "serious bespectacled females" when selecting under-graduates. Are rewards still sometimes claimed, one wonders?

*

At a time when sodomy was punishable by burning at the stake, it seems staggering that Lully was able to get away with such brazen and uninhibited flauntings of his habit, until one realises the phenomenal hold he had over *Le Roi Soleil*. Immediately after Lully's arrival at the court in 1653 as a 20-year-old "baladin" or strolling player, we find him carefully and tactfully coaching the 14-year-old dance-mad king, who would rehearse until he dropped. The two of them then danced alongside each other in the *Ballet de la Nuit*, and the *Marriage de Thétis et Peleus*. Their later artistic collaborations — between Europe's then most powerful monarch, that is, and the Florentine-born son of a miller! — included the king personally supplying Lully with the subject matter for four operas.

Although, as a lavish patron of the arts, Louis XIV had the good fortune to have geniuses working for him in every field — Molière, the painters Pierre Patel and Jean-Baptiste Martin, the architects Le Vau and Mansart, the landscape-gardener Le Nôtre, the painter and decorator Le Brun, as well as countless other outstanding practitioners — it was to music, and above all Lully's, that the king became addicted. After hearing a preview performance, for instance, of *Alceste* in Versailles in 1674, he resolved to attend every further performance when it opened in Paris.

The king had Lully's graceful and seductive music — on the violins, or the oboes, flutes and sackbutts as appropriate — in the foreground or background almost everywhere he went from the first moment of the *levée* right up to supper time: for his walks in the gardens, canal rides in the royal barge, services in chapel, and for dancing at the thrice weekly *jours d'Appartements* in surroundings like these at Versailles:

> Nothing in the world could be more beautiful, more magnificent, more astonishing. Just imagine the brilliance of a hundred thousand candles in this great suite of apartments; I thought it was all ablaze, for the sun in July is no brighter. The furnishings of gold and silver had their own peculiar lustre, as did the gilding and the marble ...
> ... I passed into a room [the Salon d'Apollon] which enchants with every object which meets the eye. The King's throne stands there. The hangings of crimson velvet embroidered with gold impose respect. The pilasters are in high relief; their bases and capitals seemed to be the work of goldsmiths: nothing could be more august or majestic ... There were many ladies, both young and beautiful and scintillating with jewellery; they were marvellously graceful. The

princesse de Conti, 'la Belle', carried off the prize for dancing ... I was astonished to see the king sitting there quite informally.
[Abbé Bourdalot]

This was just one of the sumptuous settings in which Lully worked — quite a contrast to the sordid dens he frequented afterwards. He would doff his gold-braided, richly embroidered performing uniforms and slope off, slovenly and open shirted, for slurps galore, bawdy songs, and then who knows what; a private passionate encounter, or a free-for-all in a stinking room full of writhing, slithering, whimpering, grunting, screaming debauchers.

Lully's spectacular rise to power is unequalled by any other composer. Suffice it to say that his marriage certificate of 1662 was signed by the king and queen; by 1672 his standing was such that he had absolute control over all aspects of French stage music; in 1681 he was appointed an equerry and Sécretaire du Roi, extending his control at the court far beyond music; and at his death his estate included 800,000 livres, five houses in Paris (the principal one sumptuously furnished and adorned with marquetry, Flemish tapestries, rich draperies, brocade and damask curtains, countless objets d'art and all the rest) and two in the country. His meteoric career and immunity from punishment inevitably aroused jealousy, and sparked off all sorts of plots and cabals against him, not least the bizarre and drawn-out poisoned snuff affair.

Another reason, of course, why Lully got away with so much was the rampant homosexuality in court circles, despite the dire penalties. The king's brother, "Monsieur", was a notorious homosexual, and many other aristocrats belonged to known and established gay cliques. One of the most scandalous was a "confrérie de sodomistes", headed by the Duc de Grammont, whose members had to renounce women altogether and wear a golden cross under their jerkins of a man trampling on a woman. Lully himself headed a less fanatical group known as the *communauté* including the brothers Vendôme, the Chevalier de Lorraine (Monsieur's favourite), the Comte de Fisque, "and 100 others" says Prunières. It wasn't for nothing that commentators railed against all these *débauches crapuleuses,* and when the curé Hébert of Versailles complained about them to the king through one of his mistresses, Mme de Maintenon, his reported response was "Am I then to begin with my own brother?" Sodomy was, incidentally, a great social leveller, and a prince who doted on a pauper would help him no end to make his fortune.

Perhaps such decadence was an inevitable part of a world infested with creeps and hangers-on; where fawning fops genuflected before the king's bed when he was not even in it, and where, when they bade him good night, the highest privilege was to leave the bedroom last, like clerics leaving the sanctuary.

It is worth focusing on just one documented affair in Lully's "love" life when he was head over heels because it is such a powerful epitome of his style and milieu. Lully had the right, in his capacity as Superintendent of the King's Music, to the services of a page boy "mué" — one whose voice was breaking and the dangers to these hapless creatures in Lully's case can be only too well imagined. He even dismissed one of them, Lafarge, for infidelity!

In 1684 the 53-year-old Lully became besotted with one particular page, Brunet, a talented tenor reputedly "more beautiful than Cupid", who would sing duets with Lully in the taverns. "Lully [says Prunières] didn't lose time in falling in love with his person more than his talents and was brazen enough to parade this scandalous liaison in front of his wife and children". Things came to a head when Lully had a violent row with the mother (and madam) of his current mistress, the promiscuous Mlle Certain, known as "the loveable clavichordist". Mlle Certain's mother informed the king about the Brunet affair in a letter of denunciation, and for once, the monarch had to do something. Brunet was arrested and sent in to the care of Les Pères (Abbots) de St Lazare where he was whipped and confined. In return for leniency he turned King's evidence and started naming many names in his detailed exposé of court vices.

Lully received a severe reprimand from the king, who actually loathed homosexuality as much as atheism, via the Marquis de Seignelay, the Lieutenant of Police. The only problem there was that de Seignelay's own son, so Brunet had revealed, belonged to one of the most depraved of all the sodomite circles, with an agenda which included acts of sacrilege and whore-baiting. The whole matter was therefore swept under the carpet but Lully was nevertheless threatened with a devastating exemplary sentence if he misbehaved again. True to character, Lully's sole concern in all this was the loss of the boy on whom he doted; he didn't give a damn about the bad publicity! To

Lully's extreme chagrin, Brunet, when released, was put into the care of Boesset, one of Lully's idle colleagues at the court. When Lully tried to visit his confiscated catamite, he was sent packing with a flea in his ear.

These two freely translated verses of a resulting lampoon on this scandal give the flavour of countless others:

Monsieur Lully is distressed
To see his Brunet thrashed;
He is jealous that an abbot
(Well well!)
Attends to his backside ...
If you see what I mean.

Console yourself, my dear Brunet,
Over the dirty trick Mlle Certain has played on you
And in your misfortune,
Well well!
Remind yourself that she is only a whore ...
You get my meaning.

Not surprisingly Lully was soon back in favour with the king, who was enchanted by his new opera *Roland,* though their relationship was more reserved

It has been suggested that Lully's sexual orientation may have been induced by his early background. He was born in Florence and, already an adept fiddler, tumbler, dancer and comic by the age of ten, was talent-spotted in 1646 and taken to France as a *garçon de chambre* for Mademoiselle d'Orléans, a cousin of the king. His pious mother Caterina had crossed herself when learning of her young son's ambitions to tread the boards!

For whatever reasons, Italy was notorious in France for sodomite practices and the term "Italian morals" (*horrible, exécrable, odieux* as Boileau described them) was a euphemism for raging homosexuality. Perhaps, only perhaps, his guitar tuition at the hands of a Franciscan friar and his contact with so many dancers in the marketplace of Florence during the *Carnaval* may have induced, or reinforced a homosexual preference. Even today, there are many more gays in the ballet world than in any other branch of the entertainment business, and the clerical brethren of Europe and America are, of course, continually throwing up alarming scandals: an exalted Archbishop seduces a seminarist; a humble priest fondles young lads in the confessional, sodomises them in the sacristy or the presbytery, and so it goes on.

Lully's orientation was certainly inveterate by the time he was 15 and making his way in the theatre. He was playing up to indecent suggestions from the poet and theorbo player Charles d'Assoucy, a member of a circle headed by the self-styled 'King of Sodom', Saint-Pavin, and was also possibly obliging his first musical mentor at the court, Lazarin, a leader of the *Grande Bande.*

Although the king valued the music of other composers, particularly the Italian Lorenzani, Lully's was always favourite, and it is only fair to finish with a brief word about his historically important work and his loveable personal qualities. He created French tragic opera, *tragédie en musique;* he popularised, if sometimes perhaps rather perfunctorily, all those dance forms mentioned earlier, even inventing the minuet, and introducing the bourrée into ballet for the first time. It's perhaps no surprise to discover that his composing methods were higgledy piggledy — a bit here, a bit there after ideas came to him in the middle of the night, in the pub during a debauch, or during a horse ride when he might be inspired by the sound of the wind in the marsh reeds. He would normally write out just the tune and the bass line and leave his minions to fill in the rest.

On the performance side, having inherited a bunch of "violent, coarse, drunk [and] querulous" orchestral musicians who played out of time and added endless improvised ornaments, he developed the most accomplished and disciplined band in Europe, even if his methods did include breaking players' violins over their backs! The orchestra's "premier coup d'archet" (the attack and precision of the crucial down bows), was legendary. He also directed some spectacular celebratory shows; his *Psyché* in Dunquerque, for instance, when the Royal party visited the newly constructed ramparts, featured regimental trumpets, oboes, fifes, sackbuts, crumhorns, 700 tambourines and a concluding salvo of 80 cannon shots.

His perfectionism extended to all other aspects of opera production. On one occasion he sent back the libretto for a new opera *(Alceste)* 20 times to the poet and dramatist Phillipe Quinault before he was satisfied. In spite of kicking actors up the backside when annoyed, he retained everybody's respect on stage and back stage through his own histrionic talents and detailed working knowledge of every aspect of stage craft. He even remained a supple dancer in spite of his weight, a skill doubtless also put to imaginative use in brothels and boudoirs. His spontaneous buffoonery and sense of fun were a joy to everybody, from the time when, as *garçon de chambre,* he reportedly sang an apposite popular song when Mademoiselle d'Orléans farted in her privy during the *levée*, to his clownish crashing onto the harpsichord, at the age of fifty, to escape a doctor's clyster during a comical episode in *Monsieur de Porceaugnac*.

Most marvellous of all, perhaps, was his vitality and sheer zest for life. Even his long-suffering wife Madelaine cannot have been immune to it, somehow being able to live with his promiscuity and console herself with the total trust he always placed in her to manage his vast fortune.

Life for Lully was always worth living, a brimful cup of love, fun and lust to be drained to the dregs, from his first capers in the side shows in the market square in Florence to his deathbed hoodwinking of the priest who came to administer the last rites. (His fatal gangrene, of course, developed after he bruised his toes with a large billiard cue which he banged on the floor during his *Te Deum* to keep more than 150 performers in time. He refused to have his toes cut off.) The priest, strongly disapproving of the theatre, insisted on the destruction of Lully's latest score, *Achille et Polixène,* before giving Last Rites and Extreme Unction, which Lully had only agreed to as a concession to his wife. Lully pointed to a table drawer from which the priest took the score and threw it on the fire. He little knew that the irrepressible wag had made a second copy! Even Lully's very final deathbed repentance a few days later was larger than life, more theatrical than convincingly contrite as he knelt on cinders with a rope around his neck and confessed his sins. I bet that the miller's son who took to signing himself as "fils de Laurent de Lully, gentilhomme Florentin" would repent of nothing.

One thing is certain; the more one understands Lully in his setting, the more irrelevant it becomes to judge his vices by today's standards. There is no point in delivering a posthumous sentence. In the words of a Monsieur de La Bruyère with which Henri Prunières concludes his wonderful biography: "Lully est Lully."

***

CHAPTER 3

BAROQUE BROOD
ANTONIO LUCIO VIVALDI
"IL PRETE ROSSO", OR SIMPLY "ROSSO"

BORN: VENICE, 4TH MARCH 1678
DIED: VIENNA, 28TH JULY 1741

*

Everyone knows that Vivaldi was a fast mover with his pen. He must have been to compose some 760 works on top of all his other activities: 53 or so known operas and stage works (there may well be about 40 more, lost or undiscovered); 39 cantatas; over 60 other sacred works; 478 solo and multiple concertos (some of the latter with astonishingly unusual solo combinations, such as the one for three violins, oboe, two recorders, two violas, chalumeau, two cellos, two harpsichords, two trumpets and two double basses); 90 sonatas, 14 sinfonias and a few other bits and pieces. He can't have been exaggerating very much when he boasted that he was capable of "composing a concerto in all its parts more quickly than a copyist could write them down".

Mind you, Vivaldi's irreverent detractors agree with Stravinsky that he composed "the same form so many times over". Well, why on earth not, if it worked so well, giving predictable pleasure and bringing home the bacon? Other great Italians besides Vivaldi, including Rossini and Donizetti, created music like their mothers' pastas and polentas: any number of nicely-turned tunes over the same basic forms just like mama mia's myriad sauces for the same staple dishes.

However, lovers of *The Four Seasons,* the world's most popular ever piece of "classical" music, are only now cottoning on to the fact that Antonio Vivaldi was an asthmatic, red-haired, non-officiating priest with a highly unorthodox *ménage* that included his young pupil and opera star Anna Girò, and her sister Paolina, his "nurse". Vivaldi's flexible domestic arrangements as a priest were nothing too unusual, of course, in 18th-century Italy. Some cardinals thought it their duty to take a mistress — purely, of course, to stay in touch with their flocks by sampling the earthly pleasures they had vowed to renounce. And far better, then and now, for any Catholic prelate to take a mistress than start messing about in desperation with young choirboys and seminarists.

A very widely quoted contemporary French diplomat and historian, President Charles de Brosses, pulls no punches about the worldliness, and worse, he discovered within the clerical world during his Italian journeys of 1739-40. Cardinal Ottoboni, musical fanatic and an extremely wealthy and active patron of Corelli, Handel and many others in Rome was, says De Brosses, *"sans moeurs [morals], sans crédit, débauché, ruiné, amateur des arts, grand musicien"*.

De Brosses also reported on the four renowned Venetian convents, with one of which, la Pietà, Vivaldi was closely associated. These *Ospedali* were established to bring up between them some 6,000 infants at any one time, either orphaned, or abandoned by young war widows and prostitutes. De Brosses found the teenage nuns to be very far from cloistered and much to his own taste:

> There is a furious dispute amongst the three convents of the city to decide which will have the advantage of giving a mistress to the new [papal] nuncio who has just arrived. In truth, it would be towards the nuns that I would turn most willingly if I had to stay here for long. ... They have a charming little hairstyle, a simple habit but, of course, almost entirely white, which uncovers their shoulders and throat no more and no less than the Roman costumes of our actresses.

Other travelling journalists ogled in like fashion, or uncovered even more scandal. Edward Wright found the "noble vestals" at the Celestia to be very prettily got up, with "the covering on their neck and breast ... so thin, that 'twas next to nothing at all". The philosopher and composer Jean-Jacques Rousseau found these "angels of loveliness" much less attractive but nevertheless "nearly fell in love with all these ugly girls".

Not only were the *Ospedali* marriage markets for discerning gentlemen, they also seem, according to the files of the Vatican secret agents, to have been sex markets:

Anzola Trevisana, known as *La Galinera,* a prostitute ... plies her trade on holidays, setting an example which is deplorable and scandalous without in the least enquiring whether it is allowed. Christians and Jews frequent her house, and through the mistresses of the Pietà, who act as procurators, the girls of that hospital are frequently brought in. They stay there for whole days at a time ... [G B Manuzzi, 9th September, 1740]

Be that as it may, all four convents were hotbeds of musical talent, and particularly the Pietà, where Vivaldi was first appointed as violin master in 1703 and where he worked energetically, but sporadically and in fluctuating favour with the authorities, until 1740. (He was promoted to *maestro di concerti* in 1723.) Much of his vast output of instrumental and sacred choral music was written for the talented *figlie di coro,* the small group of elite singers and players chosen from among the commoners, the *figlie commun.* The travelling journalists were as much bowled over by the ladies' musical talents as by their personal charms, though like today's music examiners and adjudicators, their judgements of the former may sometimes have been clouded by their vulnerability to the latter:

I vow to you that there is nothing so diverting as the sight of a young and pretty nun in a white habit, with a bunch of pomegranate blossoms over her ear, conducting the orchestra and beating time with all the grace and precision imaginable. [De Brosses]

Within these temples of temptation, it is hardly surprising that any priestly music master was expected or assumed to be a eunuch, as Edward Wright and also a gentleman named François Masson assumed Vivaldi to be. "They ... have concluded that a priest fitted for musick may exercise the priesthood as well as another; provided he hath his *necessities,* or, if you will, his *superfluities* in his pocket." We can safely assume that Vivaldi's *necessities* were in their divinely allotted place.

"Annina of the Red Priest"

The most readable of all distinguished music scholars, H.C. Robbins Landon (where on earth would we be without him?), has established that Anna Girò was herself a product of the Pietà. She was probably the daughter of a French wigmaker (Girò being the Italianised version of her real name Giraud). Just exactly when she became Vivaldi's protégée is uncertain, though, if his memory was correct, by about 1723 they were out on the road together working the theatres "in a good many European cities". He may have first met her a year or two earlier while he was in the service of Prince Philip of Hesse-Darmstadt in Mantua. Anna often had a "mantovana" tag to her name, which could mean she was either born there, or first hit the headlines there.

The young contralto made her operatic début in Venice in 1724 in Albinoni's *Laodice*, at the S. Moisè theatre, and in the following year she sang in her first Vivaldi opera, *Farnace*, at the S. Angelo. She was a sensation, one report mentioning "miracles" even if her voice was "not one of the most beautiful".

Did she soon become Vivaldi's mistress? There is no absolute proof but everything points that way, quite apart from the free and easy Venetian lifestyle. Although she most definitely had an independent career beyond singing in Vivaldi's operas — she sang in works by composers such as Galuppi, Hasse and Runcher — her absences from Venice coincided consistently with those of the maestro.

Vivaldi and the two ladies almost certainly lived together. One nugget of unwitting testimony to this effect just slips out during the course of a colourful and informative yarn told by the Venetian dramatist Carlo Goldoni on a visit he paid to the composer's house. In 1735 Goldoni was roped in to redraft a libretto for an opera, *Griselda*, which Vivaldi was composing for the S. Samuele theatre in Venice. (It had already been set to music by Albinoni.) Goldoni describes how Vivaldi, although an admirer of his putative librettist's own plays, was very sceptical of his ability to write the kind of aria libretto specifically needed for Anna Girò. But after persistent badgering Goldoni was handed pen and paper and given the chance to prove himself there and then — while the composer apparently read his breviary! Vivaldi was overjoyed with the result. Having stressed how Anna needed arias of "action, passion and motion" rather than static "cantabile" ones to show her off to best advantage, Goldoni's adaptation was just the ticket:

> [Vivaldi] ... got up, embraced me, ran to the door and called Signorina Annina. Annina arrived, with her sister Paolina. He read them the

arietta, shouting: "He did it here, he did it here, on this very spot!"
Again he embraced me and congratulated me ... I then murdered
Zeno's play [Griselda] as exactly as he wanted ...
[Goldoni's *Commedie*, 1761]

In his second, rather cheekier account of the same encounter (1787)
Goldoni left the fullest description we have of Anna:

She was not pretty but she had charms — a delicate figure, beautiful
eyes, beautiful hair, a charming mouth, and not much of a voice but
much acting ability. It was she who was to portray the role of Griselda.

Two years later there was further casual confirmation of the
priestly *ménage* when a spy of the Inquisition in Venice reported
that during a grand celebratory *souper* at the Spanish embassy
there was music "by the singer who lives at the house of *abbate*
Vivaldi, called la *Girò,* and at the harpsichord sat the *abbate* who
indicated the tempo to the instruments which were not many but
all excellent in both the vocal and instrumental departments. The
music went on until three o'clock in the morning, and then everybody went home ...".

We can safely assume that Vivaldi and la Girò went home together, even if the 61-year-old *abbate* would have us believe that he
and his 30-something Anna went chastely to their separate beds. Somehow, I doubt it.

Qui s'excuse, s'accuse

Vivaldi faced a crisis in 1737, a year in which his unorthodox
private life impinged disastrously on his astutely managed, not to say
mercenary one-man business as a music entrepreneur. With the help
of his mandolin-playing nobleman friend and man-on-the-spot Guido
Bentivoglio, Vivaldi was all set to mount a season of his operas in
Ferrara. But on November 16th, shortly before he planned to leave
Venice to oversee the preparations, Vivaldi received a bombshell: the
Papal Nuncio in Venice informed him that Cardinal Tomaso Ruffo of
Ferrara (which was part of Papal territory) was banning him from the
city altogether "because I am a priest who does not say Mass and
because I have the friendship of the singer Girò". Faced with heavy

contractual losses of up to 6,000 ducats, Vivaldi pleaded with Bentivoglio to intercede, but to no avail. Ruffo, a prude and a martinet who even forbade his priests from attending the annual Carnival celebrations, would not budge.

Vivaldi's defence against Ruffo's attack (in one of 13 letters to Bentivoglio spanning well over two years of frustrated initiatives in Ferrara) dodges the crucial issue:

> What troubles me most, is the stain with which His Eminence Cardinal Ruffo marks these poor women: nobody has ever done that. Fourteen years ago we went to a good many European cities, and their modesty was admired everywhere; Ferrara can give sufficient evidence of it. Every day of the week they made their devotions, as sworn and authenticated records can prove. [November 16th, 1737]

As Vivaldi scholar Michael Talbot has pointed out, it is so obvious how Vivaldi neatly diverts the issue of *his* relationship with one of the sisters into a discussion of the morals of *both* women. "Besides", continues Talbot, "it takes little cynicism to concur with the suggestion that Vivaldi would hardly have courted scandal for so long without enjoying some of the fruits."

Instead of quietly giving up, Vivaldi continued to spit into the wind two letters further on: "malicious tongues may say what they want. Your Excellency knows that in Venice I have my house for which I pay 200 ducats and the Girò sisters have another far away from me."

The whole convoluted Ferrara episode, involving much more than just the Girò scandal, was a crushing blow to Vivaldi's finances and morale, but he bounced back. On January 7th, 1738 he was in Amsterdam, where his music was already published and popular, as the principal guest for the centenary celebrations of the Schouwberg Theatre. He directed the band and played a specially composed, richly scored violin concerto (RV 562a in D).

In 1738 Anna Girò sang in all three of Vivaldi's new works for his last grand season in Venice at the San Angelo. In the autumn of 1740 she was singing in his *Catone in Utica* in Graz, very possibly with her devoted maestro in attendance.

In 1740, for reasons shrouded in mystery, "Reverend Vivaldi" quit his job at the Pietà, with which his relations had always been uneasy. By then his music had become very much passé in a very fashion-conscious city, and he set out, perhaps with Anna and Paolina, for Vienna, where he probably hoped for a position with his old admirer Charles VI. Alas, the Emperor died in October after eating a plate of poisonous mushrooms, and Vivaldi ended his days as a pauper in the house of a saddler's widow.

Vivaldi had always been money mad, and the degradation of poverty must have cut very deeply. What a turn up it is for the books that in this century at least 150 recordings of *The Four Seasons* have appeared, with Nigel Kennedy's 1990 version topping the bestseller lists for many months.

We can but hope that the devoted Anna and Paolina were actually there to comfort *Il Prete Rosso's* last days and attend his funeral in St Stephen's cathedral. Little did he know as he lay in his coffin that the nine-year-old Joseph Haydn was singing in the choir.

*

Georg Philipp Telemann
"The Operator"

Born: Magdeburg, 14th March 1681
Died: Hamburg, 25th June 1767

*

Telemann's endless experiments in cloning a cantata embryo can have left him with very little time for human pleasures. Nobody has yet painstakingly numbered and catalogued his entire output, but he makes Vivaldi look positively lazy: 1,500 cantatas; several hundred orchestral suites and concertos; chamber and keyboard pieces, Oratorios, Passions and miscellaneous serenades; *lieder,* some 25 operas and other stage works. Telemann also had his restless fingers in other pies, including pedagogic writings, publishing, engraving, and concert promotion. Never backward at coming forward, he also found time to write no less than three autobiographies, two of them at the request of another indefatigable entrepreneur, Johann Mattheson — the man who reportedly fought a duel with Handel in 1704 when the latter refused to give way at the harpsichord.

Telemann set out to write music to please as wide an audience as possible, and succeeded overwhelmingly. His music in the *style galant* — perhaps especially the programme suites such as *Don Quichotte,* the *Water Music* and the *Ouverture des nations anciens et modernes* — has a freshness, vitality and inventiveness that is only now regaining real popularity in the concert hall. However, it wasn't for nothing that the crusty though distinguished senior figure Johann Kuhnau, cantor of St Thomas Leipzig, scornfully dubbed Telemann "The Operator" after his arrival at the university there in 1701 to read law. Self-confident almost to the point of bumptiousness, Telemann started doing what he did all his active life: sussing out the musical scene and sewing it all up for himself by manipulating the authorities. But in doing so he vastly extended and enriched every aspect of the musical life of the cities in which he worked — Leipzig, Frankfurt and Hamburg. And in founding or expanding the *collegia musica* in these cities Telemann was the key figure in the development of public concerts in Germany.

For a musician he was certainly a good catch as a bread-winning husband, earning some 3,000 gulden a year in his heyday at Hamburg (1720s) — approximately three times as much as Bach was to earn in Leipzig.

Telemann's first marriage was to Amalie Louise Juliane Eberlin (Louisa), the daughter of an independent gentleman, Daniel Eberlin. Eberlin was all things to all men — one of those fiendish polymaths who upstage us all. Without going into detail, he was, so his son-in-law tells us, in various places a Papal army captain, a librarian, twice a Capellmeister, a private secretary, master of the pages, master of the mint, banker, militia captain, learned contrapuntist, accomplished violinist, deep thinker... To Amalie, even the versatile workaholic Telemann can barely have measured up to daddy when she married the composer in 1707 in Sorau. They settled in Eisenach where Telemann had recently been appointed court Konzertmeister.

Alas, after only 15 months of married happiness Amalie died in childbirth. Grief stricken, Telemann penned some verses quaintly entitled *Poetic Thoughts, by which the Ashes of the most dearly Beloved Louisa are Honour'd by her Surviving Husband, Georg Philipp Telemann, 1711.* Perhaps unable to live in surroundings with such painful memories, in 1712 Telemann left court service in Eisenach for Frankfurt, to take up the post of city Director Of Music and Kapellmeister at the Barfusserkirche.

Around the year 1714 he married the daughter of a Frankfurt council clerk. Maria Catharina Textors, whom he colourfully dubbed his "whimpering helpmeet", was to bring him scant joy in the years to come. Yet somehow she managed to distract him from his squillions of crotchets and quavers often enough to play his part in producing eight sons and two daughters (or eight children in total, according to which respectable source you read). Perhaps she had to pounce on him when he was refilling his ink well, or knew how to get him going with a goose quill feather when she took in his coffee. Or maybe (most likely) she could arouse him by stuffing handfuls of thalers down her cleavage, or even her knickers.

Whatever, Frau Telemann finally got fed up with tripping up over piles of cantatas and getting caught up in the labyrinths of exotic plants that Handel kept sending her husband from England. Having run up the family's debts to the tune of 3,000 thalers, and having kept in good shape in spite of her 10 children, she ran off with a Swedish officer.

The Hamburg town council quashed an attempt by the local theatre to stage a satirical play featuring Telemann's misfortunes. Their concern for their revered Music Director may have been misplaced, since Telemann would undoubtedly have seized the chance to compose the incidental music — for a suitable remuneration, of course.

*

GEORGE FRIDERIC HANDEL

BORN: HALLE, 23RD FEBRUARY 1685
DIED: LONDON, 14TH APRIL 1759

[He] scorned the advice of any but the Woman he loved, but his Amours were rather of short duration, always within the pale of his own profession.
[remark attributed to George III in a copy of Mainwaring's biography]

*

Mad King George, if he wasn't making it up, must have known more than anyone else has ever been able to discover about Handel's sex life. His sensual pleasures seem to have extended no lower than his stomach. Various anecdotes, bills ("Monsù Endel" 45lb "snow", for cooling wine in Italy) and jottings ("12 gallons port, 12 bottles French — Duke Street, Meels") confirm that he was undoubtedly a tippler and a trencherman, his gargantuan repasts "making the marble tables bend". There is also the cruel cartoon by his former friend Joseph Goupy in which a pig-snouted Handel is seated on a hogshead of flowing wine, facing a mirror held up to him by a satyr, in an organ loft crammed with meat, poultry and other goodies.

Such an addiction to the pleasures of the table can spell peace of mind, of course, especially to the spouses of touring celebrities. According to a recent profile in *The Guardian,* Luciano Pavarotti's wife of 33 years, Adua, never worries about her husband straying: "Luciano does not run off with women. Had you said a plate of spaghetti, I might have believed you."

Further evidence that Handel need not detain us long in our fly-on-the-wall researches comes from Dr Charles Burney, the renowned, astute and very readable 18th-century music historian:

> Handel, with many virtues, was addicted to no vice that was injurious to society. Nature, indeed, required a great supply of sustenance to support so huge a mass, and he was rather epicurean in the choice of it; but this seems to have been the only appetite he allowed himself to gratify. [1785]

Certainly the magnificent portrait of Handel in old age by Thomas Hudson exudes well-being, generosity of spirit, and inner contentment. He seems to have managed without the comforts and consolations of mistresses or matrimony.

Sex life or no, Handel gets a mention here not only because he wrote the world's most famous and best-loved oratorio. That same oratorio has earned me and countless other freelance musicians far more crusts of bread in churches and concert halls than any other single piece of music ever written, *The Four Seasons* included. Up to and including the 1980s, players throughout the length and breadth of Britian, particularly string players, could guarantee to be working their socks off in the five or six weeks up to Christmas with *Messiah* bookings, Easter likewise. The galling part about it was that on some Saturdays you had to turn down four of the five dates you were offered, because you could only be in one place at a time. One very good fiddler friend of mine assures me he once notched up a total of 19 *Messiahs* in the run-up to one Christmas, and he clearly recalls one well-known Yorkshire violinist who each year did three *Messiahs* without rehearsal on one Saturday in each December. To get the musicians, some choral societies had to put on their shows in the morning or afternoon instead of the evening.

I am just one of those many cellists who dreamed he was playing the *Messiah* and woke up and found he was! The standard performance time was two hours forty minutes, but some overly reverential or pompous conductors could take it into overtime! Believe it or not, we once even had a choral conductor who took the *rehearsal* into overtime! I'd better not say where, or I'll never go there again.

When most people think of *Messiah,* they think of their favourite solo arias and the rousing choruses. When jobbing musicians think of all their hundreds of *Messiahs* they recall armies of lathered-up conductors and their often turgid tempos; blasting *Hallelujahs* with bellowing basses, cornkrake tenors, wobbly contraltos, hooting male altos, breathy and breathless sopranos all going for broke. Besides the performances there are floods of associated memories: grand Victorian town halls, freezing churches, cramped church halls with one seriously oversubscribed loo, stewed tea in brown teapots and fish paste sandwiches kindly provided in far-flung places, cash in brown envelopes, and then long, weary journeys through the winter fogs back to base in clapped-out coaches, and then the same routine tomorrow.

Those were the days! I wouldn't have missed them for anything. Handel, incidentally, has the highest number of tunes of any composer listed in the top hundred of BBC Radio 2's vintage Sunday night programme Your Hundred Best Tunes still compèred by Alan Keith: Handel has eight, followed by Mozart (six), Beethoven (five) and Schubert and Bach (four each).

*

We had better mention "an apparent romance", during Handel's extended Italian tour of 1706-10, with the soprano Vittoria Tarquini, "la Bombace". It is mentioned in the first biography of Handel — indeed, the first biography of any composer in English — by John Mainwaring, who based his respected but sometimes erratic account on conversations with Handel's amanuensis more than 50 years later.

During the run of Handel's opera *Rodrigo* in 1707 in Florence, Vittoria Tarquini is supposed to have deserted Prince Ferdinand, her current protector and lover — and also Handel's patron for this opera! — for the composer himself. "Handel's youth and comeliness, joined with his fame and abilities in Music, had made impressions on her heart."

All perfectly possible, of course. Singers and soloists are always falling in love with their conductors. Look how Rossini pinched the divas Isabella Colbran and Marietta Marcolini from their respective protectors Domenico Barbaja and Prince Lucien Bonaparte. Further fuel is added to the fire in a letter of 1710 by the Electress Sophia of Hanover referring to Handel as "a good-looking man and the talk is that he was the lover of Victoria ...".

Handel certainly also had many very supportive and discerning female friends and admirers through times thick and thin, especially the latter when his opera projects collapsed in ruins or when his health failed. That he always bounced back with renewed vigour and optimism must have been due to their emotional support as well as to his own guts, resilience and determination. Mrs. Mary Granville (later to become Mrs. Pendarves, then later still Mrs. Delany) was one of his longest-standing friends in England, first meeting (and playing) for him in 1711 when she was 10 years old and the composer 26. Handel was clearly very much at home in her circle; on one occasion he was "in the best humour in the world, and played lessons [pieces] and accompanied Strada (an Italian soprano) and all the ladies that sang from seven o'the clock till eleven". His hostess goes on to say that "about half an hour after nine [I] had a salver brought in of chocolate, mulled white wine [in abundance, one trusts] and biscuits. Everyone was easy and seemed pleased ...".

Handel undoubtedly remained susceptible to female charms. In his late 50s he was as enchanted as everyone else by the fine soprano Mrs. Susanna Cibber, the sister of the composer Thomas Arne, who sang in the first performance of his *Messiah*. "Handel was very fond of Mrs. Cibber, whose voice and manners had softened his severity for her want of musical knowledge" (Burney).

Well, nearly every professional singer of both sexes would remain on the shelf forever if their love life depended on their ability to sight-sing music!

Handel certainly had a short fuse when handling temperamental opera stars like the fabulous but tiresome soprano Francesca Cuzzoni:

> having one day some words with Cuzzoni on her refusing to sing *Falsa imagine* in *Ottone:* "Oh! madam," said he [in French], I know well that you are a true she-devil: but I will make you realise that I, Handel, am Beelzebub, the chief of the devils. With this he took her up by the waist, and, if she made any more words, swore that he would fling her out of the window.

Being a bachelor, confirmed or otherwise, didn't mean he couldn't create the music love, of course. *Orlando,* to take perhaps his finest masterpiece, contains intensely expressive and dramatic arias of passion in Ariosto's tale of the conflicting demands of love and war complicated by a heart-rending love triangle.

*

JOHANN SEBASTIAN BACH
BORN: EISENACH, 21ST MARCH 1685
DIED: LEIPZIG, 28TH JULY 1750

Quick darling, we've just got time while the ink dries. [Anon]

*

Never as popular in his own time as Telemann or Handel — or, even, Johann Adolf Hasse, whose music is rarely if ever now heard — Bach was the greatest composer-intellectual of all time. But sometimes works like *The Art of Fugue*, fashioned in counterpoint of mind-blowing complexity and cohesion, lead us to forget how passionate a man Bach was; passionate in his devotion to God (he had a large Lutheran library) and in his expression of it through his music. He was also passionate (and often frustrated) in his pursuit of quality in every aspect of musical performance, be it the proper resources needed for competent players and singers or the construction and maintenance of fine church organs. Being wilful, contentious, stubborn and volatile, as his bullish portraits suggest, Bach was also passionate in his confrontations with the secular and ecclesiastical authorities who stood in his way. To his own detriment, he didn't have Telemann's knack of getting his own way nor Handel's worldly wisdom.

In the tradition of his assiduously fertile forbears, Bach was also clearly passionate with his two successive wives, fathering in his walnut beds the largest family by far of any great composer. There was a total of 19 children (or was it 20?), of whom only ten survived childhood, and nine survived the composer himself. No one has ever dared to suggest that he was even tempted to have a fling.

The first hint of a woman in his life comes when he was in trouble, as was to become his wont, with the church authorities during his first appointment as organist and choirmaster at Arnstadt (1703-07). Besides incorporating "surprising variations" and "irrelevant ornaments" into the hymns and committing sundry other crimes of commission and omission (he was never cut out for nor keen on humdrum schoolmasterly duties), Bach had to explain, in 1706, "by what right he recently caused the strange maiden to be invited into the organ loft and let her make music there". This maiden was probably his orphaned second cousin Maria Barbara, with whom he, also orphaned, had lived for a time with a mutual relative in Arnstadt. The cousins were married on October 17th of the following year in Dornheim by a friend of the family, Pastor Stauber, a few months after Bach had taken up a new job at St Blaise's, Mühlhausen. Bach was 22 and Maria Barbara a year younger.

Their marriage seems to have been very contented; perhaps it was especially so from 1717 when Bach embarked on what was surely the happiest period of his professional life in the service of the musically very accomplished Prince Leopold at the court of Cöthen, established in a huge turreted castle on a hill overlooking the small town. Well paid, with minimal duties to perform in the Calvinist church and a 17-piece band with eight virtuosos at his disposal, he composed the bulk of his instrumental music. By then Maria Barbara had borne him six children (two of whom, twin girls, had died) during his previous spell as court organist and choirmaster at the court of Weimar (1708-17). Bach's Weimar years, which he had ended with a month's imprisonment "for too obstinately requesting his dismissal", had also been musically very productive, especially in organ compositions.

Alas, in July 1720 the idyll was shattered. He arrived back from Carlsbad, where he and five other musicians had accompanied Prince Leopold for music making during the summer holidays, to find Maria Barbara dead and buried. He was left with four children: Catharine Dorothea, Wilhelm Friedmann, Carl Philipp Emmanuel (to whom Telemann was godfather) and Johann Gottfried.

With the eldest child only 12 and the youngest five, with floors (and ears) to be scrubbed, meals to be cooked, clothes to be darned and washing to pummelled and hung out, there was little time for extended mourning, and even less for grief counselling. After 18 months, Bach married the singer Anna Magdalena Wilcken, daughter of the court trumpeter of Prince Saxe-Weissenfels. She was then just 20, Bach 36. The Prince saved Bach 10 thalers by allowing him to marry in his own lodgings. He also boosted the Bach finances by giving Anna Magdalena a job as court singer at half her husband's salary. (Those were the days, when singers weren't always paid through the nose because they had a benevolent throat disease!) Records even tell us that feeling flush with all this money, Bach nipped down on two occasions to the local off licence and bought some cut-price booze: altogether three firkins of Rhine wine on special offer at 27 groschen instead of 32 groschen per gallon. Such is the nitty gritty of domestic life, and also of great art.

Again Bach struck very lucky. With him being irascible and Magdalena being no doormat, there must have been a few sparks flying, but that is always to the good. What real man or woman ever wanted an angel for a spouse?

That they were clearly deeply devoted to each other is shown in the two notebooks they compiled together. They completed the first, the *Clavierbüchlein,* ("A Little Clavier Book for Anna Magdalena") in 1722. The second much longer book was finished in 1725. It contains an amusing poem, possibly by Bach, linking a man's pipe and pipe smoking to his mortality. There is also a beautiful quintrain linking his love of his wife with his love of God and readiness for death:

If thou be near, I go rejoicing
To peace and rest beyond the skies,
Nor will fear what may befall me,
For I will hear thy sweet voice call me,
Thy gentle hand will close my eyes.

Also for Anna Magdalena were three versions of his tune to one of his favourite hymns, by the poet Paul Gerhardt: "Fear not, my soul, on God rely".

The spirit of family togetherness in this same second book continues with pieces written by Magdalena — marches, polonaises and minuets — for their children's keyboard and dancing lessons. On a different plane, Bach's French and English keyboard suites are also included.

The glorious lustre over musical life at Cöthen was sullied when Prince Leopold married a flibbertigibbet (according to David Mason Greene, and very probably Bach also) who resented his friendship and music making with the composer. In any case, Bach was almost certainly feeling strongly moved to compose again for the church, and he was eventually appointed (*faute de mieux,* as is very well known) to the post as Kantor St Thomasschule, Leipzig in 1723. This meant the end of Anna Magdalena's singing career, of course, since women were prohibited from church solo work. It also meant the beginning of years of irksome ructions with the church, civic and university authorities. Bach regarded the move from Kapellmeister to Kantor as a demotion — no wonder, as it involved teaching Latin as well as directing the church music.

There are very few further intimate glimpses of the Bach household, though of course they were doing more than their bit towards the survival of the human species by producing a total of 13 children, of whom only six were to survive childhood. Apart from that it was, of course, mainly a case of work, work, and more work, and Bach's supreme masterpieces from the Leipzig years are too well known to need repeating here — except, perhaps, to say that purely for me the *St Matthew* and the *St John Passions* are the two most moving choral works in the entire repertoire of music.

However, we do know that in 1739 one of their lodgers, a nephew of Bach named Johann Elias Bach, who acted as his private secretary and tutor to the young children, obtained for Anna Magdalena a singing linnet (from a certain Cantor Hiller) which she was able to train to sing; and that a family friend Mr. von Mayer sent the lady of the house a present of six carnations, which she valued "more highly than children do their Christmas presents and tends ... with such care as is usually given to children, lest a single one wither". Anna Magdalena may have been only semi-literate, since Elias Bach was her amanuensis for these transactions.

Anna Magdalena did not enjoy good health in her 40s but survived her husband by ten years. Undoubtedly the most agonising experiences for both of them during their final year together were the barbarous operations performed on Bach's eyes by the English physician John Taylor, who later operated on Handel. Apparently the routine was to force half a gallon of some anaesthetising or inebriating liquor down the patient's throat, strap him to the dining table by the wrists and ankles with leather belts, and then leave him to the mercy of the surgeon's lancet. The two horrific operations on Bach were unsuccessful and led to further complications. By July 22nd, 1750 he was perforce receiving communion in his own home, and died six days later in the wake of a massive stroke.

Amazingly, Bach left no will and his modest estate (total value 1,122 thalers 22 groschen comprising securities, cash, silver vessels, eight harpsichords, two lute-harpsichords, ten stringed instruments including a Stainer violin, a lute and a spinet) was divided up between the nine surviving children and Anna Magdalena. She was left at first with two young daughters, a halfwit son and a spinster stepdaughter from the earlier marriage. Anna Magdalena died, a frail old woman, on a pallet of straw in a garret in 1760, with nothing more than a few clothes and kitchen utensils to her name — and her husband's music. In some cases, the only manuscripts of Bach's music which survive are in her firm and hurried hand — the unaccompanied cello suites for example. She was buried in a pauper's grave at a cost to the city of two thalers and 14 groschen.

***

CHAPTER 4

THE AMOROUS HAYDN

"... A NOTORIOUS WOMANISER IN HIS YOUTH."
[H.C. Robbins Landon]

BORN: ROHRAU, (LOWER AUSTRIA) 31ST MARCH 1732
DIED: VIENNA, 31ST MAY 1809

Oh! my dear Polzelli: you are always in my heart and I shall never, never forget you. ... Actually I ought to be a little annoyed with you, because people wrote me from Vienna that you had said the worst possible things about me, but God bless you, I forgive you everything, for I know you said it in love.
[Haydn to his ex-mistress Luigia Polzelli, January 14th, 1792]

... my heart was and is full of TENDERNESS for you, but no language can express HALF THE LOVE and AFFECTION I feel for you, you are DEARER to me EVERY DAY of my life ... I shall be very happy to see you on Sunday any time convenient to you after one o'clock — I hope to see you my D'L on tuesday as usual to Dinner, [crossed out: "and all (?night ?p.m.) with me"] ...
[Letters from Rebecca Schroeter to Haydn in March and June 1792]

When the conversation fell on that excellent work, The Creation, which we had heard yesterday, she said: 'People say it's supposed to be good, I wouldn't know.' We gathered from the old lady's words that she was neither educated nor musical. They say in Vienna that Haydn's rather unhappy and childless marriage is the reason he composed so much. Haydn came, and his wife trotted off with her dogs and cats ...
[The musician Berwald recalling a meeting with Haydn's wife Maria Anna in 1799]

*

Attractive young women quite often fall for older men, some-times much older, though rarely when they are the bin man, the caretaker, or the man from the parks department. These ordinary mortals must pay on the nail for their final fantasy flings, often with junkie-whores in very seedy surroundings. The 74-year-old Elgar, for instance, would never have got anywhere, as he undoubtedly did, with the attractive young violinist Vera Hockmann if he had been the orchestral porter, or even a colleague sitting alongside her, instead of the conductor of his own work *(Gerontius)* in Croydon in November 1930. The crucial aphrodisiacs in older men for nubile young ladies seem to be charisma, kudos and clout.

The folklore of music colleges and orchestras across the globe is redolent with tales of love and lust between professor and pupil, conductor and conducted, leader and led, fixer and fixed. One mature and distinguished piano professor once confessed to me that instead of putting one of his young stars through her paces with Czerny and Chopin, they spent her lessons for a twelvemonth spread-eagled over his piano stool in an insatiable frenzy of passion. Once, in a tiny gem of a pub somewhere in the English Midlands after a Verdi *Requiem,* I was discussing with a perky young violinist the renowned generosity of an eminent professor of violin who, it seemed, was only too eager to give his pupils free extra lessons. "Well, all I have to say is that he's very generous with his willy," came her prompt reply.

A few summers ago, many of my friends in one band were amused by the sudden solicitousness of the leader, an indefatigable plodder in every running of the Casanova Handicap, in escorting home a pretty, talented newcomer to the back desk of firsts. It soon got around that during the three-week season, leader and led were taking regular rest stops in a lay-by on the way home to admire the twinkling city lights far below. After these down-payment quickies, the young lady was duly rewarded with a début in a Vivaldi double concerto in an out-of-town date — I forget where. We always wondered what his dazzling chat-up line could be, and the hapless young lady, chastened by her experience, eventually let the cat out of the bag:

> I find the chemistry of our relationship is right, so I'd like to take it
> a stage further.

And that, evidently, was that.

*

In spite of its unhealthy, marshy climate and bitter winds, the chance of working at the fairy tale castle of Esterháza, (on the edge of the Neusiedlersee, just inside Hungary and some 30 miles southeast of Vienna), in the later part of the 18th-century must have been a godsend for almost any musician, but particularly for the ageing fiddler Signor Antonio Polzelli and his 19-year-old wife Signora Luigia, a very attractive but undoubtedly mediocre mezzo-soprano. 'Papa' Haydn, then the most renowned composer throughout Europe, was a kind, patient and mainly easy-going Kapellmeister, employment was relatively secure and well paid, and Prince Nicolaus I was a musically talented and appreciative, if sometimes demanding patron and connoisseur.

The impact which Esterháza must have made on all new vocal and orchestral recruits from 1766 onwards, when the court transferred there from Eisenstadt for the long summer seasons, must have been overwhelming. The splendour and opulence of the buildings and contents (over 400 clocks, for example, many richly set in diamonds) and the roster of musical, theatrical and festive events must have stunned not only the raw young recruits but also the most hardened pros. In addition to the main castle building of 126 rooms, there was an opera theatre seating 400, the royal box being supported by red marble Roman columns decorated with golden rods; also a marionette theatre, a Chinese pavilion, a coffee house, a temple each to Fortune and Venus, a rose garden, a menagerie and a princely hunting lodge. Second only to Versailles in magnificence, Esterháza cost some 13 million gulden.

For the musicians there was not only the bread-and-butter work of operas, church music, and the twice-weekly afternoon chamber orchestral concerts in which they were contracted to appear "neatly in white stockings, white linen, powdered, and with either pigtail or hair-bag, but otherwise of identical appearance". They were also involved in state visits, illuminations, balls, masquerades, marionette performances, fireworks, and probably even the vast crowd scenes with 2,000 peasants swinging banners and singing their national folk songs.

Although the musicians sometimes felt overworked and hard done by (to wit, the famous *Farewell* Symphony), Robbins Landon's enchanting chronicles show that the working atmosphere was usually very congenial and satisfying; not least because Haydn was ever at pains to give his best players the opportunity to shine in concertos and orchestral solos. Equally if not even more important, the prince himself, adept on the cello and baryton, frequently showed his appreciation of their work by laying on post-concert binges and sometimes even handing out bonuses in cash or kind. After an opera in 1764 that must have particularly pleased the prince, each player received a present of "six bottles of white wine, one bottle of vermouth, two of champagne, one of Cyprus, half-a-bottle of muscat, three of Tokay and 26 bottles of officer's wine". Good money and plenty of booze were ever the best ways of keeping musicians happy. (Apparently the average consumption of wine in late 18th-century Vienna was about half a gallon a day.)

La Polzelli

She was quite clearly always in his mind in his music in the 1780s, and especially in Op. 33. [H.C. Robbins Landon]

There seems to be some doubt about Luigia's Polzelli's age — 19 or 29? — when she and her husband arrived at Esterháza in March 1779 but I definitely prefer the later birth date; not only because it makes a much juicier story, but also because even the kindly Haydn would hardly have written to her or any other soprano thus, in a letter from London dated January 14th, 1792, if she were 42 rather than 32:

I am relieved that you are in good health, and that you have found a position in a little theatre; not so much because of the payment but because of the experience.

Antonio and Luigia were both out of work and completely broke when they arrived. They even had to beg for an advance of 55 florins, which was granted and the repayment of which was later waived, on their first salary payment. They were probably taken on as a compromise job lot, just as orchestral fixers nowadays will often book an unequally talented married couple to get two bums on seats for the price of one phone call. The Polzellis were both undoubtedly second raters, their joint earnings being less than half the 1,000 florins paid to Luigia's colleague Matilda Bologna, for instance. Prince Nicolaus was a shrewd judge of talent and did not always accept

Haydn's recommendations of musicians for appointment. He ordered the couple's dismissal on Christmas Day 1780, with two months severance pay. Yet somehow, the Polzellis managed to hang on to their jobs for another ten years until the disbanding of the Kapelle in 1790. Antonio, a consumptive and probably now 70 years old, did not even work most of the time because of ill health.

The answer, of course, is that Signora Polzelli had cast her spell over Haydn, now unhappily married for some 20 years, who had in turn made full use of his remarkable clout to secure the Polzellis' retention. "Let's face it" said a colleague of mine when I was telling him about all this, "Haydn kept her on so he could poke her. What's unusual about that?" In a word, nothing.

There are no portraits of "La" Polzelli, but I would love to see an artist's impression based on the tantalising and graphic details in her passport and on word-of-mouth reports: narrow longish face, dark olive complexion, lively flaming dark brown eyes, chestnut or black eyebrows and hair, medium height, elegant figure. By contrast, her new maestro, however loving and loveable, was no oil painting: short-arsed, dark, with a face pitted from smallpox (as was Mozart's) and a nose disfigured by a polyp. Perhaps to compensate, Papa Haydn was very particular about his regulation dress (colour and cloth varying from summer to winter) of neckbands, waistcoats, dresscoats, breeches, hose and buckled shoes.

It takes very little imagination to picture the rapid transition in the maestro-soubrette relationship from encouraging smiles and fatherly comforting arms round the shoulder to loving looks, lingering caresses and passionate clinches over the harpsichord during their long and intensive coaching sessions. As soon as rehearsals for Anfossi's *Metilde ritrovata* were under way in 1779, Haydn would have immediately realised Luigia's limitations as she tried to cope with Nanina's demanding arias. It's all too easy to imagine the tense, wobbling head, the laboured four-square coloratura and the harsh, flat high notes that go with vocal mediocrity — and then Signora Polzelli's tears and cries of despair about the effects of the cold north winds and the swamplands on her voice. Tactfully cutting short the rehearsal, Papa Haydn would take her on one side and promise to rewrite the part — nothing could be simpler. Better still, he would even write her an aria of his own to insert into Anfossi's — a very common contemporary practice.

It would, of course, then be essential for them to spend many extra hours together, doubtless when the tiresome Frau Haydn was entertaining the clergy to dinner, going over the parts not only of Nanina, but also of her secondary roles in operas by Bianchi, Cimarosa, Paisiello, Salieri, Traetta and many others.

Luigia Polzelli took part in only two of Haydn's own operas, *L'isola disabitata* (Silvia) and *La vera costanza* (Lisetta), her parts being very carefully chosen and expertly tailored to her limited talents: light, ironic and charming, with either slow tempi throughout or with a slow introduction followed by a fast 6/8 in *parlando* style.

In all this highly customised composition Haydn was, of course, following time-honoured traditions of Italian opera composers as well as his own genital itch. Vivaldi, for instance, carefully wrote parts from 1726 onwards (*Farnace*) to suit the strengths and limitations of Anna Giró — whose exact relationship (and her sister Paolina's) with her maestro in holy orders is tantalisingly less well documented than Haydn and Polzelli. Pacini, a collaborator with Rossini, later described how a composer should serve his singers as a tailor his clients "concealing the natural defects of the figure and emphasising its good points". Mozart also made the same point in his letters.

The hoop-breaking, livery-tearing phase of the affair seems to have been in 1781. It has been suggested that the exceptionally joyful mood of the String Quartet in C major (No.3 op.33), with its frisky outer movements and astonishing violin duet in the Trio, particularly exudes Haydn's happiness in love. Robbins Landon has noted amusing evidence of a *ménage à trois,* with Haydn personally collecting and signing for the monthly pay of both the Polzellis in February 1781! One question that has bugged me in this as well as many other musical love affairs is where did they do it? Assuming they didn't tell poor old Antonio to clear off, they couldn't have regularly used either of their married quarters. Perhaps they came to an arrangement with another player or singer, or with a castle official, or built a nest in the instrument cupboard.

The vast disparity in their mental worlds makes it unlikely that their flame of passion would have blazed for more than a year or two. They seem to have settled into one of those perplexing inter-marital arrangements accepted or tolerated by the "injured" parties. Haydn was probably, but not provably, the father of Luigia's second child, Antonio, born in February 1783. He accepted responsibility for the career and welfare not only of Antonio but also that of his elder brother Petrucchio, who later went to London to live with Luigia's sister Theresa Negri, a singer at the Pantheon.

All the other glimpses we have of Haydn and Polzelli come from his letters to her after the disbanding of the Kapelle in 1790. After the death of her husband in the summer of 1791, Luigia clearly gave Haydn a hard time while he was in London, tugging relentlessly at his purse and heart strings:

> Dear Polzelli!   London, 13ᵗʰ December, 1791
> You gave me quite a shock with your last letter, because I thought my letter had gone astray, and also the money with it. I was so upset that I couldn't sleep for three days, until I received your second letter. I hope that you will never again entertain such cruel suspicions of me, for I esteem and love you as I did on the very first day. I am very sorry for you, and it pains me terribly that I can't do more for you. But be patient, perhaps the day will come when I can show you how much I love you. Write soon and let me know how your lodgings are [in Bologna]......
> Meanwhile I am your most sincere Giuseppe Haydn.

By January 1792 Polzelli had found a season's work in the opera house at Piacenza. Haydn recalled and reiterated his intense feelings for her, and even made excuses for her bitchiness:

> I wish you every possible success, in particular a good role and a good teacher, who takes the same pains with you as did your Haydn. ... perhaps I shall never regain the good humour that I used to have when I was with you. Oh! my dear Polzelli: you are always in my heart and I shall never, never forget you. ... Actually I ought to be a little annoyed with you, because people wrote me from Vienna that you had said the worst possible things about me, but God bless you, I forgive you everything, for I know you said it in love. Do preserve your good name, I beg you, and think from time to time about your Haydn, who esteems you and loves you tenderly, and will always be faithful to you ...

Two years later, Polzelli was still pressing him for, and getting considerable sums of money, as is plain in this rather whinging, and maybe even slightly disingenuous letter that Haydn wrote to her from Eisenstadt, between his two London visits:

Dear Polzelli!   June 1793
I hope you will have received the two hundred florins which I sent
via Sig. Buchberg [Puchberg] — and perhaps also the other hundred,
a total of 300 florins; I wish I were able to send you more, but my
income is not large enough to permit it. I beg you to be patient with
a man who up to now has done more than he really could. Remember
what I have given and sent you; why, it's scarcely a year ago that I
gave you six hundred florins! Remember how much your son costs
me, and how much he will cost me until such a day as he is able to
earn his own daily bread. Remember I cannot work so hard as I have
been able to do in the years past, for I am getting old and my
memory is gradually getting less reliable. Remember, finally, that
for this and many other reasons I cannot earn any more than I do,
and that I have no salary other than a pension from my Prince
Nicolaus Esterházy (God rest his soul), and that his pension is barely
sufficient for me to keep body and soul together, particularly in
these critical times ... perhaps – perhaps – I shall see you in Naples.

He had, after all, been raking it in whilst in London and he was planning to go back to make a whole lot more.

There had been many a "perhaps", of course, from Haydn to
Polzelli, but he clearly hadn't the slightest intention of marrying her.
There must have been ever longer inward groans of despair each time
another letter in the familiar handwriting arrived on his breakfast
table squeezing him for more cash and commitment. She even seriously suggested coming to sing in London, but Haydn managed to put
her off with the warning that "the Italian opera has no success at all
now". When his wife died in 1800, Polzelli even extracted a written
promise from him that if he were ever to marry again, he would take
"no other wife than the said Polzelli".

What a relief it must have been when, after sending her further
sums of money, he finally heard that she had remarried and was off
his back. He could with a reasonably clear conscience reduce her
pension in his second will by half, though her final years were sadly
penurious. "The line", says Robbins Landon, "between success/com-
fort and failure/poverty was thin throughout the century, even for
successful musicians, even for the greatest musical genius that the
world has ever known — Mozart." What was true of 18th-century
Austria also applied to early 19th-century Italy, so it is no surprise at
all to learn that the former soubrette and her husband ended their

days in poverty in Kosice, now Kaschau, in Hungary after leaving Cremona in 1820. Luigia died in 1832.

The fiery Polzelli must, of course, have been furious to learn, as she surely would have done from her sister, of Haydn's intense autumnal affair in London with a very rich and beautiful widow of around 60. In the spring and summer of 1792 Rebecca Schroeter was besieging him with adulatory and passionate letters! Luigia would also have been very resentful, had she known of it, of Haydn's devotion to Maria von Genzinger, wife of the Esterháza physician and probably his dearest friend.

*

There are one or two other fascinating glimpses into Haydn's love life before he left for London, and into other goings-on at Esterháza. Also, where on earth did Frau Maria Anna Aloysia Apollonia Haydn, née Kellner, stand with all this infidelity under her nose?

The singers, actors and musicians at Esterháza were away from home for months on end, and therefore as inevitably prone to misbehaviour as touring artists are today. Only Haydn, the leader of the band Tomasini, and the two leading sopranos were allowed married quarters. There was a vast and reassuring chasm at Esterháza between precept and practice, between the strict regulations of the castle ("officials must lead God-fearing lives", "intoxication is the greatest vice") and the "enormous sexual freedom" and heavy drinking that Robbins Landon identifies. Haydn was regularly having to bail out his musicians from all kinds of nonsense, from starting a fire and getting into debt, to a "scandalous brawl" in which a cellist blinded an oboist in one eye! Nothing changes!

Other Robbins Landon snippets include the Castle Inspector Michael Kleinrath carrying on with the bewitching actress Catharina Rössl, seemingly under the nose of her husband, who may therefore well have been involved with someone else! The authorities drew the line, though, when tenor Johann Schilling (who took the leading young lover parts in the operas) attempted to elope with the wife of troupe *prinzipal* Diwald. The punishment was imprisonment, with bread and water every second day!

Haydn had always been a ladies' man ("It's part of the business," he once told his reliable biographer Griesinger) and was ever susceptible to their charms. Here is a delightful vignette from his late 20s, when he was in the service of Count Morzin before joining the Esterházys in 1761:

> He used to like to relate, in later years, how one day he was sitting at the harpsichord, and the beautiful Countess [Princess Maria Anna, Marchesa di Lunati-Visconti] leaned over him in order to see the notes, when her neckerchief came undone. 'It was the first time I had ever seen such a sight; I became confused, my playing faltered, my fingers became glued to the keys. — What is that, Haydn, what are you doing? cried the Countess: most respectfully I answered: But, Countess, who would not be undone at such a sight? '
> [Griesinger]

He seems to have been genuinely surprised at his pulling power, claiming to Dies, another of his early biographers, that he couldn't understand how it happened that in his life he had been loved by many a pretty woman. "They can't have been led to it by my beauty," he added.

He would surely have had a definite interest in a Mlle. Catherine Csech, to whom he left 1,000 gulden in his first will of 1801. Mlle. Csech was a lady-in-waiting to Princess Grassalkovics of Pressburg, and Haydn would have met her during the Esterházy band's extended visit there in 1767. And who was Mlle. Leonore to whom he addressed his Autobiographical Sketch of 1776? And who, in September 1768, was the "lady" whose clothing for a Masquera — "one new lady's domino of glossy taffeta, velvet skirt, and lady's hat of black taffeta" — was issued personally to Haydn?

Not surprisingly, he appears to have applied the same superlatives to more than one woman; later, while in England, Mrs. Tom Shaw was "the loveliest woman I ever saw", and so also was a Mrs. Hodges!

*

The marriage between Haydn and Maria Anna Kellner, which took place in Vienna in 1760, was a non-starter. Haydn made a massive mistake in letting himself be pushed into marrying the sister of the girl of his dreams, Therese Kellner, who entered a nunnery in 1756. Some of Haydn's biographers have had a field day in pointing out Maria Anna's defects — ugly, domineering, unfriendly, spendthrift, totally uneducated, bigoted, frequently inviting clergymen to meals and having many masses said — but she could undoubtedly have been happy with someone else; perhaps with the painter Ludvig Guttenbrunn with whom, Haydn revealed, she had an affair (tit for tat?) when he came to Esterháza in 1770 to paint portraits. What can be said firmly in Maria Anna's favour is that in spite of being slagged off by her husband as "that infernal beast" who "often made me furious", Frau Haydn was totally unvindictive in her will, leaving "my dear husband" her half share in the house, and making him her residuary legatee.

Haydn hinted at their unsatisfactory sex life — "My wife was incapable of having children, *and thus* [my italics] I was less indifferent to the charms of other women" — but the most revealing glimpse of their utter incompatibility comes from a letter of Johan Frederik Berwald. Berwald recalled how as a young touring *wunderkind* he called on Haydn in Vienna, in 1799:

> When we asked if Doctor Haydn was at home, a servant said he was not but that Frau Doctor was in the garden, and showed us there. On a bench sat an old woman, surrounded by some dogs and cats, and when my father said he had learned that the Doctor was not at home she answered in Viennese dialect, 'He ain't in but he'll be back soon'. As to my father's question, if Frau Doctor had been on the trip to England from which he [Haydn] had recently returned, she said: 'No, my husband had enough to do to persuade me to go to the suburbs. I'll never leave my dear Vienna.' When the conversation fell on that excellent work, The Creation, which we had heard yesterday, she said: 'People say it's supposed to be good, I wouldn't know.' — We gathered from the old lady's words that she was neither educated nor musical. They say in Vienna that Haydn's rather unhappy and childless marriage is the reason he composed so much.
> Haydn came, and his wife trotted off with her dogs and cats ....

Enough said!

*

London and Mistress Schroeter

To say that Haydn's emotions were complicated is a mild way of putting it. [Marion M. Scott]

The woman who truly loved and adored Haydn without any thought of what was in it for her was Rebecca Schroeter, perhaps pushing 60 and the widow "of considerable fortune ... in easy circumstances" of the former Master of the King's Musick, Johann Samuel Schroeter. This is yet another of those relationships that blossomed in the intimacy of private tuition and began or recommenced with the following letter:

> Mrs Schroeter presents her compliments to Mr Haydn, and informs him, that she is just returned to town, and will be very happy to see him whenever it is convenient for him to give her a lesson. James str. Buckingham Gate. Wednesday, June 29th, 1791.

In every sense Haydn's two London visits of 1791-92 and 1794 -95, instigated by the impresario Salomon for his famed series of concerts, were the emotional and professional peak of his life, even if also the most exhausting. Never before having travelled more than 30-odd miles from Vienna, he was overawed, from the moment he left Calais for the queasy, turbulent crossing to Dover on New Year's Day 1791, by the vast differences in scenery and lifestyle he encountered. He recorded everything in his London Notebooks, and in letters to his revered friend Maria von Genzinger, with the same pithiness and sense of innocent wonder that make the symphonies so eternally fresh-minted.

He was utterly intrigued by everything: the social whirl, the colossal scale of eating and drinking at posh receptions, royalty, the national economy, the concert scene, the horse races, and perhaps especially by the British craving for large doses of smut and scandal. He noted that when the scandalous life of Madam Billington was published "in the most shameless detail ... you couldn't get a single copy after three o'clock in the afternoon". "It's even believed her own father is involved in this affair," adds the composer, noting that "such stories are common in London. The husband provides opportunities for his wife so that he can profit from it, whereby he relieves his brother-in-law of 1,000 Sterling and more." It all sounds very familiar.

Haydn had to cope not only with his heady social life, which included visits to the blue-bloods and innermost royal circles, but also with a frantic pace of work; this was, after all, his first ever chance to make some real money provided he could keep ahead of the rival concert society called The Professionals. His output was a staggering feat for a man in his 60s: six quartets, 12 symphonies, an opera, a Sinfonia Concertante, a piano sonata, piano trios, military marches and several vocal pieces — a total of 3,000 pages of music, much of it received in an "extasy of admiration".

And, of course, he had to cope with those nagging letters from La Polzelli and also some from his wife! As a man approaching old age, he was perhaps only able to cope with all this because of the adoring attentions of Rebecca Schroeter, or "Mistress Schroeter", as she was later to sign herself in the subscription list for *The Creation.*

After the first "quiver of feeling" in that polite opening letter requesting a lesson, the relationship grew within a few months into a full-blown, sometimes angsty love affair — a case of lingering hands-on tuition at the piano quickly leading to unambiguous business on the Chesterfield and in the four-poster. Here she is writing like a love-sick girl tormented by a lovers' misunderstanding:

> March 7th, 1792.
> My dear: I was extremely sorry to part with you so suddenly last night, our previous conversation was particularly interesting and I had [a] thousand affectionate things to say to you, my heart was and is full of TENDERNESS for you, but no language can express HALF THE LOVE and AFFECTION I feel for you, you are DEARER to me EVERY DAY of my life. ... Oh how earnes[t]ly [I] wish to see you, I hope you will come to me tomorrow. I shall be happy to see you both in the Morning and in the Evening. God Bless you my love, my thoughts and best wishes ever accompany you, and I always am with the most sincere and invariable regard my D: My Dearest I cannot be happy till I see you if you know, do, tell me, when you will come.

I stumbled across a wonderfully intuitive, poetic response to this letter, and its bearing on Haydn's love life at this time, by a lady named Marion M. Scott writing in the *Musical Quarterly* of April 1932. I can do no better than quote it in full:

> The persecution of the Professionals, the newspaper campaign against Haydn, the sight of him reeling beneath his terrible efforts,

must have gone to her heart; the impulse to comfort him grew unbearably strong. He on his part had feared — one sees from the later part of her letter — that she was displeased with him, or had no confidence in him. The situation had been charged to breaking point with feeling. Mistress Schroeter probably knew little of Frau Haydn; she certainly knew nothing of Haydn's relations with the Polzelli. Pathetically she attributed all she could not understand in his behaviour to her own shortcomings and stupidity — and wondered why he had parted "so suddenly last night". So suddenly! To say that Haydn's emotions were complicated is a mild way of putting it. March and April passed at the same high tension ... All through those months Mrs Schroeter continued to write love-letters with an humble adoration that is quite touching ...

Rebecca was ever solicitous, offering her lover comfort by night as well as by day if he wanted it, as is very clear in this next letter written when he had been working flat out for months, often composing for five hours at a stretch:

My D^r I beg to know HOW YOU DO? hope to hear your headache is ENTIRELY GONE, and that you have SLEPT WELL. I shall be very happy to see you on Sunday any time convenient to you after one o'clock — I hope to see you my D^{r}L on tuesday as usual to Dinner, [crossed out: "and all (?night ?p.m.) with me"] ... I long to see you my D^t H, let me have that pleasure as soon as you can, till when and Ever I remain with the FIRMEST attachment My D^r L: most faithfully and affectionately yours [etc.] Friday, June 1st, 1792.

In all there are a score or so of letters from her during the spring and summer of 1792, swooning over his music, and expressing constant concern for his health, sleep and wellbeing — and the wish to see him. Haydn didn't disappoint her. "If he was not invited elsewhere he usually dined with her," says Griesinger.

There are no letters from Haydn's second London visit in 1794 to 1795, probably because his new lodgings in Bury Street were a mere ten minutes walk via St James's Palace, The Mall and St James's Park to her place at Buckingham Gate.

Haydn's tender affection for Rebecca Schroeter is immortalised in the second set of piano trios which he dedicated to her in 1796, and which include the famous Gypsy Rondo. One of her favourite symphonies was No.102, and Haydn adapted the lovely slow movement of it for the Trio No. 40 in F sharp minor — a farewell tribute to Rebecca and to England. Yet another case of love being the food of music.

It is an open question whether he would have married Rebecca Schroeter if he could. He loved Vienna more than London, and he may have been reminiscing from a safe distance when he later said to Dies, on coming across a pile of her letters:

> Letters from an English widow in London, who loved me; but she was, although already sixty years old, still a beautiful and charming woman and I would have married her very easily if I had been free at the time.

*

Maria von Genzinger — "Nobly Born, Gracious Lady"

Haydn possibly opened his heart to the fullest in his letters to Maria von Genzinger, wife of the Esterháza physician and a talented pianist. Certainly his letters to her express some of his deepest and most personal feelings or impressions about many events: from the "monstrous high waves rushing at us" in "that mighty monster the ocean" during the stormy nine-hour crossing from Calais to Dover, to his exhausted state in London, his "English rheumatism", his wondrous delight at being the guest of the English royalty, his homesickness for Vienna and, perhaps movingly of all, his loneliness in the final years at Esterháza, when his loyalty to Prince Nicolaus overrode his urge to leave.

> ... I beg your grace not to be frightened away from consoling me occasionally by your pleasant letters, for they comfort me in my wilderness, and are highly necessary for my heart, which is so often deeply hurt. Oh! if only I could be with Your Grace for a quarter of an hour, to pour forth all my troubles to you, and to hear all your comforting words. I have to put up with many annoyances from the court here. ...

Haydn wrote a difficult piano sonata for her in 1790 (No. 59 in E flat major) which perhaps in places, suggests David Wyn Jones' hints at his ardent feelings. Are not some of the deepest feelings between men and women experienced when, or perhaps *because* there is no hope of or desire for a physical relationship?

"Oh! how happy I shall be to see Your Grace again," he wrote from London on March 2nd,1792, "to show you how much I missed you and to show the esteem in which, gracious lady, you will ever be held by ... Your most obedient servant, Jos: Haydn." Her death in 1793 at the age of 42 must have broken his heart, and there are no known further women in his life, apart from his faithful cook Nannerl, up to his death in 1809.

*

As an orchestral musician, I prefer playing Haydn and Beethoven to Mozart because the lasting impression is always so positive. In Haydn's case there seems little doubt that the wheelright son's un-complicated and unquestioning Catholic faith underpinned his opti-mism and self sufficiency; not for nothing did he sign off after so many last chords in his scores with *Laus Deo.* "Since God has given me a cheerful heart", he once said, "He will forgive me for serving him cheerfully." And what service! No less than 104 symphonies (the 30 to 40 I've played in have given me my greatest orchestral happiness), dances, cassations, divertimentos, 83 string quartets, 52 piano sona-tas, 20 concertos, much miscellaneous chamber music, 23 operas, many songs, four oratorios, many masses and other choral works — most of them completed during his 30-year stint at Esterháza.

The lovers in Haydn's life were therefore a bonus; his creative output did not essentially depend on their emotional support as was so often the case with other men. Had Haydn experienced no relief at all from his unhappy marriage, all the uplifting music would probably still be there, if not quite in the way it is.

However, his women undoubtedly provided him with a won-derful creative boost; Luigia Polzelli with her *élan vital* during the their first full flush of passion; Rebecca Schroeter with unconditional love and lots of good dinners during a period of intense activity; and Maria von Genzinger with the kind of supportive friendship that only women, it seems, are really capable of giving.

***

CHAPTER 5

WOLFGANG AMADEUS MOZART

"I WRITE AS THE SOWS PISS."

BORN: SALZBURG, 27TH JANUARY 1756
DIED: VIENNA, 5TH DECEMBER 1791

... a remarkably small man, very thin and pale, with a profusion
of fine fair hair, of which he was rather vain.
[The tenor Michael Kelly on Mozart in his late 20s]

O Stru! Stri! I kiss and squeeze you 1095060437082 times (now you
can practise your pronunciation) and am ever your most faithful
husband and friend.
[Mozart writing to his wife Constanze, April 16th, 1789]

Mozart would not take pains in giving lessons to any ladies but
those he was in love with ...
He was always in love with his pupils ...
[Joseph Henickstein and Constanze to Vincent and Mary Novello
— *Travel Diaries*, 1829]

*

Although there is much scholarly disagreement about the happiness and stability of the later stages of Mozart's marriage, it seems very probable that before it, unlike so many of his illustrious if lesser companions in the Pantheon of the Greats, he did not go whoring around. As a knee-jerk though seemingly pious Catholic in his middle 20s, his overriding reason for wanting to marry Constanze Weber was, in his very own kind of band room babble, to get his end away. Here he is, amazingly, as a lusty young man at the age of nearly 26, pleading for his father's permission to marry so that he can satisfy his craving for legal sex:

But dearest, best father, listen to me! I have been obliged to reveal my [marriage] plans to you, now please permit me to explain my reasons, very well grounded reasons. Nature speaks in me as loudly as in any other man, and perhaps more loudly than in many another big, strong brute. I cannot possibly live the way most young men do nowadays. — First, I am too religious; secondly, I entertain too high a regard for my neighbour, and have too honourable intentions, to allow me to seduce an innocent girl; and thirdly, too much horror and disgust, too much dread and fear of diseases, and too much regard for my health, to fool about with whores; therefore I can swear to you that I've never had anything to do with women of this kind... [December 15th, 1781]

Remember that at the age of 25 Mendelssohn felt he needed his father's approval even to buy a horse!

About three years earlier Mozart had already assured his father that he was "no Brunetti, no Mysliwecek! I am Mozart; and a young and clean-minded Mozart." "That coarse and dirty Brunetti", the leading violinist at Salzburg, and Mysliwecek the Bohemian composer and friend of Mozart had both caught the clap in a big way. When Mozart visited Mysliwecek in October 1777, dying in the Duke Clemens hospital in Munich, he was shocked to confront the combined horrors of severe syphilis and primitive medicine. The Bohemian's room "smelt rather strongly" and "The surgeon Caco, that ass, burnt away his nose. He has a fearful cancer of the bone".

Further evidence, if needed, of Mozart's rather pious and priggish outlook at this period of his life (it was to change markedly) was his extreme reluctance to travel from Mannheim to Paris with his bohemian musician friends the Wendlings in 1778, because they preferred the theatre to the church and one of the daughters had been the mistress of the Elector of Mannheim.

As Mozart's choice of wife, Constanze Weber was, of course, in spite of his written protestations to the contrary, very much a second best to her elder sister Aloisia. It is extremely difficult to dispel the hunch that Mozart saw Constanze as a kind of surrogate for her more glamorous and talented elder sister. He never really kicked his addiction to Aloisia, a fabulous soprano, after she turned him down in December 1778 and there was, she said much later, some inevitable continuing friction between the two sisters. Mozart sublimated his love for Aloisia in a series of stunning concert arias which he composed between 1778 and 1788.

How many other composers have married, as a second best or

surrogate, the sister of the woman they really wanted? Apart from Haydn, who spent his life regretting his marriage to the sister of his beloved Therese who entered a nunnery, there was Dvorak, who married very happily Anna Cermáková, elder sister of his first love Josefina. Come to think of it, how many males through the ages have lusted after their sisters-in-law, especially when younger than their wives? So near, yet so far, especially when on a weekend visit they emerge from the bathroom wrapped in a dressing gown with a turbaned towel round their head.

*

Cousin Maria Anna Thekla
Do go on loving me, as I love you ... [Mozart]

Mozart often bubbled over with spontaneous demonstrations of affection as a child. At the age of six, for instance, dressed in his lilac suit and moiré waistcoat both trimmed with gold braid (he was to have a life-long passion for elegant dress), Mozart jumped up on to the lap of the Austrian Empress, Maria Theresa, "put his arms round her neck and kissed her heartily". He followed this up, of course, with his legendary troth-plight to Maria Theresa's seven-year-old daughter, Marie-Antoinette, the future Queen of France. When Marie-Antoinette picked him up after his tumble on to the polished palace floor Mozart vowed that because she was good he would marry her! Within a few months he began the first of his whirlwind European tours as a grossly exploited *wunderkind*.

The first woman who appears to have touched a quasi-romantic nerve in Mozart was his cousin Maria Anna Thekla, "the Bäsle", for whom he had the most tender affection. They met in 1777 when the 21-year-old Mozart was pausing for a fortnight with his mother in Augsberg en route for Mannheim. It was probably all innocent fun between them but she sparked off some of his flightiest, freakiest and most ribald ever literary fancies:

Ma très chère niece! cousine! mère, soeur, et épouse!
Bless my soul, a thousand curses. Croatians, damnations, devils, witches, sorcerers, hell's battalions to all eternity, by all the elements, air, water, earth, and fire, Europe, Asia, Africa and America, Jesuits,

Augustinians, Benedictines, Capuchins, Minorites, Franciscans, Dominicans, Carthusians and Brothers of the Holy Cross, canons regular and irregular, all slackers, knaves, cowards, sluggards and toadies higgledy-piggledy, asses, buffaloes, oxen, fools, nit-wits and dunces! Such a parcel to get, but no portrait as yet! ...
Forgive my wretched writing, but the pen is already worn to a shred, and I've been shitting, so 'tis said, nigh twenty-two years through the same old hole, which is not yet frayed one whit, though I've used it daily to shit, and each time the muck with my teeth I've bit ...
Je vous baise vos mains, votre visage, vos genoux, et votre — enfin, tout ce que vous me permettez de baiser.

Many other letters from Mozart to Thekla are notorious for their scatological references and lavatorial obsessions (coprolalia). They provide early pointers to the composer's rare genetic condition now defined as Tourette's syndrome — "incontinence of the emotions". Perhaps just one other very mild example in a letter to his father in 1777 will satisfy most readers:

When the sonata is finished I shall send it to you and the letter as well ... Now I must tell you of a sad thing which has just happened this very moment. As I was doing my best to write this letter, I heard something on the street. I stopped writing — I got up — went to the window ... and ... the sound ceased. I sat down again, started off again to write — but I had hardly written ten words when again I heard something. I got up again — As I did, I again heard a sound, this time quite faint — but I seemed to smell something slightly burnt — and wherever I went, it smelt. When I looked out of the window, the smell disappeared. When I looked back into the room, I again noticed it. In the end mamma said to me: "I bet you have let off one." "I don't think so, Mamma," I replied. "Well, I am certain that you have," she insisted. Well, I thought, "Let's see," put my finger to my arse and then to my nose and — Ecce, provatum est. Mamma was right after all. Well, farewell. I kiss you 1000 times and remain, as always, your little old piggy wiggy.
WOLFGANG AMADÉ ROSY POSY.
A thousand compliments from us two travellers to my aunt and uncle. My greetings bleatings to all my good friends sends. Addio, booby looby.
333 to the grave, if my life I save,
Miehnnam, Rebotco eht [ht]5, 7771.

In the same year Mozart confessed to his father that whilst fraternising with the musicians of the Mannheim court he had recited rhymes "on muck, shitting and arse-licking". And he even enjoyed composing canons to vulgar texts, such as *Leck mich im Arsch* (Lick My Arse) K231.

Why is it that farting and all the rest holds such mesmeric appeal for musicians? I have witnessed and (it must be admitted) participated in scores of impromptu band room farting contests initiated perhaps by a trombonist or a flautist. Is it because the route to the divine is so utterly down-to-earth? — dodgy reeds, flawed mouthpieces, sticking valves, trapped water, sliding spikes, slipping pegs, fraying strings, sticky fingerboards, cracked ribs and all the rest; not to mention the purlies (stage fright), the pain-in-the-arse conductors, mealy-mouthed managers, countless cock-ups and empty coffers which have been the very fabric of British orchestral life for so long?

The only section that turns down its noses at such childish vulgarity is the bassoons. But then, they have to spend thousands of pounds and years of practice on expensive instruments to obtain effects their colleagues can produce effortlessly and abundantly for the price of a prawn dhansak.

Mozart's letters, of course, are intensely absorbing, sometimes as exhilarating as the music, and reveal the utterly human being which housed the godhead; they are full of sparky, racy, sometimes outrageous anecdotes and comments, sometimes in ciphers, codes and secret tongues, on all the practicalities of making a living as a musician: bum-soring post-chaise journeys, hall-hire costs, subscriptions, bent copyists, skinflint bosses, aging singers and musicians, divine divas, applause, honour and glory, hissing and booing, practical jokes, hanky panky ...

*

Aloisia Lange née Weber

I was mad about Aloisia Lange, that's true, but what doesn't one do when one is in love? — I really loved her, and she is still not a matter of indifference to me — so it's a good thing for me that her husband is madly jealous and doesn't allow her to circulate, so I only rarely see her ... [Mozart to his father 16th May, 1781, well over two years after Aloisia had turned him down]

The 21-year-old Mozart dissolved into a puddle when his eyes and ears first encountered the 17-year-old singer Aloisia Weber, daughter of Fridolin and Cäcilia Weber in the late autumn of 1777 in Mannheim. Mozart and his mother had arrived there from Augsberg on their travels through Southern Germany in search of work.

Not only was Aloisia heavenly to look at; she was also a knockout soprano. Her father Fridolin Weber (uncle of the Carl Maria Weber many people know — *Invitation to the Dance, Der Freischütz* and *Oberon* especially) was a prompter, bass singer and copyist at the Mannehim court of Prince Karl Theodor. The moonstruck Mozart was desperate to clinch an appointment there. With a string of brilliant performances and increasingly impressive compositions under his belt in almost every genre — symphonies, concertos, operas, ballets, chamber music and sacred music — this ought to have been possible but didn't happen. His father Leopold's plan was therefore to urge his son on to Paris as quickly as possible, suitably forewarned against the evils of Parisian women, serpents and wallet-vampires all.

Leopold Mozart was ever the apotheosis of prudence and painstaking planning, and when, back in Salzburg, he sniffed the first whiffs of romance and even matrimony in his son's letters he almost popped his clogs. Each heavy hint in successive letters was another thrombobuster: "[Fridolin Weber] has a daughter who sings admirably and has a lovely pure voice," Mozart wrote in January 1778; "she is only 15 [she was 17, in fact] ... the girl is persecuted with attentions ... She sings most excellently my aria for De Amicis, with those horribly difficult passages, and she is to sing it at Kirchheim-Bolanden."

Mozart went there with Aloisia to perform for Princess Caroline of Orange, where she not only sang 13 of his songs but also played some of his piano sonatas which even he himself found difficult.

"As far as her singing is concerned," Mozart wrote on February 4th, 1778, "I would wager my life that she will bring me renown. Even in a short time she has profited by my instruction ... The thought of helping a poor family, without injury to myself, delights my very soul." Mozart was now proposing to accompany Aloisia and her elder sister Josefa, also a fine soprano, to Italy with their father. The party could even drop by in Salzburg since he was sure that Nannerl, his sister, would "find a friend and companion" in Aloisia. Indeed, the whole family resembled the Mozarts. "I have nothing to worry about; I found my torn clothes mended; in short, I was waited on like a prince." Verily the sun was shining brightly out of all the Weberian arses!

In a post script, Mozart's mother Anna Maria compounded her husband's distress: "You will have seen," she wrote to Leopold, "that when Wolfgang makes new acquaintances, he immediately wants to cede his life and property to them."

Horrified by his son's infatuation and hare-brained schemes, Leopold stayed up all night before responding on February 11th. No German prima donna, he pointed out, could possibly launch herself in Italy before first making her mark nearer home. "As for your proposal (I can scarcely write when I think of it)... it has nearly put me out of my mind ... Your letter reads like a romance ... Off with you to Paris." (Leopold's concern for his son's career was by no means entirely altruistic, incidentally; he was also trying to guarantee security for his own old age, even though he must have stashed away a good many thousand gulden netted from the *wunderkind* tours. In fact many of the pressures and vetoes that Leopold piled on his son in letters often whinging, demanding, recriminatory and guilt-inducing, were self-ishly motivated.)

Leopold was hardly encouraged by more correspondence from his son praising Aloisia's taste and technique in portamento, and hinting that he would be asking his father for "a great favour". Aloisia had even knitted her admirer "two pairs of mittens in filet ... as a remembrance and a small token of her gratitude".

Leopold was to remain unmoved — "All young people have to bang their heads against the wall" — and to become ever more sus-picious of all the Webers. "Herr Weber is a man like most of his kind ... He flattered you when he needed you."

Under constant pressure from both father and mother Mozart finally tore himself away from Mannheim after a stay of four and a half months, but the Aloisia bug didn't go away. From Paris he confided his thoughts to the Abbé Bullinger (a lifelong trusted friend of the Mozart family) on "a request on which the whole happiness and peace of my life depend". However, plans to have Aloisia come to the capital to sing foundered on his own marked lack of success there.

On July 3rd Mozart's mother died after a relatively short illness.

In mid-September, having turned down the offer of a lucrative post as court organist at Versailles, Mozart set out for home, taking his time and, inevitably, paying another visit to the Webers. He finally rejoined them on Christmas Day 1778 in Munich, where Aloisia was now a well-paid prima donna in the court opera. Alas, the hapless suitor, dressed in his red mourning coat with black buttons, had a very nasty shock when he found Aloisia in a room with other people. "She seemed ... not to know him any more." With a sense of occasion even in acute distress Mozart sat down at the piano and, with a "heart full of tears" sang "I'll gladly leave the girl who doesn't love me any more". (So wrote one of Mozart's early biographers Georg Nissen, of whom more shortly. Maynard Solomon has pointed out that what Mozart actually sang was a traditional verse "The one who doesn't want me can lick my arse"!)

"Today," wrote a heartbroken Mozart to his father on December 29th, 1778, "I can only weep. I have far too sensitive a heart. ... A Happy New Year! I cannot manage anything more today." For the time being only, Leopold Mozart's worries were over.

*

The seven magnificent arias Mozart wrote for Aloisia between 1778 and 1788 speak volumes about what she really meant to him first as suitor and then as mentor. The first, *Alcandro, lo confesso* (Alcandro I confess it) K294, written in the first full flush of adoration at Mannheim, expresses the conflicting emotions of a woman's awakened love. It is a heavenly vocal stream of iridescent cascades tumbling over glistening rocks, bubbling pools and limpid shallows, and shows off Aloisia's spectacular vocal range — reaching a high E flat (two octaves plus above middle C) in the final climactic phrase.

Mozart was demonstrably enthralled by this ravishing singer! And what about the very last aria for Aloisia, ten years later, when he had been married to Constanze for nearly six years? Partly a revision of earlier versions, *Ah se in ciel, benigne stelle* (Friendly stars, if yet in Heaven) K538 is about a lovelorn girl invoking protection for a pure affection. The coloratura voice line is breathtaking in its melodic radiance and agility. Aloisia was surely not fantasising when she told Vincent and Mary Novello some 40 years on that Mozart never stopped loving her and that she had made a mistake in refusing him.

> She [Aloisia] seems a very pleasant woman but broken by misfortune — she is parted from her husband who allows her so little that she is obliged to give lessons which at her age she finds a great hardship ... She told me that Mozart always loved her until the day of his death, which to speak candidly she fears has occasioned a slight jealousy on the part of her sister. I asked her why she refused him; she could not tell; the fathers were both agreed but she could not love him at the time. She was not capable of appreciating his talent and his amiable character, but afterwards she much regretted it. She spoke of him with great tenderness and regret.
> [Novellos' *Travel Diaries*, 1829]

In October 1780 Aloisia, now 20, married 29-year-old Joseph Lange, a fine actor and portrait painter, divorced with three children. Frau Weber, by then widowed, had used husband-nailing tactics with Lange as hard-headed as those she was to use with Mozart himself. With Aloisia becoming pregnant before the wedding, Frau Cäcilia had obliged Lange to sign a document guaranteeing her, the mother, an annual income for life of 700 gulden and obliging him to repay an advance on salary of 900 gulden which Aloisia had received from the Vienna Court Theatre in 1779.

The Langes parted company in 1795 and Joseph had a further three children by his chamber maid, who had doubtless already been delivering more than breakfast in bed. Constanze considered Lange's portrait of Mozart, albeit unfinished, to be her husband's best likeness.

*

Constanze and the other women, if there were any

> She [Frau Cäcilia Weber] should be put in chains, made to sweep streets and have boards hung round her neck with the words "seducer of youth". [Leopold Mozart]

> "God greet you, Stanzerl! God greet you, God greet you; — little rascal; — pussy-kitty; — little turned-up nose — little bagatelle — schluck und druck!". [Mozart writing to Constanze]

Following their notorious quarrel, the impudent and hot-headed 25-year-old Mozart was quite literally booted out of the service of Archbishop Colloredo of Salzburg on June 8th, 1781. Mozart had been in the Archbishop's service as Konzertmeister and Court Organist since his return to Salzburg (after visiting the Webers) early in 1779. Constantly riled by his servant status and intensely frustrated by the lack of career opportunities in Salzburg, Mozart had really been spoiling for a final showdown for some time though the decisive boot must have been traumatic for the ever cautious Leopold. Leopold himself was no creep but believed in accepting and exploiting rather than fighting the patronage system: knuckle under, lick their arses and go for all you can get. His son's position, born of supreme confidence in his own creative powers, was radically different: "I shit on both," he wrote later of both the Archbishop and the city of Salzburg itself. Mozart's insolence to the Archbishop marked the first open rebellion of a musician in feudal society.

Mozart launched his career as an independent freelance from the room he rented from the now-widowed Frau Cäcilia Weber and her three remaining unmarried daughters Josefa, Constanze and Sophie in their apartment *Zum Auge Gottes* (The Eye of God) in St Peter's Square, Vienna. The Webers had moved there from Munich, and Aloisia, of course, was now married and had just given birth to her first child.

Frau Cäcilia Weber now once again became a canny husband stalker, this time on behalf of her third daughter Constanze. Becoming more successful as a player and composer by the day, Mozart was well worth trapping, but there is absolutely no question that he was a willing victim.

By July 1781 Leopold Mozart was once again having sleepless nights. Already horrified by his son's suicidal severance from court service, he was getting alarming rumours about his son and those wretched Webers.

Mozart wrote on the 27th to say that people were gossiping about his having fun and fooling around with Constanze, and that Frau Weber thought it best if he took lodgings elsewhere. He assured his father that there was absolutely nothing in it; after all, "If I had to marry all those with whom I had jested, I should have two hundred wives at least."

So much for jesting. Five months later in December Mozart was writing on the 15th to say (in the letter quoted at the beginning) that he wanted to marry Constanze; primarily to have legal sex, but also because he needed a wife to sort out his clothes and to save "many useless expenses". "A bachelor," he continued, "in my opinion, is only half alive." Then came his appraisal of the Weber daughters. The eldest, Josefa, is "a lazy, gross, perfidious woman, and as cunning as a fox". Next, perhaps still smarting from rejection three and a half years earlier, he writes off Aloisia as "a false, malicious person and a coquette", thus confirming the commonality of love and hate. The youngest, Sophie, is dismissed as too young and feather-headed, and then comes his choice, the middle one Constanze. He assesses her as though for a menial domestic position or perhaps a walk-on part:

> She is not ugly, but at the same time far from beautiful. Her whole beauty consists in two little black eyes and a pretty figure. She has no wit, but she has enough common sense to fulfil her duties as a wife and mother ... I love her and she loves me with all her heart.

By now, however, Mozart had definitely gone off Frau Weber — for the time being. "I could fill whole sheets with descriptions of all the scenes that I have witnessed in that house." Elsewhere, he commented scathingly on the mother's drinking habits and her attempts to get her daughters to drink wine instead of water.

A week later Leopold learned that Frau Weber had made his son sign another of those "heads we win tails you lose" engagement contracts whereby he had to pay Constanze 300 guilden a year for life if he backed out of marriage! To her credit Constanze tore it up, but as far as Leopold was concerned, Mozart was well and truly hooked, a turkey voting for Christmas. To Leopold, being in love was "an act of madness". His worst fears had come true and he must have seethed with rage and frustration.

It was to be only after almost nine months of repeated wearing down that Leopold was to give his grudging consent to the marriage. Is there any parallel in the history of music of a musician in his middle twenties going to such staggering lengths to obtain paternal consent to his marriage? Of a father so determined, for whatever complex and deep-rooted reasons, to resist his son's growth towards an autonomous existence?

The attempted winning over of Leopold (and also Nannerl, Mozart's older sister by five years and a brilliantly gifted keyboard player) proceeded relentlessly and artfully. Mozart sent not only some of his new compositions and accounts of his successes but also, in March 1782, a snuff box and some very fashionable watch ribbons. Constanze joined in by passing on her "devoted greetings" and enclosing for her putative sister-in-law "two caps in the latest Viennese fashion", together with a "little cross" and a "little heart pierced by an arrow". In April Constanze took the very rare step of putting a very halting pen to paper herself, adding a note for Nannerl at the bottom of one of her fiancé's letters. In early May Mozart was again offering on Constanze's behalf to send Nannerl some Viennese haberdashery: this time it was fringes in her preferred fabrics — Saxon piqué, satins and silks — and colours — "white, black, green, blue, puce etc". Constanze even appended a note to Leopold.

All this cut no ice and in fact Leopold wrote no letters at all to his son for almost three months from the end of April.

The course of true love, if such it could be called, didn't always run smoothly. Not only was Constanze chippy, in the typically Viennese way; she called off the engagement no less than three times. Here is Mozart getting very pompous and steamed up about some chap measuring her calves in a game of forfeits:

> I entreat you, therefore, to ponder and reflect upon the cause of all this unpleasantness, which arose from my being annoyed that you were so impudently inconsiderate as to say to your sisters — and, be it noted, in my presence — that you had let a young man measure the calves of your legs. No woman who cares for her honour can do such a thing ... if it was quite impossible for you to resist the desire to take part in the game...then why, in the name of heaven, did you not take the ribbon and measure your own calves yourself (as *all self-respecting women* have done on similar occasions in my presence) and not allow a chapeau [young man] to do so? ... Why, I myself *in the presence of others* would never have done such a thing to you. I should have handed you the ribbon myself. Still less, then, should you have allowed it to be done by a stranger ...

Perhaps it's worth noting, with a big pinch of salt, that Mozart's acquaintance the violinist and composer Peter von Winter put it about that Constanze was a slut (*Luder* was the word, which also means whore). Winter also tried to persuade Mozart to take a mistress instead of marrying for the sake of "that little bit of dirt called religion". Mozart reacted with "rage and fury" to Winter's "disgraceful lies".

However the engaged couple kissed and made up and Mozart continued to bombard his father with pleas for his consent. His letter to Leopold on July 27th approaches the climax of what was now a major crisis, with the couple being "tormented to death" by pressure from Frau Weber and gossip on all sides. "My heart is restless, and my head is confused; and in such a condition how can one think and work to any good purpose?" he pleaded. "Most beloved father, I am longing to have your consent. I feel sure that you will give it, for my honour and my reputation depend on it. Do not postpone too long the joy of embracing your son and wife. I kiss your hands a thousand times and am ever your obedient son ... ."

Frau Weber was now pressing relentlessly and Mozart finally took the bull by the horns. On July 31st he told his father tactfully but firmly that "All that you have written on the subject can only be *well-meaning advice* which, however fine and good it may be, is no longer applicable to a man who has gone so far with a girl. In such a case, nothing can be postponed."

Frau Weber then struck the final blow. Wrongly suspecting that Mozart was interested only in bedding and not wedding her daughter, Cäcilia Weber threatened to have the police, no less, fetch Constanze from the apartment of the couple's good friend, Baroness von Waldstädten, where Constanze had taken refuge for the second time since the engagement — either to escape from her mother's clutches, or perhaps, so that she and her fiancé could enjoy a spot of premarital nookie.

Frau Weber's ploy was immediately effective and on August 4th 1782 Maria Constanze Weber married Wolfgang Amadeus Mozart in St Stephen's Cathedral — where Vivaldi's funeral had been conducted and where Haydn had been a choirboy.

Not surprisingly, after all these months of angst and frustration there were tears of relief all round. Writing to his father after finally receiving on the day after the wedding grudging permission to marry, Mozart relates that

When we had been joined together, both my wife and I began to weep. — All those present were touched, even the priest. — And all wept to see how much our hearts were moved. Our whole wedding consisted of a souper offered to us by Baroness von Waldstädten — which was in truth more princely than baronial.

... for some time before we were married we had always attended Holy mass and gone to confession and received communion together — and I discovered that I never prayed so ardently or confessed and received communion so devoutly as by her side; — and she felt likewise. — In short, we are made for each other ...

*

What sort of a marriage was it? Undoubtedly much healthier overall than many others in the conjugal gloom which permeates these yarns. Even though Constanze knew that she was second choice to her sister, that doesn't mean that she could not be reasonably happy nor make her husband very happy. The prospect of breaking free from the confines of home and mother at *Zum Auge Gottes,* and also the lack of any alternative suitors were motives enough for Constanze to set to and make the marriage work. But her calling off of the engagement on three occasions speaks for itself and there is not a single surviving letter of any kind, let alone any love letter, from wife to husband; Constanze may have destroyed them along with Leopold's many letters to his son after the marriage doubtless deprecating his choice of wife.

Constanze's second husband Georg Nissen — who ought to have known — relates in his important biography of Mozart that Constanze was "perhaps more attracted by his talents than by his person". "Mozart magnus, corpore parvus" ("Mozart the great, small in size") was how the composer succinctly described himself. As Harold Schonberg in his *Lives of the Great Composers* has graphically revealed, Mozart was certainly not physically glamorous, being very short, with a reportedly large head, a large nose, protruding eyes, a yellowish complexion, and a face pitted from smallpox. Nor was he ever mindful of the social graces, being at times demonstrably tactless, unstable, impulsive, arrogant, giddy, temperamental, obstinate, cadging, wheedling, spiteful and deceitful even, and, not surprisingly, not without enemies. One is tempted to say a fruitcake genius, though it's important not to go over the top since there is evidence to temper many of the flaws in his complex personality and he enjoyed a very rich network of friendships and associations.

Whatever he may or may not have got up to with hot-totty maids and nubile and talented pupils, Mozart was essentially happy with Constanze for at least seven out of their nine years together — and, quite possibly, right up to the time of his death; he was still certainly expressing his passion for her ("Plumpi — Strumpi") only six months before it. There are, however, massive and bewildering differences of opinion between pundits past and present about the state of the marriage during the last two to three years. You pays your money and takes your choice, because in the end it is all a matter of conjecture. At one extreme we have a faithful Mozart dying with a devoted and grief stricken wife who, she said, tried to catch his fever in order to end her own life. (The cause of death was perhaps rheumatic fever and/or infective endocarditis, the latter a potential consequence of the former, and/or — let's leave it at that.) Or contrariwise, they were *both* having an affair, with Constanze callously indifferent to her husband's burial and commemoration, and Mozart poisoned by his lover's husband who viciously disfigured her before cutting his own throat.

There is one matter which everybody now seems to agree on, despite what you might have concluded from Peter Shaffer's wonderfully entertaining but essentially fictional biopic *Amadeus,* in which Tom Hulce's giggling brat of a musical genius is upstaged by F. Murray Abraham as his envy-ridden rival Salieri. Although relations had undoubtedly been strained between them, Mozart was not poisoned by Salieri. He did, however, according to Constanze, definitely believe that someone had done the dirty deed with an arsenic based concoction called aqua Tofana.

*

Be all that as it may, Mozart was brimming over with marital contentment in a letter to Leopold in May 1783, the eighth month of Constanze's first pregnancy. From the Prater, Vienna's pleasure gardens to the east of the city, he wrote:

We have taken our lunch in the fresh air and shall stay on until eight or nine in the evening. My whole company consists of my little wife

LOVE LIVES OF THE GREAT COMPOSERS

who is pregnant and hers consists of her little husband, who is not pregnant, but fat and flourishing. I must ask you to wait patiently for a longer letter and the aria and variations — for, of course, I cannot finish them in the Prater; and for the sake of my dear little wife I cannot miss this fine weather. Exercise is good for her.
[May 3rd, 1783]

He took a close interest in the actual birth of Raimund on June 17th and the next day was happy to report with such wonderfully typical directness that "the child is quite strong and healthy, and has a tremendous number of things to do, I mean drinking, sleeping, yelling, pissing, shitting, dribbling and so forth." The entire experience inspired one of his loveliest compositions which he rattled off while Constanze was confined: his String Quartet in D minor, K421 (one of the six dedicated to Haydn). Constanze never forgot that during each contraction of her labour Mozart would console her and then resume work on the Minuet and Trio. The final dancing Allegretto movement is proof enough that minor keys do not always indicate misery! Raimund — "our poor, bonny, fat, darling little boy" — sadly died two months later.

The Mozarts' happiness continued after he took Constanze for what was probably a rather frigid first meeting with her father-in-law in Salzburg. The *Linz* symphony (No. 36, K425) composed at "breakneck speed" (in a maximum of five days) for a concert there after the Salzburg visit, seems particularly to exude well-being, with its majestic, slow introduction, joyous, bustling, outer movements, infinitely tender Andante and stately Menuetto.

In the mid-1780s Mozart was immensely popular and successful, and making plenty of money. He was fathering one child after another (well, not quite: six in nine years of whom only two survived) and enjoying a succession of sustained highs. The year 1784 was a particular *annus mirabilis*, yielding a miraculous cluster of no less than six piano concertos, subscription concerts galore, scores of illustrious patrons, and a family move into very upmarket accommodation at Domgasse 5. (Altogether the Mozarts changed residences eleven times in nine years.) Mozart also joined the freemasons at the "Beneficence Lodge". When his sister Nannerl married in August 1784, he sent her an amusing poem with the hope "particularly that you two will live together as harmoniously as — we two!". The happy household was supplemented piecemeal by Wimperl the dog, a caged canary, a pet starling that could sing the final theme from the Piano Concerto in G (K453) with an unwanted sharp, and a horse that Mozart rode for pleasure until his last year.

Leopold visited the Mozarts in Salzburg in the winter of 1785 and was surprised against his better judgement to find his son blossoming in every way. His letters back to Nannerl are crammed with fascinating titbits about his son's glamorous and frenetic lifestyle, and it is also obvious that a pleasant enough modus vivendi was established with the much maligned in-laws. Not only did Constanze's sister Sophie look after Leopold when he was laid up with rheumatism and a bad cold, plying him with burdock tea in bed; even Frau Weber's hospitality was acceptable, including a fine plump pheasant roast which she served in a meal that was "not too much and not too little, but superbly cooked". Certainly Mozart himself by now was totally won over to his mother-in-law, having become a loved and loving member of "mama's" extended family. She was a vital prop in all family emergencies, especially Constanze's illnesses; on one later occasion she even bound up and healed a leg wound Mozart suffered after an accident with a knife.

The lovey-dovey theme between husband and wife continues right through until Mozart's last letters to Constanze in the summer of 1791, though a distinctly disturbed note sometimes creeps in from 1789. He felt it necessary to curb her flighty behaviour when she was separated from him for weeks at a time, taking her expensive health cures in Baden.

The magic of Mozart's love letters lies in their immediacy. Like so many of the others, they are so uninhibited and spontaneous — "as the sows piss" — and poetically graphic. Here he is writing on April 13th from Berlin during his financially disastrous tour of 1789:

> If I could tell you everything I do with your dear *portrait,* you would often laugh. — For example, when I take it out of its cover, I say: "God greet you, Stanzerl! God greet you, God greet you; — little rascal; — pussy-kitty; — little turned-up nose — little bagatelle — schluck und druck!" — and, when I put it back again, I let it slip in bit by bit, and always say, "Stu! — Stu! — Stu!" but with that certain emphasis which such an important word requires; and at the very end, "good night, little mouse, sleep well".

And again, on May 19th:

> Dearest, most beloved wife of my heart!
> ... Oh, how glad I shall be to be with you again, my darling! But the first thing I shall do is to take you by your front curls; for how on earth could you think, or even imagine, that I had forgotten you? For even *supposing* such a thing you will get on the very first night a thorough spanking on your dear little kissable arse; and this you may count on ...

And four days later, after a recital of his financial disasters he is as randy as a goat:

> On the 1st of June I shall sleep in Prague, and the 4th: — the 4th? *With my dear little wife:* prepare your dear and loveliest nest very daintily, for my little piece has really earned it, he has behaved very well and wants only to possess your loveliest [c—; word crossed out]. Imagine that rascal, as I write he is crawling on to the table and looking at me questioningly, but I smack him down properly — that chap is still [raging; word crossed out] and I can hardly keep that villain in his place. I hope you will come to meet me at the first post station?
> — I hope Hofer (whom I embrace 1,000 times) will be there too — if H: and Fr: von Puchberg were also to come, everybody I love would be together.

Michael Puchberg, a wealthy businessman and fellow mason of Mozart, was by this time making repeated and crucial loans to Mozart, following the very marked dip in his finances from the summer of 1788. In spite of his high earnings in previous years his lifestyle had been very costly and there were no savings in the bank. His Academies (subscription concerts) had waned in popularity due to changing fads and fashions (including the insatiable craving for Italian opera), to the disturbing or depressive vein in many of his later works (especially in minor keys), and to the reduced amount of ready money among the nobility because of the draining costs of the Turkish wars.

"Too beautiful for our ears and far too many notes, my dear Mozart" was how Emperor Joseph II put it. Fortunately Mozart was able and willing to adapt to prevailing tastes, especially in his smash hit *Die Zauberflöte* (The Magic Flute) and his finances probably took a marked turn for the better in 1791.

*

But what about those dissonant notes intruding into some letters? On top of his money worries, Mozart was rattled by Constanze's coquettish behaviour in Baden. In August 1789 he is urging her not to be so "cheap" and "free and easy" with two men whose names a later hand has deleted. He continues:

> A woman must always make herself respected, or else people will begin to talk about her. My love! Forgive me for being so frank, but my peace of mind demands it as well as our mutual happiness. Remember that you yourself once admitted to me that you were inclined to *comply too easily.* You know the consequences of that. Remember too the promise you gave to me. Oh, God, do try my love! ... Rest assured that it is only by her prudent behaviour that a wife can enchain her husband.

In the same letter he also told her that she should not torture *herself* or *him* (my italics) with unnecessary jealousy.

In a previous letter from Dresden in April he had been urging her to "conduct yourself so as to take into consideration *your* and *my honour,* but also consider *appearances.* — Do not be annoyed at this request. — You must love me the more for thus valuing honour." Yet again, in October 1790 he was urging her to "love me half as much as I love you".

*

Was the kissy-kissy marriage actually cracking up? By the strictest rules of evidence, nothing very untoward is provable; but that has not precluded speculation from the wildest to the most careful. In the latter category Francis Carr argues at length in his fascinating book *Mozart and Constanze* that during the last two years of Mozart's life Constanze no longer truly loved her husband and was almost certainly having an affair with Franz Xaver Süssmayr, who shared the family apartments in Vienna and Baden during 1790 and 1791 (and who completed the *Requiem* after Mozart's death); and that Mozart was having an affair with his talented and ravishing young pupil, 23-year-old Magdalena Hofdemel, wife of Franz Hofdemel, a chancery official at the law court in Vienna who had joined Mozart's masonic lodge and, on one occasion, lent him money. Mozart almost certainly wrote his last, and particularly intimate Piano Concerto in B flat (K595) for Magdalena, and possibly also his last two string quintets.

Carr goes so far as to suggest that Franz Hofdemel poisoned Mozart when he learned of his wife's affair, before attempting, in a fit of insane brutality on the day of Mozart's funeral (December 6th), to murder her before successfully killing himself. There is certainly no doubt that Hofdemel slashed his wife's face, neck, shoulders and arms with a razor when she was five months pregnant before slitting his own throat. Sensational contemporary newspapers and scandal sheets certainly also linked by innuendo Mozart's death with the Hofdemel drama.

Many people, including Beethoven (through reports from his pupil Czerny stemming from Czerny's father who knew Frau Hofdemel) believed that Magdalena Hofdemel was Mozart's lover, and the meticulously detailed circumstantial evidence Carr puts forward both for the alleged love affair and associated murder attempt is very persuasively presented. However, the connection is not accepted by the scholastic fraternity at large. "There is absolutely no evidence," writes Robbins Landon, for instance, in his *Mozart's Last Year,* "that the Hofdemel tragedy can be connected either directly or indirectly with Mozart." Carr's poisoning theory (along with all the many other poisoning theories) must also be discounted. The prevailing scholarly opinion, including that of William Stafford in his closely argued book *Mozart's Death: A Corrective Survey of the Legends,* is that Mozart died a natural death.

Whether or not Constanze was having an affair with Süssmayr in Baden is again titillating but unanswerable. She certainly named her sixth child (Franz Xaver) after him, though all speculation that Süssmayr might have been the father is effectively silenced by the fact of the child's malformed left ear, a hereditary deformity passed down and shared by Mozart himself.

*

Constanze remains an elusive and unfocused figure but she

does seem to have been notably indifferent to her husband's burial arrangements. True, Mozart had left her with considerable debts to clear (perhaps up to 3,000 gulden) and his third-class (not pauper's) funeral, providing for his interment only in a communal grave, was all that could be afforded. In any case Mozart would have wished for nothing fancier and, without going into the reasons, a third-class funeral was not demeaning in the context of late 18th and early 19th-century Vienna; even Beethoven's grand affair was only a second-class funeral. But in the months after the funeral Constanze neither visited the cemetery nor arranged for any kind of remembrance; not even a customary simple commemorative cross on the perimeter wall. All this was in marked contrast, as Francis Carr points out, to the elaborate obelisk surrounded by four sets of stone flowers which she commissioned in Salzburg for her second husband Georg Nissen, in 1826.

Although Constanze wrote in Mozart's commonplace book that "eight years long we were joined in the most tender and in this world inseparable bond", her claims 28 years later to Vincent Novello (the English music publisher) that after her husband died she "threw herself on the bed and sought to catch the fever of which he died but it was not to be ... that she prayed sincerely to die ... that everything was hateful to her in the world" are unconvincing. (Many of Constanze's other reminiscences have been shown to be unreliable.) Her sister Sophie, in whose arms Mozart died, makes no mention of such a dramatic gesture in her long account, admittedly written 33 years after the event, of Mozart's final hours. Indeed, Constanze proved to be singularly unsentimental and businesslike in exploiting, with great success, her dead husband's legacy of renown and unpublished works.

To their embarrassment, she was quite prepared to give the Novellos his ink stand and one of his wedding presents to her, a small gold watch.

*

Did Mozart have any other affairs? Unconfirmed reports have proliferated since his death like gossip in a Welsh village and biographers have copied hearsay from one another, though there is no hard evidence. According to several biographers including Ludwig Nohl and Arthur Schurig, Constanze admitted that Mozart had confessed infidelities with chamber maids to her. Jean-Baptiste-Antoine Suard wrote in his *Anecdotes sur Mozart* in 1804 that Mozart

> was tenderly attached to her [Constanze]; but that did not prevent him from conceiving a fancy for other women and his fancies had such a hold over him that he could not resist them ... I have heard it said that he wrote la Flute Enchantée only to please a woman of the theatre with whom he had fallen in love, and who had offered him her favours at this price ...

And Karl Friedrich Zelter, Mendelssohn's most important teacher and the musical oracle of Berlin in the early 19th-century, wrote to his close friend Goethe on August 19th, 1827:

> We remember the circumstances of Mozart's death only too well. As a result of such good training, production went so smoothly that he had time for a hundred things, time which he spent with women; in consequence it did not do him any good.

Did Mozart have an affair with the very attractive soprano Henriette Baranius, former mistress of Frederick William II, in Berlin where she was singing the part of Blonde in *Die Entführung* when he was there in May 1789? Reported contemporary gossip certainly had it so, though Maynard Solomon's close examination of the chronology shows that if it happened at all, it must have been an extremely brief fling; a one-night stand even. A much more plausible mistress for Mozart during this Berlin journey in the spring of 1789 is, according to Solomon's detailed analysis of the circumstantial evidence, the singer Josepha Duschek.

Other women who have been included at various times in the *putative* Mozart lineup are the singers Barbara Gerl, Anna Gottleib, Adriana Ferrarese, Caterina Cavalieri, Caterina Bondini, a Mlle Kaiser, Nancy Storace, his piano pupil Josepha Auernhammer ... In the case of this last lady, although she fell in love with her teacher, he most definitely didn't respond, if his comments on her to his father ("nothing but an amorous fool") can be taken at face value:

> If a painter wanted to portray the devil, he would have to choose her face. She is as fat as a farm-wench, perspires so that you feel inclined to vomit, and goes about so scantily clad that really you can read as

plain as print: *"Pray, do look here."* True there is enough to see, in fact, quite enough to strike one blind; but — one is thoroughly well punished for the rest of the day if one is unlucky enough to let one's eyes wander in that direction ... So loathsome, dirty and horrible!

*

The libretti and chosen librettist (Lorenzo Da Ponte) for Mozart's three finest comic operas certainly all indicate a radical shift in his moral outlook from his strait-laced attitudes twenty years earlier. Lorenzo Da Ponte, poet of the Court Theatre in Vienna, was a notorious intriguer, adventurer and libertine, and the moral compass of *Don Giovanni* and *Così Fan Tutti* goes haywire in the territory of compulsive womanising and fickle women. The prudish Beethoven, indeed, condemned them as "licentious"!

Another hint of Mozart's more worldly outlook, at least when off his guard, is in a letter from Prague to Gottfried Jacquin, possibly his closest friend: "I did not dance and did not try my luck. — The first, because I was too tired, and the last out of my native shy stupidity ... ." (February 12th, 1787). Mozart may also not have been immune to the libertine influence of the womanising impresario Emanuel Schikaneder, who commissioned and provided the libretto for *The Magic Flute.* Mozart is supposed to have spent the summer of 1791 working on the opera in Schikaneder's wooden summer-house at Josefdorf, drinking champagne and punch and enjoying the company of actors and actresses while Constanze was in Baden!

We might tentatively observe that as well as being gallant and flirtatious, Mozart was undoubtedly a randy so and so, and all the smoke of gossip and circumstance cannot have been entirely self-generating. Even his loving sister-in-law Sophie, who nursed him on his death bed, recalled to Nissen that "To keep him from intercourse of a hazardous kind his wife patiently took part in everything with him".

*

Whilst Constanze unquestionably inspired her husband in the bedroom, she wrought little eternal magic through his fingers and pen. All the works he wrote for Constanze were unfinished: the

Solfeggios for voice K393 "per la mia cara Constanze" break off after 62 bars; the Violin sonata K403 "pour ma très chère épouse" has only 20 completed bars in the second movement; while in the Mass in C Minor K 427 (in which Constanze was a soprano soloist at the first performance) only the Kyrie and Gloria are complete. One certainly might question Maynard Solomon's opinion, in his newly published biography of Mozart (1995), that the Mass, whose florid soprano arias were almost certainly intended for Constanze, "surely stands as one of the most sublime compositions ever written as a gift to a beloved person". Neither Constanze's singing nor her playing seemed to turn on her husband in the way the talents of some his other pupils and singers did.

With some very notable exceptions, settled relationships, marital or otherwise, do not seem to be as creatively inspiring to composers as those involving yearning or pain. The fantasy of musical adultery also seems to be a potent inspiration. Although they may never even touch each other, men and women are often essentially making love when they make music together. Mozart wrote for particular sopranos other than Aloisia Weber, and it is difficult, for instance, to resist the suggestion that his concert aria with piano obbligato "for Mad.selle Storace and me" — *Ch'io mi scordi di te?* (I forget you my dear?) K505 — is "a love letter in music" (Francis Carr). Mozart always liked an aria "to suit a singer as accurately as a well made garment", and judging by the exquisite rapport and interplay, at once intimate and dazzling, between the piano and voice lines in the Rondo and Allegretto of K505, theirs must have been a perfect partnership. In 1784 Nancy Storace embarked on an unhappy marriage with a violinist and composer, John Fisher.

*

In fairness to Constanze one must never forget that she must have had a lot to put up with in their day to day life together. Apart from anything else she was living with a man who was sometimes carrying entire works in his head before writing them down straight off. (Mozart did also use sketches and drafts and sometimes certainly found composition laborious and difficult.) According to Dr. P.J. Davies, an eminent Australian physician who has made an exhaustive study of Mozart's behaviour and illnesses and whose findings have very considerable support, Mozart was a manic depressive — a cyclothymic. "It has to be emphasised that cyclothymics are very difficult people to live with" says Dr Davies. Robbins Landon is convinced that this explains why Mozart wrote so many tormented and turbulent works in minor keys — works like "Mozart 40" in G Minor (K 550) which, though now one of the world's favourite symphonies, did nothing for Mozart's popularity in the late 1780s.

After Mozart's death, Constanze organised and sang in several performances of his works, cleared his debts (comparatively easy, especially since his last opera, *The Magic Flute,* had been so successful) and disposed competently of his estate. In 1809 she married her lodger Georg Nissen, a Swedish bachelor and diplomat whom she helped to write Mozart's second important biography. (The first was by Franz Xaver Niemetschek.) Nissen didn't live to complete the work, which Constanze took over with the help of J.H. Feuerstein.

Leopold Mozart must surely have turned over in his grave in St Sebastian's cemetery, Salzburg, each time the three Weber sisters Aloysia, Constanze and Sophie were buried in nearby plots in 1839, 1842 and 1846.

***

CHAPTER 6

LUDWIG VAN BEETHOVEN

BORN: BONN, C. 17TH DECEMBER 1770
DIED: VIENNA, 26TH MARCH 1827

It is a singular fact, certainly, that we do not know the name of any single woman with whom Beethoven had sexual relations, but it has never been suggested that he was without sexual experience.
[Martin Cooper: *Beethoven: The Last Decade*]

*

If Beethoven, through his music, is God's greatest-ever gift to humanity — is there really any "if" about it? — the mere man himself was nevertheless the Devil incarnate to his endless succession of hapless cooks and cleaning ladies. It is all too easy to imagine what a rough time they had, Therese, Nanni, Peppi, Mariandl and all the rest. They were certainly not all angels, but as a bunch they were more sinned against than sinning.

Picture them (and also the occasional menservants) trying to sort out the skunky sausage ends from the divine if illegible scraps of *Allegro con brio* on his rubble-piled desk; or retrieving his stinking chamber pot and unsavoury dirty washing from the piles of priceless chamber music under it. But that wasn't the worst of it. These brave ladies were not only the victims of his vile temper and even physical assault. They also received, jointly or severally, some flattering open testimonials to help them on their way: "heatful cattle ... terrible cows ... filthy tribe ... an unbelievable swine of a housemaid ... bad-tempered old cook ... busty bitch ... disgusting beast possessing extraordinary sauciness, wickedness and vulgarity ... horrible female". And the unlucky waitresses at two of the almighty madman's regular haunts, the *Goldene Birne* and *Zum Camel,* fared no better when struggling with his endless trances and baffling double orders: "fat overfed little pigs ... little fat ones". It was really nice to be appreciated.

Although these doomed ladies for some reason brought out the very worst in him, it requires no imagination to see why any intelligent woman would be very wary of taking on Beethoven even as a lover, let alone a husband, however much she revered him. There's no escaping the sad hunch, which even Bernard Rose's biopic *Immortal Beloved* doesn't dispel, that Beethoven had no full-blown, abandoned love affair — no corker — at any time in his life. There was no nuzzling up against a familiar and welcoming bosom in the small hours; no backwarming; no rolling over for a dreamy quickie; no rushing back to bed after breakfast; no lazy kisses after lunch; no languid siesta sessions followed by heavenly bathroom ablutions; for the most part, it seems, only knee tremblers in the Prater (Vienna's Hyde Park) or ruttings up back alleys or in sordid rooms where he almost certainly, according to Dr Edward Larkin in his widely quoted medical appendix to Martin Cooper's *Beethoven: The Last Decade,* caught gonorrhoea. This alone, not to mention his deafness, severe illnesses and dysfunctional eccentricities, reduced the possibility of an enduring and workable relationship.

*

The job of breaking in Beethoven was beyond the whip-cracking skills of the most intrepid lion tamer, let alone the resources of the sheltered, refined and extremely well-to-do ladies, sometimes a lot younger than himself, with whom he fell in love. When the moon was in the right quarter, he could be as nice as pie, but that left more than 20 days out of the 27.322 in the lunar month when anything could happen! The sophisticated and genteel poet Goethe had good reason to describe the beetle-browed Beethoven as an "untamed personality" after their meeting in 1812.

Behold him on the lunar fringe in his later years: "a red-faced man striding furiously around Vienna, hat on the back of his head, coat-tails flying and sagging with the weight of books crammed into the pockets, and singing (described as roaring) at the top of his voice"; or "striding up and down the fashionable promenade, the Helenenthal, from ten in the morning to six at night with his coat hanging on a stick over his shoulder, making the Emperor, the Empress and the Court stand aside for him" (Edward Larkin).

Many people, not just the gobsmacked herdsman whose cattle stampeded in terror from the composer's grotesque bellowings and gesticulations during his country walks at Gneixendorf, believed that Beethoven had truly lost his marbles. He was once actually locked up as a vagrant — "I am Beethoven." "Sez you. You're a bum." — and was sometimes so unkempt that he was taken for a rough peasant. From his mid-40s his eccentricities would provoke the jeering ridicule of street urchins, one occasion being when he stood composing at his open window with no trousers on.

Beethoven was also volatile and violent, coming to blows with his servants — including the women — and also with the elder of his two brothers, Carl, when they were both in their 40s. On one occasion, overreacting to some perceived insult, Beethoven attacked one of his most loyal patrons, Prince Lichnowsky, with a chair. On another he threw a badly cooked *Lungenbratel* (a lung stew) at a waiter's head in an eating house, and roared with laughter when the waiter, laden with a pile of other cooked dishes, was forced to lick the gravy from around his mouth. And everyone knows how, when he heard that Napoleon had declared himself Emperor of France, Beethoven flew into a rage and tore up the title page of his as yet-unperformed Bonaparte symphony (his Third), and threw it on the ground. He even punctured the surface of the paper while frantically erasing the word Bonaparte before renaming the symphony *Eroica*. Elsewhere, in his score of the Eighth Symphony, for instance, his helter-skelter scratchings and crossings-out almost tear the paper. And when he played, Beethoven literally demolished pianos, which couldn't stand up to his furious fortes and sforzandos.

The full story of Beethoven's pathological and manic-depressive tendencies is far too complex to go into here. So is that of his many severe illnesses, probably associated with connective-tissue disease, and the deafness that plagued him increasingly from his early 30s and which was virtually total by the time he was 47. In the end, of course, what really matters is his sheer guts, his genuine if unpredictable kindness and charm, his loyalty to a very few close friends, and, of course, the music; music that steamrolls over convention and releases new depths of feeling in new sound worlds; music that, above all, is so often healing and cathartic in its miraculous transcendence of human frailty and suffering. What, in context, is more uplifting than the so-called Shepherd's Hymn in the final movement of the Pastoral Symphony, or more joyfully triumphant than the blazing C major tune at the climax of the Fifth?

"It seems" says Martin Cooper, "that the greatness of Beethoven's music is inextricably bound up with his violent, undisciplined nature and the suffering it brought him." In the final squalor of his deathbed and the agony of his hideously swollen, pain-wracked body, Beethoven died fulfilled. He had, after all, learned in his music the secret of how to manipulate time itself. With his own typical brand of humour, he murmured "Applaud friends, the play is over", after the doctor's final visit.

Coming back to earth, from the ladies' standpoint he was certainly no oil painting even in his youth, and the first woman to whom he proposed in 1794 — the young, beautiful and talented soprano Magdalena Willmann — turned him down because, according to one of her nieces, "he was so ugly, and half crazy". Beethoven was "lacerated" by her rejection. In 1799 Magdalena married someone else but died soon afterwards in 1801.

In his early 30s, when he got down to ostensibly serious courting, *Der Spagnol*, as Beethoven was known because of his swarthiness, was lean and short, just under Napoleon's height of 5' 6". He was ugly, with a severely pockmarked skin but with brilliant blue-grey eyes (brown?) that were later to glance habitually upwards in the characteristic way of the deaf.

"Every mood of his spirit was immediately and violently expressed in his countenance" wrote one of his later portraitists, August von Kloeber. At this stage he sometimes dressed well, though he let himself go as time went on, becoming stockier and much, much scruffier in, say, his battered hat, his unbuttoned blue frock coat with brass buttons, white waistcoat and flying necktie.

Prone to spitting conspicuously in company, or even using a candle snuff as a toothpick, Beethoven was also clumsy and badly co-ordinated. He was every nice young lady's nightmare of a date, a disaster zone. If he offered her a dance or a drink it was a case of "mind your toes and keep your nice new little tulle number out of harm's way". The world's greatest composer couldn't dance (nor conduct!) two beats in time to save his life, and "he rarely picked up anything without dropping or breaking it", reports Ferdinand Ries, one of

Beethoven's pupils and devoted assistants. "Everything was knocked over, soiled or destroyed".

*

But what about the plus side, the "diamond quality" as Martin Cooper calls it, of this noble savage? Best of all, Beethoven knew and admitted his own faults and many of his acquaintances and patrons therefore forgave him a great deal. Describing a violent quarrel with an erstwhile friend, Gerhard von Breuning, Beethoven wrote to Ries: "If I happen to be irritated at a time when I am more liable to fly into a temper than usual, then I too erupt more violently than anyone else." We've already seen what he meant. In 1799 he wrote one day to his composer-pianist friend Johann Nepomuk Hummel, calling him a "false dog". The next day he took it all back: "Dear little Ignaz of my heart! You are an honest fellow and I now realise that you were right ... Kisses from your Beethoven, also called dumpling". Beethoven was very partial to jests and puns, sometimes very laboured, in his letters.

Leaving aside for the moment Beethoven's abnormal concern for his nephew Karl, it isn't hard to find instances of his human kindness and sunny disposition. Here, for instance, is the young writer and diplomat Varnhagen von Ense writing in 1811 to his regiment commander Count Bentheim:

> I have made B's acquaintance. The unruly man is very friendly and gentle towards me ... You can be all the more assured by the fact that he greets you with true friendliness and wishes keenly to be excused for his forgetfulness of the moment ... In memoirs, I found the man in him even more appealing then the artist.

But maybe it was Rossini, himself infinitely humane, who captured the most irresistible, lovable quality in Beethoven the man:

> ... but what no etcher's needle could express was the indefinable sadness spread over his features — while from under heavy eyebrows his eyes shone out as from caverns, and though small, seemed to pierce one.

*

All these baffling contradictions in Beethoven also show up in his polarised fixations about women — as Madonnas or whores. There wasn't much middle ground between idealisation and misogyny, apart from his affection for the one or two important platonic or motherly women friends in his life. The kind of women who might have taken him on as a husband — the strong, coping hausfrau types with hearts of gold — he rejected out of hand as soul mates.

Perhaps *Fidelio* enshrines Beethoven's dream of the ideal woman: youthful, high-principled, with unblemished beauty, morality and virtue. Chosen at the point in his life when he was facing up to the prospect of isolation from the world because of his deafness, the story of *Fidelio* almost certainly symbolises his own hope of rescue by a loving wife. (The heroine Leonore, in disguise as Fidelio, the jailer's assistant, helps through her tactics and bravery to save her unjustly imprisoned husband Florestan, starving and chained to a rock, from death. They celebrate their reunion in one of the most ecstatic love duets ever written, *O namenlose Freude* (Oh joy beyond expressing).

Beethoven never found Miss Right, of course; or rather, he believed he'd found her but "it had never come to a declaration". In Baden in 1816 he confided his unhappiness in love to his friend Giannatasio del Rio (for a time the headmaster of his nephew Karl). He had, wrote Giannatasio's daughter in her diary, met someone "a union with whom he would have considered the greatest happiness of his life. It was not to be thought of, almost an impossibility, a chimera — 'nevertheless it is now as on the first day' ". The lady in question was almost certainly his Immortal Beloved.

Beethoven's dream of an ideal love surfaced also in a diary entry for July 27th, 1816 or 1817, in Baden: "Only love, yes! love alone can give you a happier life. O God, grant me the grace to find her at last, the woman who will strengthen me in virtue and whom I can possess with a quiet conscience!" Even on his deathbed, Beethoven told Hummel how lucky he was to have a wife who took care of him and who was in love with him. "But poor me," he added with a heavy sigh.

Unconsciously, perhaps, Beethoven was always avoiding commitment to a permanent relationship. He gravitated to younger women who were either married or involved with other men, and also far above his social position. His attraction to the most famous of his aristocratic pupils "often seems to have thrived in proportion as it was unrealisable in fact", says Martin Cooper. Beethoven's instinctive shyness, his ever-intensifying sense of isolation, his loathing of pity or condescension, his bouts of vile temper and his overriding creative impulses all worked against his settling down with an available woman in a workable, real-life relationship of ups and downs and give and take.

*

If Beethoven never found his Madonna figure, he was certainly obsessed with the temptations of the Frail Sisterhood. He undoubtedly resorted to prostitutes for sexual relief and his attitude towards them and to both his brothers' wives reveals all the unhealthy hangups of the prudish and prurient puritan. One undated diary entry of around 1816 to 1817 powerfully reveals a guilt-ridden conscience: "Sensual pleasure without union of souls is bestial and will always remain bestial; after it one experiences not a trace of noble sentiment but rather regret."

Beethoven didn't hesitate to warn others on the dangers of the vice that fascinated him. "Abstain from decaying fortresses, the attack is more costly than from those well preserved," he wrote to his very devoted (and considerably older) cellist friend Zmeskall, in 1816. Earlier, he had warned the younger of his two brothers, Johann (then about 20), to be on his guard against "the whole tribe of bad women" when coming to live in Vienna in 1796. Then, in 1812, when learning that Johann's housekeeper (Therese Obermayer) was doubling as his mistress, Beethoven went hotfoot to Linz to try put a stop to the affair, dragging in the bishop, the civil authorities and even the police. Johann cut short his brother's meddling with his sex life by marrying Obermayer, who already had an illegitimate daughter. Peace wasn't restored between the brothers until 1822. Was Beethoven jealous, one wonders?

Beethoven's most demented rantings on sex were directed against his sister-in-law Johanna, neé Reiss, wife of his other, more favoured brother, Carl. True enough, theirs had been a shotgun wedding with son Karl being born less than four months afterwards, but Beethoven's verbal abuse of Johanna actually tells us more about him than about her. This was, after all, Vienna, where, so scholars tell us, morality has always been permissive.

Johanna was certainly no great shakes as a *hausfrau* and seems to have been feckless, hedonistic and even unbalanced. Indeed, during Carl's last illness she had a lover by whom she bore a child after Carl's death. It was during Beethoven's ensuing relentless battle for the custody of his nephew Karl that he reviled his sister-in-law with such venom.

"Last night", he wrote to Giannatasio del Rio in 1816, "the Queen of the Night was at the Artist's Ball until 3 a.m. exposing not only her mental but also her bodily nakedness — it was whispered that she was willing to sell herself for 20 gulden. Oh horror! and are we to entrust to such hands as hers, even for a moment, our precious treasure? No certainly not ... " Elsewhere he alleged that the "fat loutish woman" with her "bastards" was a whore still on the game.

Did Johanna, the "raging Medea", also arouse desires in her brother-in-law that he could sublimate only through abuse and slander?

Beethoven also had severe problems with the sexual morality of the wider world. There was the occasion when he at first refused to play in front of the pianist Magdalena Hofdemel because he thought she had been Mozart's mistress, and also his denunciation of Mozart's three great comic operas. The plot lines of *Don Giovanni* and *Figaro* were "repugnant" to him in their moral frivolity.

Here are the known main women in his life, so far as I can make out.

*

The Brunsvik Sisters

The first women to impinge seriously on Beethoven's life after his arrival in Vienna from Bonn in 1792 were the Brunsvik sisters, Therese and Josephine. In May 1799 they came from Hungary with their widowed mother for a short visit to Vienna to have "priceless musical instruction" with the man who was by then a star and doing very well for himself, with rooms and a servant in St Petersplatz. He already had two piano concertos under his belt, not to mention countless chamber works, some songs, and several knockout performances.

Beethoven was charmed by both the sisters (Therese being then 24 and Josephine 20) and took great pains with their tuition, letting the lessons run three or four hours over, and even composing a "musical offering" for their album. This was a song, with variations, for piano duet on Goethe's poem *Ich denke dein*. Beethoven became friends with other members of the Brunsvik family, especially brother Franz, and was a welcome visitor to their estates in Hungary.

Therese von Brunsvik (1775-1861)

If, as is likely, Therese could get round the intimate piano sonata which Beethoven dedicated to her (No. 24 in F sharp major op. 78), she must have been a good player! Certainly Beethoven lavished his professional attentions on her, "holding down and bending my fingers, which I had been taught to raise and hold flat". Therese was probably more of a soul mate than a romantic prospect to Beethoven, but each clearly treasured the deep affection of the other. Therese gave Beethoven her portrait inscribed with the words *To the rare genius, the great artist, the good human being, from T.B.* and Beethoven kept it in a secret drawer of his writing bureau. Her memoirs and correspondence have much to say about Beethoven, — "a stupendous spirit" — and her sister.

Josephine Deym, née Brunsvik (1779-1821)

... I love you as dearly as you do not love me ... angel of my heart — of my life ... beloved and only J ...

Beethoven seems to have had more pain than pleasure from this association, primarily because he pressed Josephine for more than she could bring herself to offer him.

During their family visit to Vienna, the Brunsviks met Count Joseph Deym, proprietor of a famous waxworks museum, who, although nearly 30 years older than Josephine, pressed for her hand. Thinking that Deym would swell the family's depleted coffers, Josephine's mother Countess Anna put pressure on her daughter to accept. The marriage was a double disaster because the aging count with whom Josephine was landed turned out to be badly in debt.

Beethoven's frequent visits to the Deyms in the wing of their 80-room museum to give Josephine free piano lessons must have been one of her very few consolations, apart from her own family and her four young children.

After Count Deym died in January 1804, Josephine resumed her piano lessons with Beethoven and the relationship intensified, though not with reciprocal feeling. In his 14 letters to Josephine over three years, Beethoven is clearly passionately in love, but in her replies Josephine, though clearly revering his idealism and his art, remains strictly "hands-off". Bernard' Rose's fleeting scene where she (or her sister) gives chase in the garden, bares her bosom, strips off and wraps herself round him perks up the film no end but is pure fantasy. So is her coy and inviting look as he enters her bedroom. In fact, they never even got beyond addressing each other as "Sie" rather than the more intimate "du".

Josephine undoubtedly caused Beethoven a lot of heartache:

> Winter 1805 ... Long — long — of long duration — may our love become — For it is noble — so firmly founded upon mutual regard and friendship — Even the great similarity between us in so many respects — in our thoughts and feelings — Oh you, you make me hope that *your heart* will long — beat for me — *Mine* can only — cease — to beat for you — when — *it no longer beats — beloved J,* I send you all good wishes — *But I also* hope — that *through me* you will gain a little happiness — otherwise I should certainly be — *selfish.*

Alas, she made her unswerving position crystal clear in one undated letter written presumably around the same time:

> ...The distinction you bestowed on me, the pleasure of your company, could have been the greater adornment of my life if you could love me in a less sensual way — Because I cannot satisfy this sensual love — you are angry with me — I would have to tear holy bonds if I acceded to your desire. Believe me — that the fulfilment of my duties causes me the greatest suffering — and that surely the motives which guide me are noble.

Even had Josephine found Beethoven irresistible as well as supremely talented, the countess in her might well have held back from any kind of commitment because of his temper, his lack of social graces and, especially, his lowly origins as the son of an alcoholic lay clerk.

Beethoven wrote the song *An die Hoffnung* (op. 32) for her and she may well have been very much on his mind while he composed the *Eroica, Fidelio* (in particular), the *Appassionata,* the Fourth Symphony, the Fourth Piano Concerto, and the Violin concerto during the period 1804 to 1806. (Can anyone who has ever been in love listen to the yearning strains of the slow movement of the Violin Concerto without going over the edge of longing into tearful grief?)

By the autumn of 1807 the unconsummated romance had come to a chilly end after sorrowful scenes and misunderstandings. "It is better for your peace of mind and mine not to see you ... nothing against you dear J, all — all in your favour — and yet it must be so — All good wishes, beloved Josephine ... ".

Like her rejected suitor, Josephine was doomed to unhappiness in love. She left Vienna in the following summer and in 1810 married a Baron von Stackelberg. They separated in 1813, and Josephine died in 1821.

According to Therese, Beethoven and Josephine were "born for each other" and in 1846, perhaps with a touch of spinsterish naiveté, she penned in her diary:

> Why didn't my sister J take him as her husband when she was the widow Deym? She would have been happier with him than S. Mother love decided her to renounce her own happiness.

There is no foundation in the rumours that Beethoven fathered Josephine's daughter Minona, born in 1813.

*

Countess Giulietta Guicciardi (1784-1856)

> I am now leading a slightly more pleasant life ... This change has been brought about by a dear, charming girl who loves me and whom I love. After two years I am beginning to enjoy a few blissful moments; and for the first time, I feel that marriage might bring me happiness. Unfortunately she is not of my class, and at the moment I certainly could not marry — I must still bustle about a good deal. [Beethoven to Wegeler November 16th,1801]

While Josephine was sitting it out with Count Deym in the waxworks museum, Beethoven fell completely under the spell of an even more nubile young enchantress, the 17-year-old Countess Giulietta Guicciardi. This ravishing, coquettish blue-eyed beauty was a cousin of the Brunsvik sisters and came to Vienna with her parents from Trieste in 1800, starting her lessons with Beethoven in 1801.

Coming from a cultural backwater (comparatively speaking) she seems to have been flattered by her prestigious teacher's attentions, and even to have fallen in love with him for a while, or at least to have egged him on. She told Therese Brunswick that she could get Beethoven to "promise me anything". Beethoven may have actually proposed to her before she beat a hasty retreat, almost certainly on daddy's say-so. By the autumn it was all over and in 1803 she married the much more eligible and considerably younger Viennese ballet composer Count Robert von Gallenberg and they settled in Naples. Their marriage was a disaster, however, and Giulietta took refuge in the arms of a certain Prince Hermann von Pückler-Muskau. It sounds like she was desperate!

Beethoven wrote the universally popular and mauled-to-death *Moonlight* sonata for Giulietta in 1801 (No 2. op.27). People are still free to read into that what they will, just as they have always done.

In 1823 Beethoven, then deaf of course, recalled in his own hand his relationship with Giulietta in one of his Conversation Books. The addressee is his ingratiating and industrious, though very unreliable biographer Anton Schindler:

> She loved me much more than she ever loved her husband. However he was her lover more than I was.

We can but hope that this was really true, though it is probable that they got no further than a few stolen kisses behind a portière, or behind a statue on a mezzanine landing. Bernard Rose allows them one passionate clench during their ride in an open landau. Once again, respected reader, it's your decision!

Beethoven kept an ivory miniature of Giulia (a love token) in his desk. With her ringlets all over her forehead she looks lovely and winsome.

*

Countess Anna Marie Erdödy (1779-1837)

You are all so dear and precious to me that it would be hard to find
a greater measure of affection — I shall be with you again as soon
as possible — Continue to be fond of your true friend.
Beethoven [c. July 1810]

A fine pianist and admirer of Beethoven's music, the mysterious Countess Erdödy, who had married Count Peter Erdödy when
she was barely 17 in 1796, was one of the composer's close and loyal
friends over a period of about ten years from 1807.

Beethoven had rooms in the Erdödys' apartment during the
autumn and winter of 1808 and 1809, and was a frequent visitor
afterwards at their town and country residences. Described as "the
most enigmatic, the least decipherable" of the women Beethoven
knew — and also as "very pretty, small, delicate" — she corresponded
with Beethoven after the family left Vienna in 1815, but none of her
replies to Beethoven's affectionate letters survive. Beethoven
dedicated two piano trios to her (op. 70, including the *Ghost*) and
also the Vienna edition of his last two cello sonatas op.102. (He
composed these for the countess's resident "chamber virtuoso", cellist
Joseph Linke, while staying at her summer residence in Jedlersee in
1815.) Beethoven must have thought very highly of indeed of the
countess: not only do these sonatas have fiendishly difficult piano
parts (much more so than the cello lines), they are also demanding,
densely-wrought connoisseur pieces.

Beethoven abandoned a piano trio in honour of the Countess's
three children when one of them, August, died in 1816. The Countess
was even implicated in murky stories surrounding his death. Utter
nonsense, if only because no one capable of playing Beethoven trios
and sonatas could ever do anything so awful!

Countess Erdödy was undoubtedly one of Beethoven's soul
mates and, of course, suitably unattainable except in his head. She
helped to put together the details of the life annuity he received (with
a few hitches) from Archduke Rudolph and Princes Kinsky and
Lobkowitz from 1809.

*

Bettina Brentano (1785-1859)

... It is incredible how she captures and spins her web round people ... She makes you feel that you have nothing more important to do than to please her ... She always wants something from the man who is with her, she wants to admire him, and use him and tease him, or be admired, used, teased by him ... [Varnhagen in his Diary]

Beethoven formed a brief friendship with the young, talented and seductive Bettina Brentano in 1810 when he was 40 and she 25. A friend of Goethe, this effusive, nicely proportioned, dark-eyed lady was prone to fibbing and exaggerating. Doesn't this letter, for instance, sound a bit far fetched in relation to Beethoven?

... and then [he] said to me, "My song is finished." He sat down by the window and sang the whole song out into the open air. Then he said, "It sounds well, doesn't it? It belongs to you, if you like it, I wrote it for you. You incited me to it, I read it in your eyes as if it had been written down ... ."

She probably invented two letters, rambling and romantic, of the three she claims Beethoven sent to her. The third, dated February 10th, 1811, is real enough and shows that Beethoven could still enjoy himself: "I did not get home until four o'clock this morning from a bacchanalia, when I really had to laugh great deal, with the result that today I have had to cry as heartily." Beethoven was no more than charmed by Bettina, and she was so flighty and flippant that what she felt for him is anybody's guess. However, she was good company while he was getting over Therese Malfatti.

*

Therese Malfatti (1792-1851)

... the flighty Therese, who treats everything in life so lightly... [Beethoven]

I know that you will not refuse a friend's request when I ask you to obtain for me my certificate of baptism.
[Letter to Franz Wegeler May 2nd, 1810]

Coming up for 40, Beethoven lost his head over this 18-year-old beauty from Lucca with brunette locks, dark eyes, and a wilful temperament. The actress Antonie Adamberger, who played in Goethe's (and Beethoven's) *Egmont* in 1810, described Therese and her sister Anna as "the two most beautiful girls in Vienna". Quite a compliment in such a bitchy profession!

Beethoven's friends knew he was dead serious when he began preening and primping himself in Bengal cotton shirts and clothes from Vienna's finest tailor and also sent for his birth certificate to provide proof of his exact age. It was all to no avail, alas, because when he popped the question in the early summer of 1810 Therese, having strung him along for a short while, turned him down. Once again, as with Giulietta, daddy took a firm line against an eccentric musician without a coach and four and all the rest to testify to his bank balance.

It seems there was no undue angst or hard feelings. In his one letter to her, Beethoven asks her to remember him with fondness, to "forget the madman" and to "rest assured that no one can desire you to have a merrier and happier life than I do even when you do not take any interest in your devoted servant and friend Beethoven". No doubt the two summer months he spent in Baden amid country sights and sounds, which he so loved, with their "echo which man desires to hear", helped him get over it all.

Therese Malfatti, who was the niece of one of Beethoven's physicians, Giovanni Malfatti, has a lot more to answer for than turning down the composer. She was the probable inspiration of that chart-busting little piano number *Für Elise,* so often nonchalantly, or even spitefully mangled by little girls (and boys, too!) when forced to transfer their attentions from their teddy bears, dollshouses and other toys to the front parlour piano.

*

Antonie Brentano née Birkenstock (1780-1869)
"Immortal Beloved"

... Unfortunately I have no wife. I have found *only one* whom no doubt I shall *never possess* ... [Beethoven May 8th, 1816, nearly four years after the Immortal Beloved letter]

Antonie Brentano, another aristocratic lady, came to know Beethoven intimately after she and her family moved temporarily from their home in Frankfurt to look after her dying father in Vienna. Beethoven became close to the whole family, showering the Brentano children with sweets when they visited him with gifts of fruit and flowers.

Antonie had married Franz Brentano, a Frankfurt merchant and banker, in 1798 and it was through Franz's half-sister, the fluffy Bettina whom we've already met, that she met the composer in May 1810. Unlike her sister-in-law, Antonie truly revered Beethoven and probably loved him, or at least became emotionally dependent on him. She is almost certainly the addressee of the endlessly mooted Immortal Beloved letter found in Beethoven's desk after his death — along with her miniature.

Sorry, Mr. Rose; your plausible fantasy about the composer's hussy of a sister-in-law Johanna Beethoven being the Immortal Beloved may make good box-office but it's a million miles from the truth. You can forget all about Beethoven's subliminal fixations and Johanna's transfiguration from harlot to holy angel and even mother of his child. Is it really responsible to make a biopic that is so deliberately misleading about one of the world's greatest composers?

There is no magic about the truth, only painstaking work in gathering threads together and weaving them into a "powerful fabric of circumstantial evidence". The distinguished American scholar Maynard Solomon published the widely accepted findings of his researches on this enigma in a *Musical Quarterly* issue of 1972 (volume lviii). By co-ordinating hard documentary evidence (including newspaper announcements and hotel and police registers) of the intended and actual movements of both the Brentano family and Beethoven in July 1812, Solomon demonstrated the virtual certainty that Beethoven was addressing Antonie Brentano and planning to meet her with her family in Karlsbad (K in the letter).

It was on July 6th and 7th that Beethoven tore his heart out over the woman who meant more to him than any of the others, even Josephine Deym. At the end of June, with the orgiastic seventh symphony completed and the eighth begun, Beethoven, on his doctor's advice, set out on a recuperative holiday that was to include a few performances and also a meeting with Goethe. He arrived in Teplitz on July 5th, and began his most impassioned love-letter ever the next day.

It was the only time he addressed a woman intimately as "du". Even in this letter, however, his ambivalence towards total commitment surfaces. He seems to be totally committed — "Love demands everything and that very justly — *thus it is to me with you, and to you with me.*" — and wants above all to live with her:

> You are suffering — Ah, wherever I am, there you are also — I will arrange it with you and me that I can live with you. What a life!!! thus!!! without you ... I can live only wholly with you or not at all ...

But then he seems to renounce the prospect of cohabitation for a man of his age (41):

> Your love makes me at once the happiest and unhappiest of men — At my age I need a steady, quiet life — can that be so in our connection?

The letter then expires in sighs of longing:

> Be calm — love me — today — yesterday — what tearful longings for you — you — you — my life — my all — farewell. — Oh continue to love me — never misjudge the most faithful heart of your beloved.
> ever thine
> ever mine
> ever ours L.

Whether Beethoven sent the letter or not (would he have bothered to make a draft or second copy?), he joined the Brentanos at Karlsbad in the same guest house around July 25th, and also later accompanied them to Franzensbad.

The "lovers" would doubtless have had the chance for more than one heart-to-heart of mutual consolation. Beethoven's deep respect for Franz Brentano would in any case have inhibited any urge to try to steal his wife, and all the composer's other expressions of love for Antonie, apart from this letter, were veiled rather than direct. Indeed, his dedication of an easy Piano Trio (Wo039) only ten days before the Immortal Beloved letter to the Brentanos' daughter Maximiliane was probably a declaration of love by proxy.

After a brief return to Vienna, the Brentanos went back to Frankfurt, which Antonie loathed, for good. They corresponded with Beethoven and remained loyal friends, with Franz even lending Beethoven substantial sums of money without ever demanding them back.

As we saw earlier, Beethoven still hadn't got over Antonie four years later when in 1816 he told Giannatasio del Rio of a lady about whom he felt that it was "now as on the first day". The song cycle he composed in that same year on the theme of the "distant beloved" (*An die ferne Geliebte* op. 98) is an exquisitely varied and integrated collection of tender love songs doubtless echoing his undimmed feelings for Antonie.

When he could bear it, Beethoven had Antonie's portrait in his drawer to gaze at: her curly hair, almond-shaped eyes, longish neck and nose, unusually curled lips... This gift in itself symbolised the depth of her attachment to him. In return she had a copper engraving of him in which his friends, he told her, "can also discern my soul quite clearly". Antonie also had the towering edifice of the 33 *Diabelli Variations*, which he dedicated to her in 1823 — a work in which strife and tension seem finally to be spent in a mood of transcendental serenity.

*

The other women in Beethoven's life were purely sisterly or motherly good friends. He met the singer Amalie Sebald (1787-1846) at Teplitz in 1811 and 1812, and valued her sisterly support after the Immortal Beloved crisis. Over a longer period he enjoyed the warm platonic friendship of Baroness Dorothea von Ertmann (1781-1849), one of the most distinguished interpreters of his piano music who could, when appropriate, make it "sound like an entire orchestra". She married an Austrian army officer in 1798 and began piano lessons, and also "an unclouded friendship" with Beethoven in 1803. When she lost her only child Beethoven consoled his "dear, treasured Dorothea-Cecilia" by inviting her to his rooms and playing to her for over an hour. ("We will now converse in music".) After the funeral "the Master spoke no words but played for her until she began to sob, so her sorrow found an outlet and comfort". Beethoven dedicated his intimate and ethereal A major sonata op.101 to her in 1816.

Poor Fanny del Rio (1790-c.1876), daughter of Giannatasio and an informative diarist on Beethoven, was open about her deep love for him. "I certainly know someone" she wrote in November 1816, "who I would really like to please, but he does not even notice my existence ... if only I could watch over him and look after him." Beethoven's response was one of gentle mockery. A pity perhaps, because her quiet and totally undemanding devotion might just have made him happier than he was alone.

Finally, Nannette Streicher (1768-1853), daughter of the revered pianomaker Stein, was another motherly friend who advised him on handling Karl and on such thorny domestic matters as sacking his servants. Beethoven wrote her more than 60 letters on the things that *really* matter in life — such as how he was locked out of his lodgings for three hours one day and caught his death of cold "in a very thin pair of breeches ... This was injurious for me and put me in a foul humour for the whole day".

*

Not surprisingly, the women who meant most to Beethoven and who loved him, even if not sexually — the Brunswick sisters, Countess Erdödy, Antonie Brentano and Dorothea Ertmann — were serious musicians, some of them extremely accomplished. In playing his piano works they were experiencing, after all, depths of emotion and feeling, a surfacing of layers of unconsciousness hitherto unrevealed, it would seem, in music.

Although these women never made love to Beethoven, they were surely in some ways much closer to him than are many love-making partners with each other.

*

"Like Button to Trousers"

After Antonie, Beethoven resigned himself to the impossibility of having a sustained live-in relationship with any woman. The traumatic effects of the Immortal Beloved crisis included a marked and prolonged dip in his creative output and bouts of deep depression, though he did enjoy sensational success in the next two years with performances of existing works. From his diary entries it is clear that he saw his future only in dedication to his art rather than to any human being: "Thou mayst no longer be a man, not for thyself, only for others, for thee there is no longer happiness except in thyself, in thy art — O God, give me strength to conquer myself, nothing must chain me to life".

Ironically, Beethoven voluntarily spent the rest of his life very much chained to a human being — but it wasn't a woman. When Beethoven's brother Carl Caspar died in November 1815, Beethoven, in many ways an emotional simpleton, was manically driven to wrest his nephew Karl from the claws of vice and corruption in the shape of his mother Johanna, "born for intrigue, well-schooled in deceit, master of hypocrisy".

There then followed four-and-a-half years of legal wrangling with Karl toing and froing between a series of private boarding schools (including Giannatasio del Rio's), his mother, and Beethoven. Not surprisingly, Karl ran away from school back home to mother more than once. In the end, in April 1820, a Court of Appeal ruled in Beethoven's favour and gave him joint custody of his nephew with another friend of the composer, Karl Peters. Beethoven had prepared his case in a draft memorandum running to 48 pages, the longest surviving document in his handwriting.

Here is just a smattering of what the 10-year-old Karl had to endure from his obsessively protective uncle in 1816:

> ... Put on a pair of under-pants, or bring them with you so that you can put them on immediately after your bath, in case the weather turns cooler again. Has the tailor been yet? when he comes, he is to measure you for linen under-pants, too, as you need them ... Your trouser button L v. Beethoven.

After leaving school in 1823 Karl, whatever his own shortcomings, slowly cracked up under the unbearable pressure of living with his neurotic guardian. Beethoven, in his self-assumed role as the boy's "true bodily father", was by turns jealous, suspicious, over-strict, querulous, rejecting and suffocatingly affectionate, clinging pathetically to him "like button to trousers".

In July 1826 Karl bungled an attempt to shoot himself in the head with two pistols, one bullet missing, the second only injuring him. He then finally found the strength to break free from his "imprisonment" and later that year joined the army. He left in 1832 to get married and spent the rest of his life as a private citizen. Though Beethoven was shattered by the loss of his "son" they remained on good terms.

Experts and many others have had a field day speculating about this very unhealthy relationship. Besides being a surrogate son, was Karl a surrogate Immortal Beloved? A surrogate wife? Or was it all to do with Beethoven's repressed sexual obsession with the wicked Johanna, the "Queen of the Night"?

And how on earth did Beethoven manage to compose the *Missa Solemnis,* the Ninth Symphony, the *Diabelli* variations, the late quartets, overtures and all the rest through all these Karl years?

Next Question?

*

Perhaps the key to all Beethoven's personal relationships lies with the woman least known about in his life: his quiet and serious mother, Maria Magdalena, to whom he was devoted and whom he lost at the age of 16:

> She was such a good, kind mother to me and indeed my best friend. Oh, who was happier than I, when I could still utter the sweet name of mother and it was heard and answered; to whom can I say it now? [September 15th, 1787]

***

CHAPTER 7

GIOACHINO ROSSINI

BORN: PESARO, 29TH FEBRUARY 1792
DIED: PARIS, 13TH NOVEMBER 1868

Monsieur Rossini ... abused Venus from his earliest youth. That is why he frequently contracted gonorrhoeas that he almost always treated with astringents and more often with mild laxatives and purges. At the age of 44, he tempered his passions for women, stopped the abuse of liquors and heating foods.
[Bologna physician's report]

*

Nothing can be said with complete certainty about Rossini's love life before his marriage to the stunning and voluptuous Spanish soprano Isabella Colbran in 1822, except that she became his mistress some time after they started working regularly together in 1815.

Although Rossini was truly mega-popular, and easily the most prestigious and wealthy of all composers in the first half of the 19th-century, there are very few written pointers to his personal life as a young man, especially to his love life and first marriage. Certainly there are no romantic, uninhibited and revealing letters in the manner of so many other composers in this volume. The first ever biography of Rossini, published as early as 1824 when the composer was only 32, was written by the French writer, free-lover and posthumously very popular novelist Stendhal. His *Life of Rossini* makes compulsive reading for its period detail and atmosphere, but the Rossini data are unreliable. Rossini's own reminiscences related in his old age to his friends are also subject to flights of fancy and faulty memory.

However, it seems odds-on that as a result of womanising or whoring from his early teens, Gioachino Antonio Rossini first contracted gonorrhoea at the age of 15 or 16, with acute and depressing later consequences, especially in his 40s and 50s. In addition to the "lady-friends and patronesses" whom he recalls, perhaps fancifully, cultivating for his pleasure and professional advantage from the age of 13, there were, after all, swarms of prostitutes plying their trade in Venice, Milan and the other cities where he worked during his exhausting periods on the road in his late teens and early 20s. And from the time of his first indisputable hit at the age of 20 (*L'inganno felice*, his fourth opera, premièred at the San Moisè theatre in Venice in 1812), there would unquestionably have been many obliging singers and adoring groupies at the ready wherever his roving eye twinkled and homed in. *L'inganno* led to many other commissions, and between 1812 and 1815 he wrote and directed no less than 11 of his own operas in Venice, Ferrara and Milan before basing himself in Naples in 1815 — and, sometime afterwards, settling into a steady relationship with Isabella Colbran. In October of that year Colbran starred in the title role of his *Elisabetta Regina d'Inghilterra*, the first of a string of *opera seria* he was to compose inspired by her special talents.

Theatres throughout Europe seem to have inevitably been knocking shops as much as venues for stage performances. The offer of or consent to sex by singers and actresses in return for work on the stage was part and parcel of the general in-fighting and bitchery, and certainly out-of-work actresses and singers had to resort to high-class prostitution or mistressing. (Even Hollywood film star Clark Gable did shifts as a male prostitute before he hit the big-time.) For the duration of a run, the leading lady was, according to the author Henri Blaze de Bury, the mistress "[by] right of every self-respecting theatrical director". Way back in 1720, the composer Benedetto Marcello mentioned similar goings-on in his satire on operatic life, *Il teatro alla moda* (The Theatre in Fashion).

One such case in the very early stages of Rossini's career, when he was playing harpsichord at the age of 13 at the theatre in Sinigaglia, was the young soprano Adelaide Carpano and her "protector", the Marchese Cavalli, who ran the theatre. Cavalli was a wealthy roué who was in it more for the women and the kicks than for money or art. (Rossini, incidentally, sparked off giggles all round during one show by bursting into laughter at Carpano's off-key cadenzas.)

Also, in Italy at least, there was hanky panky during the show, usually between the big show-piece arias, behind closed curtains in the boxes of the auditorium, if the English poet Samuel Rogers, who arrived in Milan in 1814, is to be believed: "Sometimes", he tells us, "the curtains are drawn and you may imagine what you please." Byron also noted that audiences in their boxes might "chatter, play cards ... or anything else".

By the time of his *Italian in Algiers,* the wackiest of his operas, at the San Benedetto theatre in Venice when he was 21, Rossini's fame was assured and his pulling power with women was on a par not only with theatre directors but also princes. That's at least according to Stendhal, who tells us that Marietta Marcolini, the prima donna in *Italian Girl*, in order to stay on Rossini's good side gave up her affair with Prince Lucien Bonaparte.

Rossini's appetite for all aspects of the good life besides beautiful women could now be enjoyed as a package in elegant surroundings. No need normally to pull rank with chorus girls nor to comb the back streets, even for a one-night stand.

*

Whether Rossini had designs on Isabella Colbran before *Elisabetta* in 1815 (he then being 23, she seven years older) is speculative. He had almost certainly already met her two or three times when their paths crossed, and it seems that she had asked him to write an opera for her.

Whatever, the die was cast when Rossini arrived in Naples at the invitation of the legendary and brilliant impresario Barbaja to write and direct operas in his two theatres, a move sparking off a lucrative and artistically productive partnership between the two men lasting seven years. Barbaja not only boosted Rossini's finances enormously by forming with him a till-busting gambling business run in the foyer of the Teatro San Carlo; he also seems to have been happy enough at some point to hand over the luscious Colbran, who almost certainly was or had been the impresario's mistress as well as his prima donna. According to Stendhal, Barbaja presented Rossini, *gratis,* "a carriage, food, lodgings, and his mistress". Colbran, by the way, had also had a thing going with Prince Wablonowski.

Given all the circumstances of theatrical life, the transfer would be almost inevitable now that Rossini, entranced by Colbran's singing and beauty, was not only composing for her but also coaching her. Barbaja probably decided that what was good for them would be good for his business. There were, after all, many other fish in the sea for a man with his enormous clout.

During his seven years based in Naples between 1815 and 1822, Rossini wrote no fewer than nine *opera serie* geared to Colbran's specific gifts as a dramatic soprano specialising in tragic roles and elaborate *fioritura* — vocal embellishments craved by the audiences and invariably improvised on the spot. Indeed, after his comic operas *Il Barbiere di Siviglia* and *La Cenerentola* (an enchanting, effervescent fantasy based on the Cinderella fable) premièred in Rome in 1816 and 1817 respectively, Rossini's next significant *opera buffa* was not to hit the boards until 1828 with *Le Comte Ory*. Rossini's last *opera seria* for Isabella was to be *Semiramide,* premièred in Venice in 1823.

Rossini pundits seem to differ markedly over whether the composer's switch from comic to serious opera, because of his relationship with Colbran, was more of a gain than a loss artistically, and this is not the place to go into the fascinating arguments. The general public might invariably consider it a loss, since all they really know and love are the overtures — vintage musical bubbly, to be sure — and, of course, *Il Barbiere di Siviglia,* surely still the world's most popular comic opera. The exuberant rhythms, hypnotic, roller-coaster crescendos and perky tunes provide an enormous lift to the spirits and we could have done with many more *Barbers,* please. On the other hand, one of the world's most readable music columnists, Tom Sutcliffe, has suggested in *The Guardian* that Rossini's two Voltaire-based serious operas, *Tancredi* (with some judicious cutting) and *Semiramide*, could become "a new seam of gold" for those poncy (my word, not Mr Sutcliffe's) summer opera festivals in places like Glyndebourne and elsewhere.

The one enduring favourite from the serious operas of this period is, of course, the stirring and justly famous Prayer from *Mosè in Egitto* (1818), Verdian in its majestic dignity and originally added to distract the audience's attention during the technically very tricky parting of the waves.

*

It is hard to build up either a revealing or especially loveable picture of Isabella Colbran. She had a fine figure and her beauty, according to Stendhal, was

> of a most queenly kind: noble features which on stage radiated majesty; an eye like that of a Circassian maiden darting fire; and to crown it all, a true and deep instinct for tragedy.

In her prime she had a range of almost three octaves. The daughter of a trumpeter in the royal court at Madrid, she made her concert début in Paris in 1801 and later consolidated her operatic career in Italy before being engaged — and "protected" — by Barbaja.

Like many other divas from time immemorial (and, for sure, to the end of time) Colbran was also, apparently, imperious and difficult. By the time Rossini started working with her in Naples she was, at the age of 30, already past her peak though still thriving. "She is rather inferior to Catalani in voice and lacks her mechanical perfection, but sings with true feeling and acts with passion," wrote the violinist and composer Spohr in 1817 after hearing her sing in *Elisabetta.*

The marriage took place in 1822 near Bologna when the couple were en route from Naples for a mammoth Rossini festival (with Barbaja's company) in Vienna. Cynics do seem to have some case for saying that Rossini married Colbran for what she was worth. Others have said that he was looking for a mother figure, in which case he was doomed to disappointment. He certainly did well for himself, with his share of her properties (a castle at Modica, and a villa at Castenaso, near Bologna) and assets being worth 40,000 scudi — perhaps some three quarters of a million pounds in today's terms (let's call it $1.5 million US, give or take a few thousand). Herbert Weinstock sums up the marriage soberly but tellingly:

> Nothing discoverable about either Rossini or Isabella Colbran suggests that theirs was a prolonged, impassioned romance. For better or worse, however, they lived together for about eight years after their wedding. Their eventual separation was brought about, in part, by Rossini's prolonged absences, during which Isabella, then no longer an operatic star, was left either alone or in the company of her aged father-in-law. Meanwhile, she had developed a passion for gambling and had become insistently, if fruitlessly,

demanding. But Rossini, even when irritated by the sharp edges of her later character and by her often rash behaviour, treated her respectfully. She never lost her steady affection for him. On the whole their marriage was a calm and dignified one. It faded out rather than foundering during a tempest. To picture Rossini as having married an ageing nymphomaniac so as to acquire her money is nonsense. His motives — and hers — were humanly mixed.

Certainly, the more one reads about Rossini, the more complex and elusive he becomes; light years away from the simplistic and enduring misconception of him as a sluggard retiring at 30, lying in bed all day and getting up only to gorge himself on food and drink. Perhaps Rossini was as pragmatic in his choice of women as he was in his approach to composing, where self-plagiarism, patchwork and corner-cutting were ways of meeting deadlines.

Weinstock makes the marriage sound depressing. The damage to a star's ego and morale when she — or he, of course — is finally passé and has no inner resources or satisfying pursuits can obviously be devastating. No more idolatry, no more fixes for the junkie-diva, no more ecstatic encores and curtain calls, no heaps of bouquets, no more diamond necklaces, princely admirers, popping corks, caviar and quails eggs; an emptied life of boredom and resentment, and a wounded feeling of neglect. Isabella was in such a hole and Rossini was not the sort of man to lift her out. He had neither the will nor the capability.

Their eight ensuing years together were very eventful for Rossini, but shed little further light on their marriage and must be glossed over. Immediately after the wedding they continued towards Vienna and the already-mentioned Rossini Festival in 1822, where Isabella starred in *Zelmira* in April and in a further six operas until July. (While he was there, Rossini met Beethoven, who rather condescendingly advised him to stick to *opera buffa* — rather a rebuff given that Rossini had been writing mainly *opera seria* for five years.)

After Vienna the Rossinis quit with Barbaja and returned to Italy. In December Isabella was whistled off the stage in Venice during a revival of *Maometto II. Semiramide,* Rossini's last opera for Italy — and Isabella — was premiered (also in Venice) in February 1823. In the autumn they set out for Paris and London. Rossini was now un-doubtedly the most important and popular composer of his time, having written 34 operas, the best of them forming the core repertory of opera houses throughout Italy. (On the international scene, within another six or so years his operas had reached London, Brussels, Frankfurt, Berlin, Graz, Vienna, Brün, Madrid, Prague, Budapest, Odessa, Algiers, New York, Mexico, Buenos Aires, Rio de Janeiro, Havana and Philadelphia. By 1844 they had reached every inhabited continent including India and Australia, and by the time of his death Rossini had collected honours and decorations from Italy, France, Germany, Belgium, Spain and Mexico.)

They stopped off only briefly in Paris, where, royally fêted and popular as any modern pop star, Rossini began negotiations for official appointments there, and then continued to London. The Rossini season in London at the King's theatre was unsuccessful, with many singers not up to the job and poor Isabella now definitely overdue for retirement. Lord Mount Edgecumbe, composer, writer and amateur violinist, described her as "entirely passé". Nevertheless, the Rossinis in London laughed all the way to the bank! Isabella was paid £1,500 for her stage appearances and Rossini was able to charge a standard fee of £50 for appearing at each of some 60 soirées. Even more astonishing, he gave private lessons at up to £100 a time to Lady Holland, the Duke of Wellington and the spoiled daughters of the rich and famous.

The Rossinis then returned to Paris in the summer of 1824, where they lived together for nearly five years. Rossini had already while in London signed a contract agreeing to become director of the Théâtre-Italien and to produce his existing operas there. He was also to write and produce new operas for both the Théâtre-Italien and the Opéra-Comique, and also introduce Italian operas by other composers. The breathtaking payment he had stood out for and got was 40,000 French francs per annum.

But he did not deliver all the goods as contracted, winding down his workload and enjoying the life of a popular and wealthy gentleman of leisure. "May one be so bold as to ask this illustrious man what has he done up till now for the good Parisian public which is so fond of him?" asked Stendhal in 1826. He was "in great repute in Paris, and mixed a great deal in society, to which his social and happy temperament inclines him. He spent his time in agreeable union of the occupations of director and bon-vivant". By 1826 Rossini had tired of his responsibilities at the Théâtre and accepted a govern-ment sinecure offered as an inducement to stay on in Paris: Chief Composer to the King and Inspector General of Singing in France, worth 25,000 francs a year. He certainly knew how to coin it.

Overall, however, Rossini's achievements during these five years were considerable enough for someone addicted to the good life and with his eyes now set on retirement. He introduced some fine Italian singers to Paris in two of his most advanced existing operas, *La donna del lago* and *Semiramide*. He also radically recast and renamed two others, mounting them as *Le Siège de Corinthe* and *Moïse*. And he wrote two new operas, *Le Comte Ory* and *Guillaume Tell*. Some connoisseurs hold the latter to contain some of his most inspired music.

Against this background of work and leisure, the Rossinis may have rubbed along, though Isabella's ego must have been knocked by the prospect of new divas taking on roles especially created for her, such as the title role in *Semiramide*. The couple's age difference may also have also told in bed, Rossini being in his mid-30s, and Isabella in her early 40s. If she was difficult and imperious in her prime, she must have been even harder to live with now. In spite of the cushion-ing of luxuries and good friends — they were, for example, the fre-quent guests of the Spanish banker Alejandro Aguado at Petit Bourg — they were almost certainly stale as a couple. They took a holiday in Dieppe in November 1827, where Rossini "was horribly bored".

After launching *Guillaume Tell* in 1829 and cannily fixing him-self up with a pension for life from the government of Charles X, Rossini and Isabella returned in August to Bologna for a vacation — soon to be shattered by the news that following the dethronement of Charles X all contracts under the old regime were suspended.

*

Rossini needed to sort out his pension with the new regime and left for France in September 1830 — alone. Relations had become strained with Isabella. She had been spreading it around that she had been driven to giving singing lessons because of Rossini's meanness, when in fact the teaching money was needed to fund her extravagances. She was increasingly addicted to gambling and high spending.

Apart from a few brief trips, including one to Spain, one back to Castenaso and another to Germany where he met Mendelssohn, Rossini was to remain in France for six years, sorting out the pension problem and writing nothing apart from about half of his *Stabat Mater* (the rest was completed by his friend Tadolini) and the *Soirées Musicales*. The marriage was effectively dead and letters from his father Giuseppe and Isabella (who were stuck with each other in the same house in Bologna) during these six years speak for themselves. Giuseppe's successive references to Isabella show ever increasing disenchantment: *the dear Isabella ... your wife ... your lady ... my lady the duchess of Castenaso ...* So do these short extracts:

> ... and on Christmas Day our table was made up of your wife, me, and her two maidservants. You can imagine with what happiness that was. [December 31st, 1830]

> ... if things go on in this way, I too shall go crazy. You are lucky to be far away, and may God always keep you thus so that you can always be tranquil and enjoy your peace, which you probably could not enjoy near her ... [August 4th, 1833]

Isabella, for her part, was soon to be forced to confront the eternal triangle when her husband acquired a mistress. For a short while at least, she coped with some dignity — not least because of Rossini's considerate and careful handling of the matter.

*

Rossini's inactivity as a composer from the time of his return to Paris in 1830 was not just a matter of laziness, though this in itself is understandable as the aftermath of his exhausting earlier years on the move, slogging it up and down Italy in small hired coaches or in mail coaches. (These coaches rumbled along rough, rutted, bandit-ridden roads at about five to six miles an hour, from one dirty inn to the next through a succession of endless toll-gates and frontier posts.)

Besides being tired, he was also out of sympathy with new trends in Romantic opera, especially grand opera, and he deplored in particular the demise of *bel canto* singing. Beauty of sound and brilliance of execution were now less important than powerful dramatic presentation. For Rossini, the tidal waves of emotion in people like Wagner and Meyerbeer were swamping the defences of good taste. Most crucially of all, Rossini was having to contend with severe waterworks problems and by 1832 he had entered a phase of morbid sickness, with manic-depressive symptoms, which plagued him for the next 25 years, especially from 1839 onwards up to 1857. Were it not for his extreme good fortune in meeting Madame Olympe Pélissier, he may well have never recovered to enjoy a much happier old age. Their prolonged affair was to culminate, after the death of Isabella in 1845, in a happy marriage lasting 22 years until Rossini's death.

Rossini probably met Olympe Pélissier in Aix-les-Bains in 1832, where he went to try to ease his debilitating urethritis. She was then 33, seven years younger than Rossini, and had, as they say, been around. As the daughter of an unmarried mother there were few opportunities open to her other than posh prostitution. Her mother helped matters along by making sure the young Olympe was duly introduced to a series of wealthy 'protectors' to ensure a steady supply of rent money.

Gossip about Olympe's front-ranking artistic and aristocratic punters, short or long stay, abounded. The list included the popbusting novelist Eugène Sue, Balzac, the renowned military painter Horace Vernet and the Duc de Fitz-James, whoever he was. Balzac is supposed to have proposed unsuccessfully to her and drawn her portrait in his early novel *Le Peau de chagrin*. Rossini met many of these people, of course, and one wonders whether he knew of Olympe's alleged history. If he did, he probably didn't give a damn.

So much for gossip. What matters is that she was willing to take on Rossini in spite of his catheters and acute depressions. She must inevitably have been more of a nurse than a mistress, and may have found it hard to cope with a sudden curbing of her sex life. She had at last, however, found someone whom she could love and who truly needed her. She must have been overjoyed by one of Rossini's very early presents: a "Grande scena — Giovanna d'Arco. Cantata for solo voice composed expressly for Mademoiselle Olympe Pélissier by Rossini". When it was later performed at one of his celebrated soirées the guests were enraptured.

The relationship blossomed in the happiest way. Olympe was prepared to take him as she found him, to be his devoted protectress and motherly nurse.

One person who seems to have resented Olympe's arrival on the scene was Rossini's crony Edouard Robert, director of the Théâtre-Italien. Deprived of Rossini's company on a "man-to-man basis", Robert referred to her as *Mme Rabatjoie No. 2* (the second Mrs. Spoilsport). Doubtless, their nights on the tiles in Paris hadn't always ended in a gentlemen's club with brandy and cigars. They were probably Rossini's final flings and can only have aggravated his gonorrhoeal condition.

This delicate situation

There was, of course, the problem of Isabella to sort out, and it seems that for a time a civilised triangle existed when Rossini, having finally clinched his pension from the new French government, returned to Bologna in November 1836. Olympe arrived there the following February, brave in the circumstances and expecting a dignified response from Isabella. As Olympe wrote to her friend Hector Couvert:

> Rossini never having ceased to deserve her esteem and recognition, she must now learn to make for her husband the sacrifices that all women resign themselves to making, she must receive me in her home as an accepted fact ... if his wife is even a little good to me, I shall sacrifice myself to the proprieties.

The "proprieties" presumably meant that until Isabella died, divorce being out of the question, Olympe would have to live alone in Bologna, and in fact she lived at three successive addresses until they married in 1846.

Rossini wrote to his friend Severini that everything was hunky dory:

> Olympe lunched the other day with Mme Rossini, who, furthermore, was friendly with her, and everything goes well ... [Olympe] has been very well received everywhere, and Isabella is behaving herself very well in this delicate situation. [March 12ᵗʰ, 1837]

Not surprisingly it didn't stay that way and, according to Antonio Zanolini, one of Rossini's close friends and biographers, "one day they separated in a rage, and they never saw each other again".

The strain of all this may temporarily have led Olympe to seek comfort in other men's beds. She was, after all, used to having active lovers and Rossini can't have been much fun in that department. She wrote to Hector Couvert:

> ... the sacrifices I must make to create an honourable position are beyond my moral strength, so that he has no right to criticise me because I seek happiness according to my own tastes.

The triangle must have been very awkward for papa Giuseppe as well as everyone else, and in September 1837 a formal separation was arranged to the apparent satisfaction of both parties. Rossini left Isabella well provided for.

Rossini and Olympe now left for Milan where, when his health permitted, they settled into a congenial lifestyle of musical parties and fine dining, with Olympe doing the honours well as mistress of the household.

The only discordant note came, somewhat hypocritically, from Liszt's mistress, the snooty Comtesse Marie d'Agoult (future mother by him of Cosima Wagner) who, nonsensically, said that "not a single woman of respectable standing" attended the Rossini soirées.

Rossini returned to Bologna on the pleas of his 79-year-old father in the spring of 1838, and was offered the post of perpetual consultant at the Liceo Musicale in Bologna. He eventually accepted in April 1839, but was in no fit state just then to do very much, not least because of the trauma of his father's death in the same month.

Although there were respites, the story of Rossini's life between 1839 and 1855 makes distressing reading, driven as he was to the brink of madness by his black depressions, and by urethral and bowel disorders and their prolonged and often painful treatments.

These treatments involved injections into his urethra of, among other things, sweet almond oil, milk, mallow and some sort of gum. For his haemorrhoids the physicians prescribed leeches and doses of sulphur with cream of tartar. As a purgative, caster oil replaced the saline solution that Rossini himself had decided to take. Not content with that, a Bologna doctor's medical report notes, Rossini for several years had himself regularly inserted a catheter into his bladder, for fear that his urethra might become contracted.

To all this Olympe adds a glimpse of bloated lethargy: "We are unwell," she wrote in 1840, "from eating too much. The Maestro and I live to eat and we acquit ourselves of this duty religiously". After eight years of living with Rossini, she admitted, "I am neither proud nor gracious, I am a fat woman who is occupied from morning to evening with digesting".

One respite from all this was the performance and ecstatic reception of his revised *Stabat Mater* in 1841, which he had resolved to complete himself, dispensing with Tadolini's contributions. Donizetti, who was conducting, reported that

> The enthusiasm is impossible to describe. Even at the final rehearsal which Rossini attended, in the middle of the day, he was accompanied to his home to the shouting of more than 500 persons. The same thing the first night, under his window, since he did not appear in the hall.

A visit to Paris in 1843 for treatment by the distinguished surgeon Jean Civiale must also have given Rossini a boost, if only because so many admirers clamoured to see him. During the first and last of the four months he was there some 2,000 visitors beat a path to his door — musicians, writers, diplomats, painters. During the middle two months, Civiale forbade all activity. When asked by the celebrated singer Duprez to write a new opera, Rossini's reply was "I came upon the scene too early, you too late".

Rossini remained inactive on his return to Italy, his morale taking another nose-dive with the news of Isabella's impending death in September 1845. He spent half an hour alone with her — their first private meeting since the bust-up with Olympe eight years earlier — and emerged in floods of tears. Isabella died on October 7th, having called his name several times in her last moments — almost 30 years after their first dazzling collaboration in *Elisabetta* in Naples. Rossini never lived in the Castenaso villa again and later sold it.

On August 16th, 1846, Rossini, now 54, and Olympe 49, finally married after almost 15 years of living together. Masters and mistresses often make a mess of converting to husbands and wives, but Rossini and Olympe were exceptions. They were to enjoy 22 years of mutual affection together — a heartening tale and one turn up for the books in the litany of tormented musical marriages and love-lives.

Although buoyed up by Olympe and capable of rallying round with humorous outbursts — such as the marvellous thank-you letter to an admiring sausage maker for a package of his products — and also the odd musical trifle, Rossini was still wading in the Slough of Despond. The revolutions of 1848 ("nothing but barricades and assassinations" grumbled the maestro) made things even worse; attacked by many Bolognese for being unsympathetic to the cause of national unity, he became even more depressed and moved to Florence in 1851.

In 1854 he wrote of "the deplorable state of health in which I find myself for five long months, a most obstinate nervous malady that robs me of my sleep and I might say almost renders my life useless". In the same year his friend Filippo Mordani referred to Rossini's "truly miserable life ... pallid face, the eyes languid and deep sunk, the cheeks hollow, the head drooping".

A most moving and powerful portrait of Rossini's condition at its blackest is that of Emilia Branca Romani, who with her husband Felice Romani was a member of the Rossinis' close circle in Florence. Rossini, she wrote, was suffering from

> a neurosis which, altering his fibres, rendered him almost monomaniac ... Rossini truly was sick, disturbed, nervous, very much weakened and depressed in spirit. According to him, the world had forgotten him, and he would have liked to forget the world, by removing himself from it ... Sometimes the altered Maestro moved around the room with agitated steps, struck his head, and, fulminating against his adverse fate, exclaimed: "Someone else in my state would kill himself, but I ... I am a coward and haven't the courage to do it!"

*

But thanks to the tender ministrations of Olympe, and the infinitely patient and sympathetic support of his intimate friends, who included some of his finest divas, Rossini was nursed lovingly out of his moods of black despair — by means of his own music. Olympe organised regular musical soirées in their darkened drawing room, with the maestro himself "drawing forth magical sounds" as he accompanied his divas at the piano. It was as though, wrote Signora

Romani, "far from being sluggish, he did nothing but practise on the keyboard".

On Olympe's insistence the Rossinis once more, in April 1855, set out for Paris in a further search for a medical cure and a rejuvenation of the maestro's morale. Although he continued to be very poorly for a time, defended against all comers by the concierge, his male servant Tonino, and Olympe ("The first is a small fortress, the second a formidable bastion; as for the third, to get past it, one needs to be invincible"), Rossini slowly recovered in body and spirit, his sense of fun and humour revitalised, and his urge to compose re-fired. He rented spacious and sumptuously appointed quarters on the rue de la Chausée d'Antin and started his series of famed *Samedi Soirs,* Saturday evening concerts that were the most sought-after diary dates in high Parisian society. The greatest artists of the day living in or passing through Paris performed there.

Rossini's first composition on recovery was for Olympe, without whose loving attention he would very probably by then (1857) have been insane or dead:

> Musique Anodine
> I offer these modest songs to my dear wife Olympe
> as a simple testimonial of gratitude for the
> affectionate, intelligent care of which she was prodigal
> during my overlong and terrible illness
> (Shame of the medical faculty)
> Gioachino Rossini
> Words by Metastasio

He also wrote her an exquisite piano miniature, tender and ardent, entitled *Une caresse à ma femme.*

Contrary to the persisting popular mythology, other compositions now poured forth. There were over 150 delightful and inventive piano pieces, enjoyable songs, and small ensemble pieces that he dubbed collectively his *Péchés de viellesse* — his *Sins of Old Age.* (These are only now gradually gaining ground in the concert hall.) There was also the lovely and much better known *Petite Messe Solennelle.*

Rossini and Olympe remained happy to the end, in spite of — or more probably because of — some wonderful touches of henpeckery. "Sh, sh, sh … that's my wife coming back," he once said to his publisher Ricordi after receiving a wodge of royalties and throwing them hastily into a drawer, "I'll keep these for my pocket money … I'll send you the receipt tomorrow." Inevitably, some high-society snobs looked down their noses at Olympe, as this revealing domestic vignette from the memoirs of Lille de Hegermann-Lindencrone (a Massachusetts-born beauty, who attended one of the soirées in 1864 with her American banker husband) makes clear:

> Rossini's wife's name is Olga [sic]. Someone called her Vulgar, she is so ordinary and pretentious, and would make Rossini's home and salon very commonplace if it were not that the master glorified all by his presense.

In her own way Olympe was as vital to Rossini as was Cosima to Richard Wagner, enabling him to rebuild his life and to revive his creative embers.

*

Rossini became seriously ill in the autumn of 1868 and died in his villa in Passy, a suburb of Paris, on November 13th. He was surrounded by close friends including the three singers Adelina Patti, Alboni and Tamburini. Herbert Weinstock, reffering to the Abbé Gallet who administered Extreme Unction, reports the last moments:

> Sobs came from all parts of the room: one would have said that a desolated family was gathered at the deathbed of the best of parents… At about ten o'clock that night, lying with his spent eyes wide open, Rossini said "Olympe." At quarter after eleven, Dr. D'Ancona said to Olympe: "Madame, Rossini has stopped suffering." Olympe threw herself upon her husband's body, exclaiming: "Rossini, I shall always be worthy of you!" She could be pulled away only with difficulty.

His funeral was attended by some 4,000 mourners and memorial services were held throughout France and Italy.

Olmpe, who had wanted to be buried with him, was persuaded to let his remains be removed to Italy, where they were finally laid to rest at Santa Croce church in Venice. Olympe died at the age of 81 in 1878.

***

CHAPTER 8

FRANZ PETER SCHUBERT
"MUSIC ON THE RIM OF DEATH"
[Conductor Nikolaus Harnoncourt]

BORN: VIENNA, 31ST JANUARY 1797
DIED: VIENNA, 19TH NOVEMBER 1828

Schubert ailing [he needs 'young peacocks' like Benv. Cellini].
[Eduard von Bauernfeld's diary, 1826]

Would to God I did know how to practise so noble an art, for one reads that Jove practised it with Ganymede in paradise, and here on earth there use it the greatest emperors and the grandest kings in the world. [Benvenuto Cellini's response to being called "a dirty sodomite": *Memoirs* 1558-62]

*

Although Schubert, unlike Mozart and Beethoven, has not yet had his life essentially re-invented for the big screen biopic by Milos Forman, Bernard Rose or whomever, he has nevertheless been assiduously, if innocuously, metamorphosed and caricatured for the musical stage.

It started with Willner and Reichart's *Das Dreimäderlhaus* (The House of the Three Sisters), which soon spawned such offspring as *Lilac Time, Blossom Time* and *Chanson d'amour*. The storyline has our dear Franz, a hopelessly tongue-tied swain, dreaming of romance with "a fair maiden all of his own with lilac blossom on her swelling breast". She appears in the shape of Hannerl, one of his lovely young pupils, who, alas, "may learn more from the petals of a flower as to what he really feels for her" than anything the poor fellow says. In the end Franz loses Hannerl to his friend Schober because of his shyness, and those contrived misunderstandings that are the lifeblood of stage and screen storylines. For Schubert there is "nothing for it but to find comfort in his music". After first appearing in 1916 in Vienna, *Das Dreimäderlhaus* has appeared in countless guises in London, Paris and New York, the two most notable fingers in the musical pie being those of Sigmund Romberg and Richard Tauber. There were also at least four film versions between 1921 and 1958.

In the case of Schubert, inventive image-making for stage or screen has been inevitable, even unavoidable, since so little is known even now about his private life. As John Reed, one of Schubert's leading biographers, has written recently in the journal of the Schubert Institute (UK), "It does not seem possible to study Schubert's life in any detail without becoming aware that there is a conspicuous gap at the centre of the story".

The gap still exists, but it has been narrowed very significantly by the recent researches of that most distinguished of musicological private eyes, the American scholar Maynard Solomon — the gentleman who effectively solved the riddle of Beethoven's Immortal Beloved in 1972. In the spring 1989 issue of *19th Century Music,* a journal from the University of California, Solomon suggests that Schubert and his intimate reading circle of like-minded friends including musicians, poets, painters, actors, writers and civil servants may have developed, from 1816 onwards, into a coterie consisting mainly of practising homosexuals or, in some cases, bisexuals.

The circle had been founded in 1814 by Schubert's older school friend Joseph von Spaun, a government official who almost certainly wasn't gay. Over the ensuing years the innermost members included (not necessarily concurrently) Schubert's most loved friend, the dissolute dilettante Franz von Schober, an actor, poet, librettist and archhedonist; the distinguished and rampantly gay painter Moritz von Schwind; the dramatist Eduard von Bauernfeld; the rich patron Franz von Bruchmann; the artist Leopold Kupelweiser; the poet Johann Mayrhofer, one of Schubert's most important song collaborators; and the distinguished baritone Michael Vogl, the "Greek bird" and oldest member of the coterie. Many others came and went at different times.

Solomon also believes that Schubert probably contracted syphilis from one of the many "young peacocks" these men used. In gay-speak, peacocks were one of many euphemisms for "beautiful boys in extravagant or feminine dress". Indeed, the unknown "girl" who was seen with Schubert in a Grinzing tavern by the alarmed poet Heinrich Hoffman on August 15th, 1827 may well have been a peacock. "[Schubert] came to join us and did not show himself again," noted Hoffman laconically.

Other quarry terms that had been in use since the Italian Renaissance among homosexuals (including, notably, the Italian sculptor Benvenuto Cellini) included pheasants, hazel hens, nightingales, pigeons and pea-hens. (In ancient Greece the gift of an adult game bird to a youth was evidence of amorous interest.) The euphemisms were necessary, of course, because even in the morally permissive climate of the Vienna of Mozart, Beethoven and Schubert, homosexuality was definitely illegal and therefore driven underground along with many other clandestine or subversive fraternities.

*

At least Schubert's appearance has never been an enigma, with contemporary descriptions matching and supplementing the pencil drawing of 1821 by his friend Leopold Kupelweiser and an anonymous portrait painted in 1827. Jestingly likened by Schwind to a "drunken cabby", Schubert was physically unprepossessing, apparently neglecting his teeth and clothes, and smelling of tobacco. He was a very stumpy 4' 11½", much smaller than Beethoven's Napoleonic height of just under 5' 6". Nicknamed *Schwammerl* (Tubby, literally "little mushroom"), he had soft, sparkling grey-brown eyes, bushy eyebrows, curly brown hair, a round face, snub nose, prominent dimpled chin, domed forehead, and a pale but bright complexion.

*

Because Schubert probably became a practising homosexual doesn't mean that he had always been indifferent to women. It is well established that at the age of 17 he fell in love with 15-year-old Therese Grob, whose widowed mother ran a silk business. After a year at training college (1813-14) Schubert had returned very unwillingly to the classroom as a sixth assistant teacher in his father's flourishing in-house school, apparently not averse to giving his pupils a clip over the ear if they played him up. Even if he kept up with the marking, he can only have been a very middling teacher because all he ever wanted to do was compose. To wit, by the end of 1814 his tally of compositions already included the first symphony, six string quartets, a good quantity of church music, including his first Mass in F, and his first flawless "poem-in-music" *Gretchen am Spinnrade* (Gretchen at the Spinning Wheel). This was Schubert's first setting of Goethe, whose impact on him was explosive.

On October 16th Therese, then barely 16, sang the soprano solo part in the first performance of the Mass, with Schubert conducting, his brother at the organ and his teacher Salieri, no less, in the audience. The occasion was the centenary celebration of the parish church in Liechtental where he had been baptised and had sung as a choirboy. From there he had moved up as far as you could go in the choral world to become a "Vienna choirboy" at the Imperial and Royal Court Chapel between 1808 and 1812.

During the night following the first performance of the Mass, Schubert composed what was surely meant to be a love token for Therese when he set to music Schiller's *Das Mädchen aus der Freunde*, (beginning: Blissful was her nearness/and all hearts opened ...). The remarkable surge of further settings of love poems during the next two years suggests that Therese was at the heart of them. The titles seem to speak for themselves: *Love's Intoxication, Frustrated Love, Yearning of Love, First Love, All for Love, The Secret* and many more. Perhaps he was unable to stammer out his feelings directly to her during their Sunday afternoon walks together — if they even got that far — and so they all went into his music. Wonderful for us, if sad for the young swain at the time.

As Peggy Woodford has shown so clearly, July 1815, in fact, proved to be the most musically bountiful month of Schubert's entire life, with some 17 song settings composed (to Goethe, Kosegarten and Stadler) plus a *Salve Regina*, a *Hymn to the Eternal Spirit*, and the completion of the Third Symphony. The year 1815 as a whole was an *annus mirabilis*, generating over 200 works, of which 150 were songs. These included one of his most popular ever, the spine-chilling *Erlkönig*, and also one of the most beautiful and briefest of all his love songs, a setting of Goethe's *Nähe des Geliebten* (The Beloved's nearness):

> I think of you when the sun's lustre
> Shines from the sea;
> I think of you when the moon's gleam
> Reflects in wells ...

The following year was almost as prolific, with over 160 compositions.

Therese was no belle, but then neither was her shy suitor a beau. His older friend from schooldays Anton Holzapfel paints a picture of two young people wrapped up in music and each other:

> ... Therese was by no means a beauty but she was well built, rather plump, and with a fresh, childlike round little face; she had a lovely soprano voice ... Schubert wrote several things for her and in particular an enchantingly lovely Ave in C ... the Grob household opened its doors and became of importance to our Franz ...

Therese's mementos of Schubert included a songbook, which he lovingly compiled as a farewell keepsake for her in 1816 and which remained in the family for many years.

Anton Holzapfel, at this time one of the composer's friends from their school days, mentions a lost letter Schubert wrote him in 1815, waxing long and lyrical about his feelings for Therese. The elder man's reply advising the composer to forget all about his "ridiculous infatuation" turned out to be sound if inevitably pointless. Schubert, never really cut out for the grind of regular employment, was a more than welcome visitor to the home of the musical Grob family, but he most definitely didn't measure up to the widowed Frau Grob's idea of an eligible son-in-law. In due course Therese married into her own class, becoming the wife of a master baker Johann Bergmann on November 21st, 1820. Frilled silk shirts, neckties, waistcoats and stockings in exchange for limitless supplies of scrumptious *vienoisserie!* Did the rather plump 21-year-old Therese fill out into a very matronly hausfrau, one wonders?

Schubert had to stop "seeing" Therese in 1816 and may have taken some while to get over her. She seems to have been still on his mind in the summer of 1819 while on a holiday in Steyr. Writing to his brother Ferdinand, who lived near Therese, Schubert asked him to forward "the enclosed letter" — unidentified, just to tease biographers — and concluded: "As you can see, I am not quite so faithless as you imagine."

If we could believe Schubert's friend Anselm Hüttenbrenner writing some 40 years later, Therese had been keen to marry Schubert and waited three years for him to find a proper job, which he searched for in vain. Nonsense, of course, because Schubert actually had a job and desperately wanted out to devote himself to the pursuit of beauty and pleasure. After Therese, he very definitely renounced the idea of marriage; not primarily because of his homosexuality (marriage indeed was often used as a convenient front for it); more because he rejected what he saw as its limitations. "To a free man," he wrote in his diary in 1816, "matrimony is a terrifying thought these days; he exchanges it [his freedom] either for melancholy or for crude sensuality." In 1827 Schober reported that when he suggested that Schubert enter into a marriage of convenience with a certain well-disposed dancer called Gusti Grünwedel, the composer "rushed out without his hat, flushed with anger ... and let himself go to pieces".

*

Upstairs, Downstairs

Many biographers have mentioned another woman in Schubert's life, a chambermaid named 'Pepi' Pöckelhofer, with whom he may have enjoyed a brief fling. In 1818 Schubert packed in teaching for good and spent the summer in Hungary as music tutor to the two young daughters of Count Johann Karl Esterházy, Marie and Karoline, at their summer castle of Zseliz (now Zeliezovce in Czechoslovakia, some 300 miles east of Vienna). Schubert was, of course, employed as a servant and seems to have got on very well with the downstairs crowd after giving lessons upstairs. In a letter to his closest and most-loved friend Schober on 8th September, Schubert describes the field of play:

A companion of the count, a gay old fellow and a capable musician, often keeps me company. The cook, the lady's maid, the chambermaid, the nurse, the butler, &c, and two grooms are all good folk. The cook rather a rake; the lady's maid 30 years of age; the chambermaid very pretty and often my companion; the nurse a good old thing; the manager my rival. The two grooms are more fit for traffic with horses than with human beings.

According to Maynard Solomon this can be read *two* ways. Everybody assumes that the manager was Schubert's rival for Pepi, but in view of the accumulation of evidence pointing to Schubert's homosexuality, the object of the rivals' attentions could equally be read as the count's companion! Perhaps he, rather than 'Pepi' kept both rivals on the go; doing a turn in the wine cellar with the manager between swigs of Pócs-Megyer, when Schubert was upstairs correcting the finger action of the young ladies; then another with his fellow *Musiker* in the barn when the manager was inspecting the estate.

Either way, Fraulein 'Pepi', who never in her wildest dreams imagined she would be immortalised in biographies and very learned journals, remained friendly enough with Schubert years later to deliver his letters home on her visits to Vienna. But neither she nor the count's companion provided any kind of compensation for Schubert's separation from his family and Viennese circle. "Not a soul here," he wrote to his brothers, "has any feeling for true art, or at the most the Countess now and again (unless I am wrong) ... Have no fear, then, that I shall stay away longer than is absolutely necessary ... "

By the time of his second summer visit to Zseliz in 1824, Schubert was an established composer and was treated accordingly, with his own rooms, decent fees and the privilege of dining with the Esterházys. This time some kind of deep, idealised *amitié amoureuse* developed between the composer and the younger of his two pupils, the impressionable Countess Karoline, now 18-years-old. Music was undoubtedly the binding force between them, and Karoline must have been enraptured by the magnificent series of piano duets he wrote for them both to play while he was there: the so-called *Grand Duo* (Sonata in C), the *Variations on an Original Theme* (one of the classics of the duet repertoire), and the *Divertissement a l'hongroise*. Karoline must indeed have been a good player to get round the tricky keys and triplet passages in even the second player's part of the *Grand Duo*.

Karoline must have been stunned by the way her teacher could, in the words of one of the house guests Baron von Schönstein, "shake the most glorious things out of his sleeve"; during the September of his stay Schubert composed a 14-page vocal quartet called *Gebet,* for performance by members of the house party, within a day. (Like Mozart, Schubert was one of the fastest writers in musical history.) And at parties she will have no doubt adored his improvised minuets, Ländler and waltzes as they flowed through his fingers as effortlessly as the bubbly from the bottles.

Countess Karoline was probably Schubert's ideal woman or distant beloved. As John Reed has so succinctly pointed out, "Schubert's reference to 'the attractions of a certain rising star' in a letter to Schwind sums it all up, for a star is by its nature beautiful, remote and unattainable". And such an attraction to a woman is surely perfectly consistent with a primarily homosexual orientation.

Schubert still thought enough of Karoline four years later to dedicate his greatest work for four hands to her, the F minor Fantasy, with its beautiful opening *cri de coeur* in the repeated descending fourth figure. Although supposedly retarded, according to Solomon, she must have been a fine enough musician. She married when she was approaching 40 but an annulment soon followed.

It would surely be too simplistic to suggest that Schubert's relationships with Therese and Karoline were unimportant to him simply because he may have become a practising homosexual.

**

Anyone who knew Schubert knows how he was made of two natures, foreign to each other, how powerfully the craving for pleasure dragged his soul down to the cesspool of slime.
[Josef Kenner, 1830]

The co-existence of the sordid and the sublime, the tacky and the transcendental in the same human beings never ceases to baffle. We don't know exactly when Schubert may have started using "peacocks", but by the end of February 1823 at the age of 26 he was house bound, in the family home in the Rossau district of Vienna, for five months and suffering from the secondary-phase symptoms of syphilis that were to recur for the rest of his life: rashes, anaemia, inflammation of the glands, blinding headaches, aching bones, nausea, giddiness and loss of hair.

The same young man had been living two different lives. There he was, perhaps in the company of the incorrigible Schober, or the insatiable Schwind, slinking into one of Vienna's gay pickup taverns, in the *Halbwelt,* to choose one from any number of transvestite rent boys. This was the same man who, although inevitably dwarfed by Beethoven, had already established his reputation in Vienna as a composer of consummate songs and fine instrumental music.

One landmark on his rise to fame had been a decisive move by his influential barrister friend Leopold von Sonnleithner, an important figure in Vienna's Philharmonic Society; after hosting a private performance of the *Erlkönig* in 1820, Sonnleithner took the lead in setting up a scheme to publish Schubert's songs privately. In March 1821, the final public seal of excellence had been stamped on Schubert's reputation after one of the finest baritones in Vienna, Michael Vogl, having already enthusiastically promoted Schubert's interests, performed *Erlkönig* at a charity concert at the Kärntnertor (Court Theatre).

In that same year the *Schubertiaden* were also under way, evenings in fashionable salons where Schubert's friends and admirers gathered regularly for performances of his works alone, followed by "grand feeding and dancing". In 1822 a review in the posh paper *Wiener Zeitschrift für Kunst* (The Vienna Journal for the Arts) referred to him as a "genius" and in the following year as "this popular master".

By the time his syphilis had taken hold in 1824, Schubert's most enduring and best-known achievements included the high-spirited and ever-fresh Fifth Symphony; the *'Unfinished'*, still one of the best-loved and most frequently performed of all his works; the magnificent *Wanderer* fantasy for piano, whose opening, with its pounding rhythms and brilliant passagework Schumann later described as "a seraphic hymn to the God-head"; the Fifth Mass in A flat major, the ever-popular *Trout Quintet*; his first impassioned and headily lyrical song cycle, *Die schöne Müllerin* (The Fair Maid of the Mill); and countless other sublime songs set to the poems of Müller, Mayrhofer, Goethe, and many others. There were also many other lesser-known works, including operas, choral works, piano and chamber music.

But the writing was already on the wall. By the end of March 1824, even if he didn't know the precise nature of his illness, Schubert was facing a period of "fateful recognition of a miserable reality" and becoming increasingly subject to bouts of melancholy:

> Think of a man whose health will never be right again, and who in sheer despair over this always makes things worse instead of better. Think of a man, I say, whose brightest hopes have come to nothing; for whom the happiness of love and friendship have nothing to offer, but, at the best, pain; whose passion for beauty (at least the

sort that inspires) threatens to forsake him. I ask you, is he not a miserable, unhappy being? — "My peace is gone, my heart is sore, I shall find it never, nevermore." I may well sing this every day now, for every night, when I go to bed, I hope I may not wake again, and every morning only recalls yesterday's grief.
[Letter to Kupelweiser, March 31st, 1824]

*

Schubert's Circle

Nobody disputes that the young men in Schubert's circle loved each other ardently and demonstratively, in the extravagant, *Schwärmerisch* (gushing) style of the period. This ending of one letter from Schubert to his beloved Schober in 1823 during their two-year separation is a very mild example of epistolary affection between members of the circle:

> For the rest, I hope to regain my health, and this recovered treasure will let me forget many a sorrow; only you, dear Schober, I shall never forget, for what you meant to me no one else can mean, alas! And now keep well and do not forget
> Your eternally affectionate friend,
> Franz Schubert

A later letter also grieves over their separation, and recalls the "sweet time ... when one inspired the other and thus united striving after the highest beauty enlivened us all". Although the discovery of these kinds of letters in the pocket of a British soldier or sailor today might well result in a discharge, such expressions of affection were then no evidence of homosexual behaviour.

There is, incidentally, no extant letter written by Schubert to any man, or woman, which could be described as passionate. Other members of the inner circle, however, were very much less inhibited, especially Schwind the painter. Take this "middling" letter of his to Schober, one of many definitely suggesting something more than warm affection:

> I see myself in thy heart's love like an angel, who binds us together and I rejoice that you speak to me, to me, who rests calmly and with

total love in thy arms, as I do ... I want to dance naked, but in the highest sense and in front of everyone ... O if I could once again possess thee, then I would know all and be capable of everything.

Schober, who assumed the manner of an oriental prince in his exotically furnished rooms, was the circle's undisputed leader, bewitching (or in some cases appalling) the others. Although he lived with Schubert for several extended periods between 1816 and 1828, he shunned the idea of exclusive relationships. Several members of the circle blamed him for luring Schubert into debauchery; unfairly so, because in the end, Schubert was very definitely his own man.

The hottest hints of what they all got up to burn holes in the pages on which they appear. Schwind, after advising Schubert in 1825 to conceal his "fleshly and spiritual needs — or rather your need for pheasants and punch" if he wanted to obtain the post of Court Organist, went on to bemoan the dearth of "wind music" at Wasserburger's café in the winter. "We will have to play on our own pipes," he concludes. Since there was never any music at Wasserburger's the *double entendre* becomes unmistakable (thanks to Maynard Solomon, of course).

Two or three years later a certain "Nina" invited Schubert and Schober to a party promising them heavenly entertainment in a letter seemingly crammed with allusions to pretty boys, penises and condoms:

The snowed in nightingales of the Alleegasse will, not withstanding all the cold rinds, flute with all their might ... We expect implicit obedience on the part of our vassals.

The various cross-age and possible "Queen" relationships within the circle are surely the very stuff of future American doctorates. What is also interesting is the ultimate fate of the circle, which started to disintegrate in 1824 because so many of its members got married or engaged.

Some of these enigmatic relationships endured, others withered. Schwind's engagement to Anna Hönig was broken off by her family because of his non-conformist behaviour and "lack of piety"; Schober's engagement to Justina Bruchmann, after their clandestine affair, was similarly aborted. Schubert had, revealingly, been fiercely opposed to both these relationships. Schober did actually marry later, when he was 60, but the arrangement was short-lived. But the marriages of the "Greek bird" Vogl, of Spaun and Kupelweiser endured, as did Bauernfeld's long-term liaison with "Clothilde", whoever she (or he?) might have been. Vogl's marriage, however, at the age of 58, was a cause of great merriment for Schubert and many others. Had Schubert, wonders Maynard Solomon, been an "ephebe" or pederastic object for his "second father" Vogl?

Finally, in this orgy of speculation, Schubert seems to have been moved in a particularly personal way by the verses of the homosexual poet August Graf von Platen. Platen provided him with the text for two songs which, according to John Reed, "seem to carry a special weight of subjective emotion". The text of one of them, *Die Liebe hat gelogen* (Love has lied), reads:

Love has lied;
Sorrow lies heavily upon me.
Everything, alas! has conspired to delude me.
Hot tears continually
Flow down my cheeks.
Beat no more my heart!
My poor heart, beat no more!

*

It seems apt to focus last on the poet with whom Schubert shared rooms for well over two years between 1818 and 1821, Mayrhofer. As early as 1814 he led an informally structured group of quasi-political radicals, including Schubert, Kupelweiser and Schober, which published two volumes of a journal embodying their "true and mainly patriotic sentiments".

Mayrhofer, who somewhat ironically was a state censor, provided Schubert with the poems for 50 lieder, which included some of the composer's greatest works. Mayrhofer's melancholic temperament and preoccupation in his poems with suffering, death and "the happier land" of the after-life influenced and reinforced Schubert's own very similar perspective, which reached its apotheosis in his song cycle of 1827, *Die Winterreise* (The Winter Journey).

The cause of the breach between them in late 1820 remains a

mystery, but Mayrhofer's pervading melancholia eventually got the better of him in 1836 when he committed suicide.

*

Schubert's hedonism and debauchery were evidently as inseparable from his prodigious creativity as was Lully's infinitely more depraved behaviour nearly two centuries earlier. Look at Schubert's phenomenal output in the year of his death: the F minor Fantasy dedicated to Countess Karoline, the Mass No. 6 in E flat, the song cycle *Schwanengesang*, (Swan Song), three piano sonatas together with other piano pieces, any number of solo and part songs and religious works — and one of the supreme works of the entire chamber music repertoire, the String Quintet in C major (a string quartet with an extra cello). Generations of string players have often experienced from "within", as it were — however imperfect their execution(!) — the heart-rending melodic cries and sighs in the slow movement, at times infinitely tender, at others unbearably anguished. And what a disturbing, curiously busy second cello part that same movement has.

Maynard Solomon even suggests that Schubert's insatiable pursuit of "peacocks", "pheasants" and "punch" "represents [his] drive towards physical extinction, his way of hastening death even while seeking to delay it, of bringing on the shadows by a total immersion in the sensuous moment". It may have been a kind of heroic defiance of orthodoxy and fear of death, "the ultimate sign of the exertion of Schubert's free will". The man who in the penultimate year of his life had sublimated and transfigured his suffering into the world's greatest song cycle on the theme of despair and death, *Die Winterreise,* was ready to face his end, ready to throw in his lot with the lonesome, uncomplaining, long-suffering old organ grinder.

Ferdinand's account of Schubert's final hours surely reinforces the composer's total readiness for death: "Schubert looked fixedly into the doctor's eyes, grasped at the wall with a feeble hand, and said slowly and seriously: 'Here, here is my end!' "

***

CHAPTER 9

GAETANO DONIZETTI
"MAESTRO ORGASMO"

BORN: BERGAMO, 29TH NOVEMBER 1797
DIED BERGAMO, 8TH APRIL 1848

His character has become either irritable or taciturn; the excitement of his genital organs no longer allows M. Donizetti to resist the impulse of his desires, and he more and more compromises his health in giving reign to partly unhealthy needs ...
[Paris, January 28th, 1846, Calmeil, Mitivié, Ricord]

His talent is great, but even greater is his fecundity, which is exceeded only by rabbits. [Contemporary critic Heinrich Heine]

*

The physical and mental decline of Gaetano Donizetti — the man who dominated Italian opera between the death of Bellini in 1835 and the emergence of Verdi with *Nabucco* seven years later — is probably the most harrowing of the many stories of syphilitic affliction in this volume. For well over two years, Donzetti was little more than a decaying human cabbage — increasingly inarticulate, incoherent, immobile and incontinent. The poor man had arrived at this state after a descent into uncontrollable eroticism: compulsive masturbation certainly and, very likely, insatiable whoring.

The justly sung heroes and heroines of Donizetti's distressing finale are his longtime closest friend Antonio Dolci, and also his selfless hostesses, Countess Rosa Rota-Basoni and her daughter Giovannina, who so lovingly and unstintingly took care of him in their family palace in Bergamo.

There is also an unsung hero in the piece: Donizetti's male nurse Antoine Pourcelot, who so devotedly and repeatedly changed his soiled clothes and cleaned him up for well over two years right up to his death on April 8th, 1848. Monsieur Pourcelot tended the composer during his 16-month confinement in a mental asylum in Ivry (outside Paris) and then elected to stay with him to the end, nursing him during the weary 18-day rail and stage coach journey from Paris, via Brussels, to Bergamo. Donizetti died from the combined effects of fever and a series of strokes, common in the terminal stage of late syphilis.

Donizetti makes you realise how fortunate his compatriot Rossini was in only catching gonorrhoea. There seems little doubt that after catching syphilis in his late teens while studying in Bologna (1815-17),Donizetti passed it on to his adored wife Virginia (née Vassellani) immediately after they were married in June 1828. The tragedy compounded remorselessly. Virginia gave birth to three children — two boys and a girl. The first son was two months premature, deformed, and died in less than two weeks:

> ... it had a very long vein on top of its head, crossing over the head and reaching from one ear to the other. The fact is that after seven days it began to have convulsions, its eyes were twisted, and after the little life kept in it by spoonfeeding it milk, it remained for two days with its mouth shut, and died ...

The second child, a girl, was a month-and-a-half premature and stillborn; and the third child, a son, died almost immediately after birth. Virginia herself died soon after her third labour at the age of 29 in 1837. She was never to enjoy the thrill of driving in style around Naples in the coach and pair that her husband had just purchased along with an elegant and larger up-market apartment on the strada Nardones.

The coach and pair were Donizetti's first real status symbol as a hugely successful composer. His international career had first taken off in 1831 when performances of his tragic opera *Anna Bolena* were staged in London and Paris after several very successful runs in Italy following its première in Milan in 1830. And with his triumphant *Lucia di Lammermoor* at the Teatro San Carlo in Naples (1835) Donizetti had established his pre-eminence among his contemporaries, epitomising the Italian Romantic spirit in that golden age of voice-worship, especially of diva-heroines warbling clusters of trills, arpeggios, scales, and scary high notes.

Donizetti was never really to recover from the loss of Virginia, and much of his subsequent "abuse of Venus" (to transplant the quaint whoring euphemism from Rossini's medical report) can be seen as attempts to block out his grief as much his syphilis-induced lechery:

There are moments when I would put myself in the hands of a hundred women if they could distract me for half an hour, and would pay as much as I could.

Donizetti never realised the most likely cause of Virginia's death. It was put down to "measles", "German measles" or "scarlatina", or the effects of an untimely bath after her labour. (Although there was a severe cholera epidemic at the time, there is no direct evidence that this contributed to her death.)

The year 1837 was indeed a grievous one for Donizetti. In nine years he had lost two sons, a daughter, both his parents and now his wife. He would be unable in future letters ever to bring himself to write her name; and even unable to enter the room in which she died.

*

1805-1837

Although Donizetti's student days were productive musically, they were obviously fatal for his future health and long-term career. His earliest and dearly revered mentor and teacher, Johannes Simon Mayr, then an important composer, and *maestro di cappella* at Bergamo's Santa Maria Maggiore, spotted Gaetano's talent and admitted him into his free music school, funded by a local charitable institution, in 1805. Well grounded in the technical basics, Donizetti in due course (1815) moved on, with Mayr's support and financial help, to Bologna to study counterpoint under the very efficient but, by comparison with Mayr, uninspiring Padre Mattei. Mattei had, incidentally, numbered Rossini among his distinguished former pupils.

It was doubtless to relieve the arduous rigours of producing four-part fugues, two or three prentice operas, and bulging basketfuls of other fledgling creations, that Donizetti first strayed into the back streets (probably with his mates), nervously anticipating his first lessons in the school of life. ("I will if you will." "OK, you go first." "No, after you." "Mamma mia, come come signori, don't be wimps, I'll teach you both together.") Donizetti sadly picked up more than he bargained for, though it was to be some 30 years on before he appears, if at all, to have had an inkling of the true cause of his then rapidly advancing cerebro-spinal degeneration.

After completing his formal education in 1817 Donizetti, just like Rossini, soon made the most of his ability to produce serviceable operas to order at lightning speed, usually in trying circumstances. He began turning out the vocal equivalents of five-finger exercises like hotcakes or scones on a griddle-iron, or pizzas in an oven. After composing four prentice operas for the impresario Zancla in Venice, in January 1822 Donizetti premièred in Rome his first significant success, *Zoraida di Granita* — not, as far as one can make out, an opera about an ice-cream goddess, but if you're burning to research the storyline, please feel free.

Between *Zoraida* and his first operatic triumph with *Anna Bolena* in 1830, the most important event in Donizetti's life was falling in love with and marrying Virginia Vasselli. Operatically he was very active but not illustriously so. The success of *Zoraida* led to a summons to Naples from that supremest of impresario supremos whom we have already met — Domenico Barbaja, who needed a replacement for Rossini. Between 1822 and 1830 Donizetti produced between two and five operas a year, mainly for Naples, but also for Milan, Rome, Palermo and Genoa. He was still finding his own voice, relying often on Rossinian formulas and having to make do with some very inferior librettos.

In 1826 Donizetti fell in love with Virginia, a lively 18-year-old dark-haired beauty. They were engaged in May 1827 and married in June 1828. Donizetti's father, Andrea, was none too pleased at this ecstatic event, though more because of the loss of his son's financial support than disapproval of Virginia, who came from a well-to-do lawyer's family in Rome.

The marriage, albeit cruelly aborted after nine years, and overcast by the repeated loss of children and Donizetti's bouts of syphilitic ill health, was a very happy one. Donizetti's work often entailed periods of separation, and there is very touching evidence of Virginia's concern for her husband's morale and well-being, especially on his first nights and the run-up to them. "You can imagine the agitation in which I live," she wrote to her father-in-law before the première of

Anna Bolena, "the more so because I know the sensitivity of his character; for that reason I commend myself to you so that you may keep me company during the days when he is about to go on the stage."

Donizetti's health also gave her cause for anxiety. Soon after their marriage the composer was writing to his father about his ailments and treatments — "convulsions and bile, and internal haemorrhoids; therefore bleedings, baths, purgatives, treatments" — and she was adding her own concern:

> I assure you that this illness of poor Gaetano's has made me suffer much, but much. Now, however, I thank God that He has showed His grace, and I hope that he will be perfectly recovered in a short time.

Happily married though they were, it seems that Donizetti was unable to resist the opportunity for at least one brief fling with a singer during his enforced absences from home. An early biographer, Alberto Cametti, tells us that while twiddling his thumbs in Florence in the summer of 1833 waiting for a libretto before he could dash off *Parisina,* Donizetti "occupied himself with the contralto of the company, Giuseppina Merola, in a way that certainly would not have satisfied his distant wife".

"Nothing about this story is intrinsically unbelievable," says the cautious but fascinating and hugely knowledgeable Donizetti scholar Herbert Weinstock, in one of his characteristically belt-and-braces double negatives. That must mean he thinks Donizetti *did* misbehave.

*

Two years after the success of *Anna Bolena* in 1830, Donizetti broke his contract with Barbaja in Naples to be free to take on more work in other theatres, and launch his lucrative business in intensively reared, factory-farmed operas. Up to the time of Virginia's death, his most notable successes, among a string of lesser works now rarely if ever heard of, began with the especially delightful and ever-popular rustic romp *L'elisir d'amore* (Milan 1832), reportedly dashed off in two weeks. In 1833 there were *Il furioso all'isola di San Domingo* and *Torquato Tasso* (Rome), and *Lucrezia Borga* (Milan), which remained popular for half a century. *Maria Stuarda* appeared in 1834 (Milan), and in September of the following year came the powerful and resoundingly triumphant masterpiece *Lucia di Lammermoor* (Naples), one of the most popular operas of the century. After *Lammermoor* there was no let-up. Hold your breath for *Belisario* (Venice 1836), the one-acters *Il campanello* and *Betly* (Naples 1836), then *The Siege of Calais* (Naples, November 1836) and *Pia de Tolomei* (February 1837).

No, you're not the only one who hasn't ever heard of these last five operas. I certainly hadn't either until recently! Donizetti was to compose more than 30 more before his death (around 70 all told), though you'll be relieved to hear we're giving most of them a miss.

Overwhelming grief at Virginia's death temporarily dried up his pen. He was then 39 and had no one. He wrote in agony to Virginia's brother Antonio on August 5th, 1837:

> Oh! my Totò, let my grief find an echo in yours, for I need someone to understand me. I shall be unhappy forever. Don't drive me away, think that we are alone in this world. Oh, Totò, Totò write me out of pity, for love of your Gaetano.

And again on Aug 12th:

> Without a father, without a mother, without a wife, without children ... Why then do I labour on? Why?

He shut the door to the room where Virginia died and probably never re-entered it again.

*

1837-1848

For the workaholic Donizetti, the only possible distractions from suicidal grief were the writing-desk and the opera house. Soon after Virginia's death came the successful *Roberto Devereux* in October 1837 (Naples), and then *Maria di Rudenz* (Venice, January 1838), said to have been too weighed down with the composer's personal sorrow.

Donizetti decided to get away from Naples, not only from his heartbreaking memories but also from other slings and arrows of outrageous fortune at this time. He had been finally turned down in favour of Saverio Mercadante for the post of director of the Naples Conservatory. (For a time, Mercadante was to become the only serious rival to Verdi after Donizetti's death.) To rub salt into his wounds, the royal censor had banned his next opera, *Poliuto*, because of its depiction on stage of the martyrdom of a saint.

*

Donizetti arrived in Paris in October 1838 and was instantly successful. Much to the jealous annoyance of Berlioz, he mounted his operas in four Paris theatres, including revamps of his Italian successes, and a specially Frenchified *Lammermoor*. But he suffered from inevitable bouts of depression, homesickness and renewed grief, aggravated by his syphilitic condition.

In 1840 three other operas followed: *La Fille du Regiment,* a definite favourite with audiences if not the critics; *Les Martyrs*, an expanded version of *Poliuto* that had a lukewarm reception; and *La favorite,* which gradually became popular.

Donizetti's health now began to deteriorate markedly and he reacted by plunging into ever more frenzied activity. He made separate trips to Rome and Milan for stagings of *Adelia* (February 1841, with overbooking and pandemonium on the first night!) and *Maria Padilla* (December 1841, successful enough for 24 performances, then soon forgotten forever).

In March 1842 he went to Bologna, where his conducting of the première of Rossini's *Stabat Mater* received a rapturous reception and was marked by a gift of four diamond studs from the ecstatic composer. From Bologna he continued to Vienna, where he launched *Linda di Chamonix* (May 1842 — not many more to come, promise!), and conducted the *Stabat Mater* again. While in Vienna he landed the handsomely paid post of *Kapellmeister (Maestro di Direttore di Concerti Privati)* to the Austrian court — 2,000 lire a year "for doing nothing and many months of freedom". Like Rossini, he had an unfailing flair for racking up his credit balance.

During these frenetic years in Paris, Italy and Vienna (1840-42) there was plenty of steamy gossip about the composer's premature aging and love affairs, not all of it well informed. Relaying tittle-tattle by the yard about Donizetti's womanising in Rome for instance, a writer named Franco Abbiati, one of Verdi's biographers, went to town:

> The widowed Donizetti habitually became inflamed with abrupt amorous sympathies: as if out of a frenzy to search anxiously and indiscriminately for a companion who might serve to cool the illogical sultrinesses of his body and, at the same time drive from him his sad and, alas, not unjustified forebodings of an approaching complete loss of mind.

Donizetti certainly often joked about finding a new wife, though all the supposed affairs with a whole string of women whom Appiati then goes on to mention were quite possibly apocryphal — nothing more than warm friendships with favoured divas and admired beauties within his social circles. The list includes a signora Giuseppina Strigelli-Appiani, "still a noted beauty at the age of 45", who was supposed to have reminded the composer of Virginia; a young marchioness Sterlich cultivated for the same reason; the wife of the famed baritone Magrini; and the soprano Sophie Löwe, for whom he wrote the role of Maria in *Padilla*. However, the most interesting mention of all is the stunning, young and majestically independent Giuseppina Strepponi (future mistress and wife of Verdi), for whom Donizetti had created *Adelia*. We may never know the truth.

Donizetti himself denied any womanising, though how convincing he is here to his brother-in-law Vasselli on the fifth anniversary of Virginia's death (July 1842) is perhaps debatable:

> What is this that you speak to me about concerning other women? Oh really, laugh, and believe me that I still weep as on the first day ... Oh, if I could find distraction! Believe it! ... I am trying to numb myself! Enough!

*

Back in Paris in the fall of 1842, Donizetti continued with his self-imposed, by now crushing workload. In early January 1843 came *Don Pasquale,* given the thumbs down, strangely, at the dress rehearsal in the Théatre-Italien by the musicians in the pit, who even drew rude pictures of the composer in the margins of their band parts. (Orchestral graffiti are still a flourishing folk art, of course.) One of these waggish cartoons was apparently very close to the bone, showing Donizetti being given an enema! Pit musicians or no, *Don Pasquale* was a clamorous success and is assuredly his comic master-piece, equal to Rossini in invention if not in compressed energy. It was also one of the crowning glories of the massively corpulent and charismatic Luigi Lablache in the bass title role.

Later in the year, back again in Vienna, there was the powerful and melodramatic (so they say) *Maria de Rohan,* and then finally, back in Paris, there was *Dom Sebastien, roi de Portugal* at the Opéra. Although a flop at the time and uneven in quality, enthusiasts claim it contains some of Donizetti's finest music.

Well, at least I've only mentioned less than half of them.

*

It was during the fraught rehearsals of *Dom Sebastien,* in Octo-ber and November 1843 in Paris, that Donizetti's by then decidedly wayward and cantankerous behaviour and deteriorating physical condition started to cause real alarm. Later, during his final Vienna season (1844-45), lurid tittle-tattle proliferated, one famous singer, Felice Varesi, claiming (according to the gossipy writer Raffaelo Barbiera) that he had seen "the idol of Vienna shun the delightful precincts of the Royal Palace in order to wander at night through the dark paths of the Prater, trailing dreadful phantoms".

Donizetti scholar Alessandro Luzio describes unedited letters written by the composer at this time, including a lengthy one in versified code language to his publisher. They contain "excessively free language, which skims the pornographic" and which makes no bones about his desire to "distract himself" with bouts of "digitalis", (no, not the drug, but what one might call solitary five-finger exer-cises), nor about his cravings for group sex with "the florid and acces-sible Viennese beauties":

> ... the composer of L'Elisir (d'amore) was not satisfied to celebrate his aphrodisiac rites with one girl alone, but hankered — we'll say it this way — to drive a tandem.

Compulsive masturbation! Cravings for sex in tandem with goodness knows how many tarts at once! Mind and body literally rotting away! The mind boggles even when one realises how common syphilis was, and how violent its effects could be.

*

After the Vienna season of 1844-45, Donizetti turned down the invitation of his close and concerned friends in Italy to take peaceful refuge there, and returned to Paris, whence he wrote deranged letters, especially about his colossal workload. His last letter to his beloved brother-in-law Totò, on August 11th, 1845, written in a quivering hand and descending into total incoherence, mentions that doctors had placed "twelve leeches at the place of defecation". And on October 7th he wrote to a friend Tommaso Persico:

> My nerves are so aroused that I fall from bed at night, and it seems to me that the bed rolls over on me. I don't know whether I'm still alive, as I fall head down, without helping myself with my hand, as if strangled. I have a manservant in my room now while I sleep. But a night, and I won't fall out any more? No! Silence! I commend the tombeau to you!

His decay reached the point where his friends contacted his brother Giuseppe, who was Chief of Military Music to the Ottoman armies, in Constantinople. Giussepe eventually sent his son Andrea to take charge of the composer and a medical consultation was arranged on January 28th, 1846. The lengthy report of the same date mentions that:

> Often during the night when M. Donizetti abandoned the horizontal position to make some movement of his arms, a sort of commotion operating in the interior of the cranial box caused him painful terror; it seemed to him that the floor sank beneath him, that something traversed his brain from front to back, and that the house had fallen into ruins. On the morning after one such shock, M. Donizetti was found stretched out on the floor, and it was only after being suitably relieved that he was able to return to full consciousness.

The report concluded that committal to an asylum "for mental alienations" was necessary and by a series of necessary ruses organised by his distraught nephew, Donizetti was manoeuvred into Mitvié's sanatorium, where he spent much time weeping, believing he was in jail. At least then he was out of the clutches of a mysterious but unidentified scarlet woman who appeared on the scene at this time; a *Circe* figure who, Weinstock tells us, either had a "powerful psychosexual attachment" towards the composer, or who was "artfully sinister" and possibly after his money.

Even the often-querulous Heinrich Heine, the German critic, poet and polemicist, was now moved to eloquent pity in his portrait of Donizetti's pathetic state:

> The news about the sick condition of Donizetti becomes more saddening from day to day. While his melodies ravish the world with their happy accents and are sung and trilled everywhere, he himself sits, a frightening image of insanity, in a sanatorium not far from Paris. Only in the matter of his dress did he maintain up until a short time ago a puerile ray of reason, and therefore had himself dressed carefully every morning in complete court gala, the habit adorned with all his decorations. Thus he sat, immobile, his hat in his hand, from early in the morning until late in the evening. But that too has stopped. He recognises no-one. Such is the fortune of poor mankind.

Eventually in October 1847, after a bewildering sequence of tableaux involving police objections, counter-objections, plottings, schemings and suings that would in themselves form a riveting night at the theatre, Donizetti was escorted back to Bergamo.

The rest of the heart-rending story concerning his terminal care has been touched on, but one observation in the autopsy report, signed by eight doctors, provides interesting evidence of the state of medical ignorance at that time. Having no real knowledge of the central nervous system, the physicians observed that the composer's brain "showed very highly developed circumvolutions corresponding to the locality of the organs of music, of mentation, and of genius". They may not have known what they were talking about, but they said it with conviction!

*

The story of Donizetti's remains is macabre. They have been disturbed twice. The first exhumation, carried out in 1875 when his bones were moved to the Santa Maria Maggiore from a cemetery in Lower Bergamo, revealed that the cap of his skull had been stolen. After being quickly recovered from the director of a nearby asylum it was not fitted back on to the skull but placed in an urn in the Museo Donizettiano. In 1951, however, the Bergamo Municipal Council decided that the cap should rejoin the skull. At a second exhumation, on July 26th of that year in the presence of town officials and church authorities, the outer copper casket was opened, and the cover of the inner wooden coffin removed. The 83-year-old devoted and long-time Donizetti scholar Guido Zavadini fitted the cap snugly back on to the skull with three pieces of transparent adhesive tape. The remains were then covered with a fresh piece of hand-washed linen, and the coffin and copper casket were resealed.

Let's hope the poor man can now lie in peace.

*

All told, Donizetti wrote around 70 operas, and clearly the vast majority will forever remain no more than names on a sheet of paper, no more relevant than the archived stock-lists of the parks department. These days we are, in theory at least, a bit more fussy about what we pay to hear. Gone are the Rossini and Donizetti days when operas were essentially alternatives to the casinos or elegant *caffè,* providing customers with a chance to dress up to the nines in sable, mink and ermine, or frilled shirts and silk-lapelled coats, diamonds or decorations included. They supped and gossiped like mad (or made love behind closed curtains) until a favourite diva appeared on stage with her show-piece aria. What the hell, they knew the story anyway.

Nevertheless, Donizetti's premature decay and early death at the age of 51 have almost certainly deprived us of potential masterpieces. There seems to be little doubt among the scholars and aficionados that had he lived on in good health, he would have grown further in operatic stature. At his best, he never quite equalled Rossini, Bellini or Verdi at their best. But had he lived longer he might well have done so with a masterpiece excelling *Lammermoor* or *Don Pasquale.*

CHAPTER 10

FELIX MENDELSSOHN-BARTHOLDY

BORN: HAMBURG, 3RD FEBRUARY 1809
DIED: LEIPZIG, 4TH NOVEMBER 1847

I have your portrait before me and ever repeating your dear name, and thinking of you as if you stood at my side, I weep ... Every morning and every moment of my life I shall love you from the bottom of my heart, and I am sure that in doing so I shall not wrong Hensel.
[Fanny Mendelssohn to her brother Felix on her wedding day, 1829]

Their correspondence sometimes reads like a series of love letters.
[Mozelle Moshansky on Mendelssohn and his sister Fanny]

When he is lying at her breast and tugging away, they both look so happy that I hardly know what to do with myself for joy.
[Mendelssohn to his friend Ferdinand Hiller after the birth of his first son, Karl Mendelssohn, 1838]

*

1809-1830

Being the whizziest and most well-heeled of all young whiz-kid composers, Mendelssohn was perhaps the most eligible bachelor of them all by the time he was 21. He could have picked his bride from any number of nubile young ladies on the proverbial cherry tree — or alternatively slipped into the boudoirs of the married ones already plucked. No wonder the great Goethe was worried that his head might be turned by gushing female flattery!

Mendelssohn may sometimes have been a bit snooty, tetchy and priggish, but he was also very athletic, dapper and good-looking with his high forehead, dark brown (*not* black) curly locks, refined features, silk and cashmere cravats, smart frock coats and gold-nobbed chains. On top of all this he was an undisputed genius — and stinking rich. The style to which he had become accustomed is neatly etched in the vast travelling entourages assembled for the Mendelssohn family holiday journeys to Paris, Switzerland or the Italian Lakes: a procession of three coaches crowded with servants, secretaries, tutors, governesses and the family physician in the train of the splendid four-horse family carriage.

On the face of it, no young prodigy ever had so much going for him. For, although hard-driven and never spoiled, Mendelssohn was provided with the best teaching, tackle and expertise that money could buy. From the age of 14, for instance, conducting on a stool, he could actually try out his compositions with professional musicians whom his father engaged for regular Sunday morning concerts on the first floor of the elegant and spacious family house on the Neue Promenade, Berlin. (The ground floor was given over to the family bank.) On other occasions Felix would play the piano or the violin; Fanny, his very talented elder sister with "Bach fugue fingers", would also play the piano, the younger sister Rebecca would sing, and the younger brother Paul would play cello.

As a child Felix could rattle off at the piano all nine of Beethoven's symphonies by heart. It was even said that he could remember any piece of music after hearing it just once, though that was admittedly before he had come across Berlioz's cataclysmic *Symphonie Fantastique* and Wagner's interminable *Tannhaüser*. Between the age of nine when he made his début in a private concert and the age of 16, he turned out masses of compositions, several of them still in today's concert repertoires — 13 string symphonies, two concertos, three double concertos and some glorious chamber music, including the Piano Quartet in B minor No. 3, which he dedicated to Goethe. This quartet so impressed the crusty but respected guru Cherubini, Director of the Paris Conservatoire, that on his advice Abraham Mendelssohn, the composer's ever cautious and vigilant father, consented to Felix's pursuit of a musical career.

While still 16, in 1825, Mendelssohn created two of the finest works of his lifetime. The first was the thrilling Octet for Strings, the second the overture to *A Midsummer Night's Dream*, which Fanny described as "the incarnation of Felix". Neither Mozart nor Beethoven nor Schubert nor anyone else ever showed such brilliance at the same age. Before his 21st birthday, the composer had also — hold your breath — paid several substantial visits to the all-admiring and welcoming Goethe; had travelled extensively; had read aesthetics, geography and politics at Berlin University after matriculating with a translation from the Latin of Terence's comedy *Andria;* and had taken London by storm with his piano playing and own compositions, including his first symphony, the *Dream* overture and the Double Piano Concerto in E major. (He was to remain a lifelong darling of English audiences and choral societies.)

This severely abridged litany of Mendelssohn's pre-majority achievements finishes with his epoch-making revival performance of Bach's *St Matthew Passion* in 1829 at the Berlin *Singakademie.* And just after his 21st birthday he was offered the new chair of Music at the University.

In his "spare" time Mendelssohn had also written reams of letters and produced some notable, rather than inspired, poems, drawings and paintings — it can only have been while he was shaving at his normal rising hour of 5 A.M., or sitting on the loo!

Mendelssohn's talents within the humanities and fine arts seem particularly to have come from his mother's side. Lea Mendelssohn came from a family of brilliant Berlin Jews and, besides being an exquisite line-drawer, could read Homer in the original and was conversant in French, Italian and German. Abraham Mendelssohn was also cultured and literate, and the head of an enormously successful and prestigious Berlin banking house — the end product of stupendous family talent, toil and opportunism applied by two generations of Mendelssohns from grandfather Moses's degrading origins in Berlin's ghetto Jewry. The composer proved definitely to be a chip off the old block in being incapable of kicking the workaholic habit.

In the summer of 1825 Abraham Mendelssohn moved his family from the Neue Promenade to 3 Leipzigerstrasse, turning it, after vastly expensive renovations, into a palatial mansion of some 40 or more rooms, set in seven acres of parkland on the very edge of the city, and requiring vast armies of butlers, maids, cooks, gardeners, grooms and coachmen to service it. There was also a Garden House seating 200 to 300 people for concerts. Needless to say, the family's salons, soirées, magnificent dinners and glittering balls became a must for everybody who was anybody. (No wonder Mendelssohn was also something of a gastronome and wine connoisseur.) Notable salon habitués with whom young Felix rubbed noses included the philosopher Hegel, Jacob Grimm (he of the *Fairy Tales*), the poets Heine and Müller (one of Schubert's collaborators) and the famous naturalist Alexander Humboldt and his brother Wilhelm.

One of Mendelssohn's admirers from afar, Frau Elise Polko, who first met the composer only two years before his death when she was a little girl singing as an elfin in his *Midsummer Night's Dream,* records in her collection of her own and other people's *Reminiscences of Felix Bartholdy* that at these gatherings there were plenty of nice young ladies present as well, "an ever-blooming *Flora* of the most attractive fair forms".

*

To what extent Mendelssohn, in his teens and 20s before his marriage at the age of 28, explored these "fair forms" beneath their swirling hooped skirts is very unclear. Mendelssohn wrote in total some 5,000 letters, but the family books have been cooked or burned to make him look as clean as a whistle, and nobody else has unearthed or at least published any titillating tales of trysts and intrigues of the kind that were so rife amongst his contemporaries Liszt, Chopin, Berlioz, Wagner and many others.

However, there's no real harm in inventing Mendelssohn's sex life in a novel if you make it clear that's what you're doing. The most entertaining fantasies about Mendelssohn that I have come across, thanks to leads by a Mrs. Peter Talbot-Willcox and Wilfrid Blunt, are to be found in *Beyond Desire* by Pierre La Mure, a gem of a novel in which the period detail (which I have pinched here and there) is wonderfully evocative even if his facts are gleefully made up.

In *Beyond Desire* Mendelssohn has two or three steamy affairs, including one longer-term pre and post-marital scorcher with the fiery diva Maria Salla. This sultry and volatile beauty plays very hard to get before her sudden and abject surrender to our young Felix — a surrender which is in the finest tradition of those genre romances that millions read or watch and handfuls look down their noses at:

> "You are too strong", she said. A smile drifted across her face. Her limbs turned limp, relaxed into acquiescence. "Long time I fight because I have much fear of love ... But now I fight no more ..."

Gently he caressed her hair, trailed his fingertips over her bare shoulder with the tranquil assurance of undisputed ownership. She was his, she had told him a hundred times, his to do with whatever he wanted. For instance, he could beat her, if he felt like it ... He could also take her whenever the urge was upon him, whatever the place or hour. He was the *padrone*, the master.

Wonderful stuff. But returning to Mendelssohn's real pre-marital life, the woman at the very heart of it was undoubtedly his sister Fanny — who, though rather plain-looking, had beautiful eyes, and a ripe figure slightly warped by a spinal curvature. Although Mendelssohn's marriage was to be a very happy one, Fanny's ever-watchful doppelgänger nevertheless seems to have hovered in the marital wings. As he said after her death: "She was part of me every moment of my life. There was no joy I experienced without thinking of the joy she would feel with me."

Nobody has ever made any murky insinuations about brother and sister, but the degree of closeness between them is certainly startling. Dysfunctional even? Or does one really need to be Jewish to understand this degree of attachment between brother and sister? (The family's conversion to Christianity in their childhood was essentially strategic; Felix objected to the "Bartholdy" tag to his name and soon dropped it. In any case, Jewish blood is a lot thicker than ink.)

Fanny was another version of the Immortal Beloved, or in the words of Mozelle Moshansky, "the luminous Madonna, the 'mother confessor', the eternal woman, the sounding board and the yard-stick against which he could measure his ideas, his hopes and his fears". The bond between them was unshakeable and life-long. "The evidence for this love", says Moshansky "is everywhere to be found. Its strength — its passion, even — is unmistakable, on occasion highly charged. Their correspondence sometimes reads like a series of love letters."

When Cécile Jeanrenaud married him in 1837 she was thus taking on a lot more than a husband. The same was even more true in reverse when Fanny's suitor, the prestigious but comparatively penniless 33-year-old painter Wilhelm Hensel, was finally allowed to marry her in 1829. (Frau Mendelssohn had banished him to Rome for five years in order to prove his devotion and eligibility.) The Hensels lived their entire married life in the house at the bottom of her family garden, which must have been a bit trying for the son-in-law in spite of the perks of rent-free living and a newly built studio.

Was young Felix jealous of Fanny's courtship and marriage? At first, perhaps, but not in his heart of hearts, surely, because he knew he had no need to be. From London, where his injuries from a coach accident had scuppered his plans to attend her wedding, he wrote his last letter to Fanny as "Fraülein Fanny Mendelssohn-Bartholdy", confessing to her that the prospect of change made his thoughts become "unclear and half wild", but bidding her to be happy and "stay the same as you were". He knew that "whether I call my sister Fraülein or madam is unimportant. The name is unimportant".

As for Fanny, a bridegroom was "no more than a man". Many people had jested that the siblings really ought to marry, and Fanny sent this breathtaking classic of a letter from a sister to a brother on her wedding day:

> I have your portrait before me and ever repeating your dear name, and thinking of you as if you stood at my side, I weep ... Every morning and every moment of my life I shall love you from the bottom of my heart, and I am sure that in doing so I shall not wrong Hensel.

Close as brother and sister were, they nevertheless both seem to have enjoyed unusally happy marriages in what Fanny later described as "double counterpoint".

*

The powerful influence in his life of both Fanny and his parents does seem to have stunted Mendelssohn's emotional and spiritual growth. Even at the age of 25 he felt he needed his father's approval to buy a horse, and his prime motivation in later searching for a wife was to honour his dead father's wishes. There are many who feel that for all the poise, serenity, intense poignancy, vitality and brilliance that characterise Mendelssohn's music at its wonderful best, it never plumbs the spiritual and emotional depths that are the ingredients of greatness. And at its worst, of course, it descends, for many, into mawkish sentimentality. When Elijah sings *It is enough,* six numbers into Part Two of the oratorio, there are many besides orchestral musicians who feel the same way!

As for Fanny's artistic growth, this was quite simply never an an issue. The notion of a respectable woman in Mendelssohn circles in those dark ages pursuing a career was a non-starter. Although as a pianist she could have rivalled Clara Schumann and Marie Pleyel, she was never allowed to play professionally, nor even encouraged to develop her considerable gifts as a composer. Even her devoted brother Felix would not, when first asked, sanction her plans to publish her compositions, reminding her of "her first duties" as a wife and mother!

Not only talented female musicians had a hard time of it, of course. When Charlotte Brontë sent her poems to the Poet Laureate Robert Southey in 1837 for his opinion, he dismissed them on the grounds that "Literature cannot be the business of a woman's life and it ought not to be. The more she is engaged in her proper duties, the less leisure she will have for it". It took her ten years to recover from this "damping" rejection before she produced *Jane Eyre*.

*

1830-1837

[Mendelssohn] did not go out of his way to avoid adventures ... There was a young girl-friend of Rosen, gifted in painting, whose temperament, aggressive in the erotic sense, charmed Felix. He seems to have had success with her, too.
[From Eric Werner's *Mendelssohn*, quoted in Wilfrid Blunt's *On Wings of Song*]

As far as I know and believe, his whole life was one of singular purity. [J.C. Horsley, one of Mendelssohn's close English friends]

Mendelssohn's *opportunities* for romance were legion. After turning down the chair at Berlin University early in 1830 he was constantly on the move until his highly prestigious appointment as Chief Conductor of the Leipzig Gewandhaus orchestra in 1835.

He first had a cultural binge over some two years on the obligatory Grand Tour, composing steadily and concertising as he felt fit — though never, of course, having to stoop to knocking off pot-boilers in order to pay for his own and his family's bills à la Rossini and

Donizetti. This spree took him to Italy as far down as Naples, then to Paris, where he met those known heart-throbs Liszt, Berlioz and Chopin (and many other distinguished musicians) during the winter of 1831 -32. Over the next three years he flitted about endlessly between Berlin, Düsseldorf, London and elsewhere.

The main career landmarks included his première of the *Italian* Symphony in London on May 13th, 1833 and the first of his many appearances as Director of the Lower Rhine Festival in Düsseldorf later that same month. (Particularly interesting here was a revival of Handel's oratorio *Israel in Egypt* with background presentations of *tableaux vivants*.) Such was the success of this festival that he was immediately offered a three-year contract to lead Düsseldorf's theatrical and church music, to do a winter season of orchestral concerts and direct the annual festival.

For many reasons, including Mendelssohn's own lack of diplomacy and the Düsseldorfers' resistance to his adventurous and innovative programmes, the appointment proved to be mutually disagreeable. When a more prestigious offer came from Leipzig to conduct the Gewandhaus orchestra he eventually accepted it, though continued his association with the Lower Rhine Festival. From 1835 until 1841 he spent most of his time in Leipzig.

Thanks to the streak of pyromania in his future wife Cécile and to the scissors and blue-pencil frenzies of his brother Paul, most of Mendelssohn's so-called "adventures" during his bachelor years are unknown. The truth may be just the opposite, but even if he was no plaster-cast saint, it is hard to imagine such a model son and such a darling of the adoring and respectable choral society ladies of Düsseldorf and Leipzig (maidens and matrons alike only too ready to festoon him with flowers and laurel wreaths) getting up to very much hanky panky. We can be certain he never used whores; when he and John Calcott Horsley (son of Mendelssohn's glee-composing friend Dr. William Horsley) passed a street-full of them lolling out of their windows in downtown London, Horsley blushed scarlet with horror and embarrassment and Mendelssohn said "My dear, dear, John, God grant that you may always feel as you are now doing."

He seems to have been more of "a dear" "a love", "a sweetie", a mummy's-boy charmer, bringing out the maternal instincts, for instance, of the the Horsley sisters. Fanny Horsley wrote during

Mendelssohn's first London visit that "Mama and Mary think Mendelssohn will never marry. I do, that is if he doesn't plague his mistress to death before the day arrives. He was dressed very badly, and looked in sad want of the piece of soap and nail brush which I have so often threatened to offer him." Later, during a family visit to Düsseldorf, she wrote: "He wants to compose a great deal I believe, and I think at the same time he had better compose himself, for his mind wants settling in my opinion. He is looking much handsomer than he has yet, for, his hair is long again like it was last year, which is so very becoming."

The undoubted prudish streak in Mendelssohn may also have inhibited his urges for *amourettes* (casual flings) — though of course behind the mask of the prude sometimes lurks the rampant lecher. While in Paris in 1832 he and his friend Hiller (a pianist and then-noted composer) enjoyed going to the *vaudevilles* at the Gymnase Dramatique, but deplored the "degree of immorality that almost passes belief" intruding into every piece. He sounded every inch the priggish parson when writing about Auber's *Fra Diavolo,* and also Meyerbeer's *Robert Le Diable*, in which decidedly dissolute nuns dance in the graveyard. "The nuns come on, one after the other, trying to seduce the hero, until finally the Abbess succeeds. In another opera (*Fra Diavolo*) a young girl undresses while singing that this time tomorrow she will be married. It made a sensation; but I haven't any music for such vulgarities, and if *that* is what people want nowadays, then I shall stick to church music."

One young lady who, Mendelssohn later admitted to Schumann, had been "dangerous" to him and whom he followed around "like a pet lamb" was the brilliant and very beautiful 16-year-old pianist Delphine von Schauroth. He met her in Munich on both legs of his journey to and from Italy and dedicated to her his Piano Concerto in G minor, premièring it on the return visit. It is a wonderful romp of a piece, with its whirlwind first and typhoon third movements, and gorgeous, schmaltzy slow movement featuring the veiled cantabile sounds of divided cellos and violas (a favourite Mendelssohnian colouring).

"We flirted dreadfully," he wrote to Fanny on the way out, "but there isn't any danger because I'm already in love with a young Scotch girl whose name I don't know." Paul Mendelssohn actually banned this depraved letter from his publication of the composer's letters!

Other suppressed correspondence from Mendelssohn concerning Delphine referred to King Ludwig I's suggestion that Mendelssohn might make an "excellent match" with her, a suggestion that the composer found impertinent. Delphine's parents seemed to be all in favour but Mendelssohn was not then, at the age of 24, ready to settle down. In any case he was extremely choosy and his eyes were easily caught by other nymphs, such as his Munich pupil Josefine Lang, "one of the sweetest creatures I ever saw".

Mendelssohn seems to have been attracted to older women, and it would figure that if he had affairs, the women would make the first move. Another crumb of naughtiness we have is that according to his biographer Eric Werner, Mendelssohn got involved with a "widowed aristocratic lady" in the summer of 1834 in Aachen, where he was once again directing the Lower Rhine Festival. The affair was supposed to have been passionate for a time but then to have fizzled out for lack of common interests. Perhaps, after fun between the sheets, the finicky Felix's post coital plunge was intensified on discovering that his *amourette* was unable to recite Terence's *Andria* by heart, or sing the second viola line in the slow movement of his Octet. Apparently even Frau Mendelssohn got wind of this affair, probably via the Woringens, who were staunch Mendelssohn groupies and choir members, and friends of the entire family. Rebecka actually met this unnamed widow a year later and, not surprisingly, was not impressed. It's a good job the soon-jilted lady never met Fanny. Nothing shop-soiled for her Felix!

*

1837-1847

Cécile

> There can be no doubt that [Mendelssohn] was deeply in love with
> her and that the marriage brought great happiness, but it did not
> diminish the very strong influence of his own family background,
> and indeed it may have seemed to him to be a kind of extension of
> it. [Philip Radcliffe: *Mendelssohn*]

It was the death of his father — "my only true friend, my teacher in art and in life" — in November 1835 that undoubtedly spurred Mendelssohn into finding a wife, since that was one of his father's repeated wishes. With Fanny feeling likewise, marriage became an obligation.

In the summer of 1836 after conducting the première of his *St Paul* Oratorio at the Lower Rhine Festival in May, Mendelssohn did himself a favour, as well as one for his indisposed friend Johann Schelble, when he deputised for him as director of the *Cäcilienverein* (St Cecilia's Society) in Frankfurt. Mendelssohn stayed in Frankfurt with the Jeanrenaud family who were relatives of a friend in Leipzig. Now aged 27, Mendelssohn was at first attracted to his lively and attractive 40-year-old hostess Mme. Elisabeth Jeanrenaud (née Souchay), the widow of the pastor of the French Reformed Church there and, says Wilfrid Blunt, very "county". However, the parson's widow clearly didn't fancy herself in the role of a passing motherly fancy, and Mendelssohn soon developed a keen but initially reticent interest in her younger 19-year-old daughter, Cécile.

Naturally the whole family in Berlin had to be informed, but in varying degrees. He wrote to his mother that he had met "a particularly beautiful girl" of whom he wanted to see more. This was all too much for mother, and Fanny, also all agog, had to calm her down:

Dear Mother, I do beseech you not to worry, at the age of sixty, because you think that Felix is in love! Couldn't Dr W. give you a sedative to calm such youthful feverishness? I feel just as you do and the suspense is upsetting me too; but we mustn't worry: Felix has good taste. I've got a vague idea that it may be a Mlle Jeanrenaud or a Mlle Souchay ...

Fanny was only too keen to see her brother settled and properly looked after and expressed her deep interest in Felix's "bride", hoping it wouldn't all fizzle out. "It occurs to me that I have never before seen you truly in love. All your great amours were ... superficial," she wrote.

Mendelssohn wrote to Rebecka (his younger sister), fearing that Fanny might be jealous and pouring out his heart:

I am more desperately in love than I have ever been in my life, and I don't know what to do. ...But I haven't any idea whether or not she likes me, and I don't know what to do to make her like me. ... O Rebecka! what shall I do? I can't settle to anything all day long. I can't compose or write letters or play the piano; all I can do is to sketch a little ...

Both Hiller and a Dr. Speiss were also subjected to similar moonstruck monologues.

Frau Polko left us with an evocative description of Cécile in her characteristically *Schwärmerisch* (gushing) mode:

Her figure was slight, of middle height, and rather drooping, like a flower heavy with dew, her luxuriant golden-brown hair fell in rich curls on her shoulders, her complexion was of transparent delicacy, her smile charming, and she had the most bewitching deep blue eyes I ever beheld, with dark eyelashes and eyebrows.

Everyone else seemed to think that Cécile was charming, serene, stable, and ordinary — but not boring.

Being the son of Abraham, Mendelssohn didn't rush into a proposal, but went to take the cures at Scheveningen and, doubtless, think over what father would have advised. Cécile waited confidently for the decision: "Mother and I have made a little bet ... I hope I win!" she wrote to a cousin. After returning from Scheveningen he proposed during a picnic in the Taunus and was accepted. "Oh, how wonderful and happy I feel!" he wrote to his mother. After a trip back to Leipzig for a Gewandhaus concert, he returned to Frankfurt to make the required 163 courtesy calls to all and sundry.

Neither family was madly thrilled, thinking that their darlings could have done better for themselves. Frau Mendelssohn fretted and Cécile's granny was difficult. Fanny became openly jealous and neither she nor her mother attended the wedding on March 28th, 1837. Admittedly, the journey was a difficult one.

Their two-month honeymoon through the Upper Rhineland and Swabia was, according to Pierrepoint in *The Romance of the Mendelssohns,* "a fairytale journey of unforgettable happiness". Actually, there was one tiff. Cécile was insanely jealous when Mendelssohn admired a very pretty flowergirl, going into a sulk before confessing all in their joint diary. Felix added: "Don't be angry with me, dear C." and wrote her a "delightful allegretto" — still, alas, unpublished.

Honeymoon happiness inspired Mendelssohn to compose some wonderful music in between bouts of rumpy pumpy and sightseeing: Psalm 42, the Quartet in E minor No. 2 op. 44, and the Second Piano Concerto in D minor op. 40, written, like the previous one for Delphine, in honour of the woman with whom he was now in love. Six years later the concerto was to be applauded for 10 minutes in London. The E minor quartet exudes love and well-being, particularly in the slow movement with its radiant soaring melody in the first violin and cello.

Cécile, not surprisingly became pregnant. That's what marriage was all about in those days, and in total they were to fulfil familial obligations and expectations by producing three daughters and two sons, four of whom survived to adulthood.

By all known accounts the marriage was supremely happy. Whenever Mendelssohn was away (he visited England alone six times after their marriage, the first soon after their honeymoon) he missed her dearly. Like Cosima Wagner and, later, Caroline Alice Elgar (wife of Sir Edward), Cécile devoted her entire life to her husband and children. This, she said, "was enough of a life's work for any woman".

Here they are, each missing the other:

Felix to Cécile: I can only write to you today and would like so much to speak to you, to kiss you, to spend the whole day with you, to gaze at you, to enjoy [your birthday], to celebrate my happiness and to wish you happiness. If I were with you I'd kiss you ever so often.

Cécile to Felix: Time hangs heavily till you announce your return. My treasure, why don't you write a few lines ...

Here he is writing to his mother-in-law:

When I am with her I do not understand how indispensable to my life, every moment of it, she is. But every time I am away from her, the absence becomes heavier to bear, more insupportable. I patiently count the hours till I shall see her again, her without whom I no longer know gladness or happiness.

And here is the young first-time father over the moon, writing to Hiller in 1838:

When he [Karl] is lying at her breast and tugging away, they both look so happy that I hardly know what to do with myself for joy.

Having been unable, even in correspondence, to conceal her jealousy of her new sister-in-law, Fanny finally met her in the autumn of 1837 and approved. She sent her character appraisal to Karl Klingemann, Mendelssohn's lifelong friend with a very cushy job at the Hanoverian Legation in London:

> At last I know my sister-in-law, and feel as if a load were off my mind, for I cannot deny that I was very uncomfortable and ill at ease at never having seen her. She is amiable, childlike, fresh, bright, and even-tempered, and I think Felix is very lucky; for though inexpressibly fond of him she does not spoil him, but when he is moody treats him with an equanimity which will in time probably cure his fits of irritability altogether. Her presence produces the effect of a fresh breeze, so light and bright and natural is she.

Relations between wife and sister later deteriorated, however, the families being at too close quarters following the Mendelssohns' move to Berlin in 1841. After the accession of King Wilhelm IV, Mendelssohn accepted a lucrative royal appointment there as director of the Royal Orchestra, composer to the Royal Theatre, director of the music class at the Academy, and conductor and organiser of the Cathedral choir. In spite of paying so handsomely, the job proved to be something of a white elephant and the Mendelssohns returned to Leipzig in 1844.

*

The pattern of Mendelssohn's life after marriage continued in a frenzy of work. It was really no wonder that he burned out within ten years. Take as just one example what he packed in to a fortnight in England only months after the honeymoon: organ recitals at Christ Church, Oxford, and St Paul's cathedral; a performance of *St Paul* at Exeter Hall in London; then up to Birmingham for the Festival (in the new Town Hall) of four main concerts (Handel's *Solomon, St Paul,* his new Piano Concerto and a Bach organ recital) plus an impromptu extra recital. Then there was a mad dash back to Germany for the first Gewandhaus concert of the new season on October 1st. This meant travelling through the night to Dover, crossing the channel (and getting sea-sick) to Boulogne, going straight on through Belgium to Cologne, and thence by boat down the Rhine to Frankfurt. But instead of resting on the boat he had to abandon it in a fog and catch a stage coach at Coblenz for the 12-hour journey to Frankfurt where Cécile was waiting for him. It then took three more days to get to Leipzig, where they arrived after lunch. At six o'clock sharp he was on the box for the down beat. He actually confessed after the concert to feeling "a little *kaput*".

The pace of his life throughout the middle 1840s was unrelenting: a whirligig of composing, conducting, concerto playing, teaching and administration (he became the first director of the Leipzig Conservatory in 1844) and travelling. He played a key part in founding music festivals in Cologne, Schwerin and Birmingham. And he also took seriously his obligations as a father.

His last working months were crippling. In the spring of 1847 he conducted *St Paul* in Leipzig, then went to England for the tenth and last time. In addition to recitals and functions galore, including another royal audience (Queen Victoria was deeply distressed when he died), he conducted four performances of *Elijah* in London and one each in Birmingham and Manchester. "One more week of this unremitting fatigue," he said when pressed to prolong his stay, "and I should be killed outright."

But it was Mendelssohn's achievements at Leipzig that tower above everything else. He transformed the Gewandhaus into a thriving, pioneering powerhouse and centre of excellence. He directed revivals of works by Handel, Bach, Haydn and Mozart and promoted the work of newer composers such as Liszt, Schumann, Berlioz, Spohr, Cherubini, Moscheles, Schubert (mounting the first performance of the newly discovered Great C major) Rossini and Gade. Until Mendelssohn arrived, the Leipzig repertoire had been largely a boring diet of unknowns, no more meaningful now than random names in a telephone directory: Eberl, von Seyfried, Reissiger, Fesca, Neukomm, Ries ...

Mendelssohn also achieved dramatic orchestral improvements, securing pensions for the musicians and raising playing standards from ropy to record high. He was the first conductor to use a baton — in whalebone, covered in white leather — though never made more gesture than was necessary. "His movements," said Hiller, "were short and precise, and often barely visible, for he stood with his right side towards the orchestra. A glance at the leader, a quick look in this direction or that, was all that was needed." Sounds too good to be true!

*

Jenny Lind

... a slender girlish form, with luxuriant fair hair, dressed in pink silk, and white and pink camellias on her breast and in her hair, in all the chaste grace of her deportment, and utterly devoid of all pretension ... [Jenny] only looked beautiful when she sang.
[Frau Polko]

... as great an artist as ever lived, and the greatest I have ever known.
[Mendelssohn]

In this ceaseless round of work, Mendelssohn had neither time nor seeming inclination for naughtiness. The only frisson of concern for Cécile was the arrival on the scene of the controversial and temperamental "Swedish Nightingale" Jenny Lind, "as moody and capricious as she was charming", in 1844. She was described as "a soul singing" with a voice "of virginal purity". When she made her début in Meyerbeer's *Robert le Diable* "the crush was so great that men were pushed over, women fainted and dress suits torn to tatters". Nothing changes!

The attraction between Mendelssohn and Lind was immediate and mutual. "That she fell in love with Mendelssohn is beyond doubt" says Blunt, though she is said to have "clamped down on her feelings". Although she didn't sing in his first performance of *Elijah* in 1846 at the Birmingham Festival, he had definitely built the part round her voice.

Mendelssohn wrote it at a time when they were in almost daily contact, when the sound of her voice was ringing in his ears. He had studied her voice minutely, knew the timbre of every note. each had a quality of its own. Of them all he loved best the upper F sharp, and often spoke admiringly of her *wunderbares Fis* (wonderful F sharp).

It is for her that the F sharps ring out in the opening bars of 'Hear ye, Israel!' [Joan Bulman]

Was this another case of musical adultery, like Mozart with Aloisia Weber and, perhaps, Nancy Storace? That's as far as it got, though they spent hours of time together, even taking journeys down the Rhine during the Lower Rhine Festival at Aachen in 1846. The composer's love token to her was a manuscript album of his songs, and his portrait painted by Gustav Magnus.

"A less honourable man than Mendelssohn might have made an 'affair' out of this love," writes Werner, "and entered into an adventure with the adoring young girl. Who knows whether, in the interests of music, we should not regret Mendelssohn's integrity?" Food for thought, certainly.

*

Brother and Sister

A messenger arrived with an urgent letter from Berlin; he opened it, read it, and "with a loud fearful shriek, fell senseless to the ground". [Wilfrid Blunt]

The final crunch really came on May 14th, 1847 after Mendelssohn returned from his final London visit. The exact details of Fanny's sudden death at the age of 42 differ alarmingly, but she had been rehearsing for one of her Sunday concerts when suddenly her hands went limp and fell from the keys. Then or soon afterwards her whole body was seized with a paralytic stroke and by 11 o'clock that night she was dead.

To all intents and purposes, Felix died with her. It was the greatest blow of his life and when he came round after collapsing at the news he cried ceaselessly. Life was essentially meaningless. "What's the use? I'll not be here" he would suddenly say in mid-sentence.

Fanny's death wrung two grief-ridden masterpieces from him while he tried to recover with Cécile and his brother's family in Interlaken: the F minor String Quartet, which he inscribed as "Requiem for Fanny", and one of his finest songs, *Nachtlied*. Werner describes the quartet as "one of the most impassioned outpourings of sadness existing in instrumental music". Mendelssohn's friend and mentor the pianist Moscheles later listened in "a deeply agitated state of mind" to the bereaved composer playing through the quartet at the piano. Nowhere, even in the slow movement, does there seem to be a moment of repose.

With Cécile's devoted support Mendelssohn's condition improved in Interlaken — he even produced 13 splendid water-colour sketches — though he never regained his vitality. The English music critic H.F. Chorley, who had become a close friend, remarked after meeting him that "he was too much depressed and worn, and walked too heavily". Then in September came the beginning of the drawn-out and agonising end, when Mendelssohn called in at 3 Leipzigerstrasse before the German première of *Elijah*. After being shown Fanny's room with her music still open at the piano, he broke down and cancelled all further engagements.

The final few weeks are a story of brief cheerful respites between periods of agonising pain, with headaches, paroxysms, and piercing screams. On November 3rd he had what was probably a brain haemorrhage, and died the next day at 9.24 pm. He was buried in the family vault beside his alter ego.

"Life lasts so long" said Cécile at his deathbed, "how shall I live it alone?" Within six years she herself was dead. It surely isn't over the top to suggest that she died of a broken heart.

***

CHAPTER 11

ROBERT ALEXANDER SCHUMANN

BORN: ZWICKAU, JUNE 8TH 1810
DIED ENDENICH (BONN), JUNE 29TH 1856

Are you musical too? What instrument do you play?
[Royal host to Schumann after his wife's recital in Holland,
December 1853]

*The separation has again made my strange and difficult situation
more palpable. Ought I to neglect my talent so that I can be your
travel escort? Have you or should you let your talent go to waste
because I am tied to the newspaper and my piano? ... Yes, it is
absolutely necessary for us to find a way to use and develop our
two talents side by side.*
[Schumann writing to his wife Clara, 1842]

*Dear Clara, I will throw my wedding ring into the Rhine. Do the
same and both rings will then be united.* [Schumann, suicide note]

*

It seems as though you really need to be well versed in psychol-
ogy, psychiatry, psychoanalysis, psychotherapy, psychopathy and
psycho-goodness-knows-what-else in order to write anything with
confidence about Schumann's personality and love life. A knowledge
of venereology and neuropathology would also come in handy. However, Schumann's personal relationships, and his courtship and marriage in particular, were so musically productive that it's worth diving
in. Nowhere else, certainly in this volume, are there so many intimate
and explicit links between a man and his woman and his music.

At least we can be thankful that such a tortured and twisted
soul, who was haunted by fears of insanity from his student days and
who ended up literally starving himself to death in an asylum after
unsuccessfully trying to drown himself by plunging into the icy waters of the Rhine, was so often somehow able to channel his neuroses

and psychoses into the creation of so many inspired, exquisitely expressive compositions. No other composer conveys the essence of Romanticism so completely as Schumann in his small-scale songs and piano pieces with their intriguing programmatic titles (which sequentially form a sort of spiritual diary) and impulsive, quixotic shapes.

The poet Grillparzer (who had written the oration for Beethoven's funeral), reviewing Schumann's *Papillons* and the *Abegg Variations* in 1831 put his finger on the matter:

> He follows no school, but draws inspiration only from himself ... he has created a new and ideal world for himself, in which he revels almost recklessly, and sometimes with quite original eccentricity.

At times it seems that the more stressful his situation was, the more frenziedly he composed. Indeed his most loved and enduring large-scale work, the intensely rhapsodic Piano Concerto in A minor, was completed in 1845 during a period of severe depression. Mind you, the last movement of that same work has driven many conductors to similar depths of despair when trying to conduct the second theme, which is really in six-four but perversely written out in three-four. Generations of orchestral musicians and quite a few solo pianists have also inevitably been screwed up in the same process.

Dr Peter Ostwald's intensely absorbing study, *Schumann: Music and Madness,* ends with a professional diagnosis of the "patient" whose life he has so carefully and sympathetically analysed, whose music he so much loves, and whose chamber music in particular he loves to play as a violinist. He concludes that Schumann, whose parents were occasionally severely depressed, and one of whose sisters committed suicide, was a manic depressive with schizophrenic and paranoid tendencies. His condition was exacerbated at various stages in his life by physical disorders: acute alcoholic intoxication, malaria, meningitis, anal problems, rheumatism, severe fatigue, cardio-vascular disease, dizziness and fainting spells, paroxysms, rare auditory disturbances, migraine attacks, labyrinthitis, tuberculosis — and so on.

Dr Ostwald is more hesitant than many other biographers and medical experts in believing that syphilis (terminating in organic brain disease and general paresis) was a possibility rather than a probability.

Given a lifetime of endless introspection that also included several mental breakdowns, it sometimes seems amazing that Schumann ever managed to crawl out of bed and compose one bar of music; or even turn over in it and play his part in producing four sons and four daughters! Yet during the few years he lived in Düsseldorf, for instance (1850-54), when he was plagued not only by deteriorating mental and physical health but also burdened with his many administrative and performing duties as Director of Music, he actually completed about one third of his entire output of important compositions, which spanned some 25 years.

The Düsseldorf bonanza included the *Rhenish* Symphony, Scenes from Goethe's *Faust,* the Cello Concerto in A minor, Songs, Overtures, Piano Trios, Violin Sonatas, piano pieces, Cantatas, a Mass, a Requiem, and the suppressed Violin Concerto. No wonder his beloved friend and protégé the virtuoso violinist Joachim said, "He is constantly so filled up with music that I really don't blame the man for preferring not to be disturbed by the sounds of the outer world". And Dr Ostwald adds that "some of his best work was written under the pressure of inescapable inner voices": the *Spring* Symphony, for example, his early songs, the piano pieces *Kreisleriania,* and the *Manfred Overture.* Some people feel that the intensity of the later orchestral works foreshadows his final breakdown.

Schumann's sons, incidentally, were tarred with the same genetic brush without the blessing of concomitant genius: Emil died in infancy; Ludwig became hospitalised in his 20s and died at the age of 51; Ferdinand became a morphine addict, dying at 41, and Felix died at 24 of tuberculosis. For some reason the daughters fared much better, three out of the four living long and active lives.

*

Many other events and pressures interacted with and exacerbated Schumann's own disorders. During his childhood, the Napoleonic invasions and his mother's illnesses caused prolonged separations from his family. He lost his father at the age of 16, only months after the suicide, at the age of 29, of his psychotic sister Emilie, who had a distressing skin infection. He became severely suicidal after hearing in quick succession of the deaths of his sister-in-law Rosalie and his brother Julius in the summer and autumn of 1833. He even transferred himself from his fourth-floor Leipzig apartment to the ground floor and persuaded a friend to sleep in the same room to stop him doing anything desperate.

In his 20s an injury to his right hand, arising possibly either from mercury treatment, which was then standard for syphilis, or from some unidentifiable but crazy "finger-torturer" device for cultivating finger strength and independence (a "cigar mechanism", sling-and-pulley arrangement or whatever) put paid to his career as a concert pianist. (That didn't actually seem to bother him very much, as he found performance too nerve-racking.)

His editorship of the *Neue Leipziger Zeitschrift für Musik* (The New Leipzig Music Journal), which he co-founded with a group of friends in 1834, made very heavy demands on his time and energies when he soon found himself running it single-handedly, as well as writing many articles for it. (Schumann's passion for writing and for literature, devouring Homer, Cicero, Sophocles, Schiller and Goethe in his childhood, came from his father, who became a very successful writer, publisher and bookseller.)

Other external pressures on Schumann included the sustained hostility of his piano teacher Friedrich Wieck towards the composer's marriage with his daughter Clara, causing the notoriously bitter and drawn-out legal battle before the marriage finally took place in 1840. After the marriage there were financial problems and an unending conflict between Clara's professional goals as a brilliant pianist and Schumann's need for a settled domestic setting in which to compose. There was the trauma of the death of Mendelssohn in 1847, at once his model, friend and rival, and also the entry into his life of his beloved Brahms, who probably intensified his feelings of inadequacy!

Schumann's real undoing, though, was his acceptance of the offer of the post of Director of Music at Düsseldorf, from which he was eventually eased out because of his sad incompetence as a conductor. Finally, his two-and-a-half years of voluntary committal to the asylum at Endenich, instead of rehabilitating him, finished him off. The doctors were unable to do anything for him and his suicide was the seemingly inevitable finale to a life that had been recurringly obsessed with death and insanity.

*

Some of the treatments Schumann received at the hands of the still mainly bumbling medical fraternity are even more mind-blowing than the problems themselves. The most astonishing is probably the time-honoured "animal baths" he agreed to in his early 20s. These were for his hand problem, which he may, consciously or unconsciously, have exploited in part as a cop-out for his failure as a concert pianist. (His contemporaries Mendelssohn, Liszt and Chopin were, after all, already streaks ahead of him in their pianistic careers in their early 20s.) The animal bath routine involved visiting a butcher's shop, obtaining a newly slaughtered calf, lamb or pig, and inserting the ailing members into the animal's moist belly. The warmth of the entrails, blood and faeces was supposed to be curative, but it probably did Schumann more harm than good. Ever a self-confessed hypochondriac, he feared that "something of the cattle essence might get into my system". With their punitive and even necrophiliac associations, animal baths were a particularly weird form of treatment for what were probably inflamed tendons.

His depressions, hallucinations and suicidal impulses were treated with any number of other remedies including hydrotherapy, hypnotherapy, cold plunge baths, electromagnetic charges, Dr. Portius's psychometer, opium and so on.

*

Schumann's ailing, self-pitying and neurotic widowed mother Christiane must come first in any overview of his love life. Until he had a woman of his own, Christiane remained the main focus of his craving for acceptance, and her disapproval of music as a career caused him a lot of distress. But although Frau Schumann took a lot of persuading before she let her son drop the law, which he began studying at Leipzig University in March 1828, for music, she invariably fell for his cajoling and emotional blackmail when he pleaded for more funds "as soon as possible as much as possible". "I am living like a dog," he wrote on one occasion. "My hair is yards long and I want to get it cut, but I can't spare a penny. My piano is terribly out of tune but I can't afford to get a tuner. And so on and so on. I haven't even got a pistol to shoot myself with."

Much of the money was squandered on his colossal consumption of booze, champagne included, and cigars. (His father had left him 10,000 thalers in trust to be administered by his appointed guardian Gottlob Rudel.) Frau Schumann's reluctant "on your own head be it" agreement to the switch to music (a "breadless art" as she called it, with good reason) came after she had written to his piano teacher Wieck in 1830 for his candid opinion of her son's prospects in music. The reply was that Schumann had the talent to succeed and that even though his capacity for methodical application was a moot point she should give her son her blessing.

Schumann's filial love seems to have been alarmingly fervent. During his second student binge in 1829, around Switzerland and Italy with his friend Rosen, he continually longed for her: "Travel with me now across the dozen laughing lakes, and climb with me to the top of the mountains," he wrote. "Sit next to me now, and let me squeeze your hand. Take a map so that somehow you could come along... "

On this same trip Schumann did not, of course, mention to his dearest mother encounters he recorded in his diary that would have given her kittens: "Voluptuous scandal during the night [in Milan] with the naked tour guide and the naked waitress... The homosexual who thrust himself on me, and my sudden departure... Coffee-house and the girl constantly looking around, certainly a whore... real fear of ladies." *If* Schumann did actually contract syphilis by using prostitutes, it was probably during this second vacation, or his earlier one in 1828.

*

Schumann's premarital experiences with women veered between the rarefied and the randy in ways already familiar in this saga of love lives. Not counting a few childhood crushes, his "first fiery love" as a teenager was Nanni Patsch. The charms of this young lady inspired him to exotic hyperbole in the manner of his literary hero Jean Paul Richter, whose passionate and popular sentimental novels, essentially autobiographical, ranged from morbid obsessions with death to humorous portraits of family life:

> O friend! were I but a smile, how I would flit about her eyes! were I but joy, how gently would I throb in all her pulses! yea, might I be but a tear, I would weep with her, and then if she smiled again, how gladly would I die on her eyelash, and gladly, gladly, be no more.

So he wrote to his friend Emil Fleschig, adding also that he wanted to sink to his knees and pray to her like a Madonna. At the same time his diaries record such less spiritual activities as dancing, hand squeezing and sexual arousal — and, of course, an essentially Schumannesque anxiety about the whole adventure: "My hands shook, my voice trembled, I grew dizzy."

The same neurotic fretting permeates his next partly concurrent adventure with a young lady named Liddy Hempel. When she stood him up on one occasion he got smashed out of his brain in the nearest tavern, oblivion into which he was so very frequently to plunge when depressed or under stress. He saw Liddy's role in his life as being his "guardian angel" and had recurring anxiety dreams of being unacceptable to, or rejected by her. He was to have similar hangups all through his marriage.

At 17, Schumann next invested maternal and erotic fantasies in an adored and unavailable love-object, eight years older than himself, a soprano named Agnes Carus whom he first met in 1827. This distant beloved was the wife of Doctor Ernst August Carus. Schumann accompanied Agnes at the piano, especially in the songs of his god Schubert. "Sitting alone at the piano with her for two hours, it was as if all dormant depths woke up mightily; she must have seen it in my eyes," says his diary. He often dreamed "beautiful, beautiful dreams" about her and imagined what she would be doing: "She's probably asleep right now; I've been having good fantasies, because she was alive in my fantasies and with her the entire firmament of sounds." And inevitably, as an arch-Romantic he would gladly die after "only one kiss from her". Equally inevitably, of course, Agnes was wasted on her "boorish", "bungling" and "sleepy" husband. Four songs composed about this time to poems including ones by Byron and himself were probably intended for Agnes.

It was at a Carus music party on March 31st, 1828 that Schumann first met the two people who overwhelmed his adult life: Freidrich Wieck, his future piano teacher, and Wieck's eight-year-old child prodigy daughter and pupil, Clara, whom he was to marry 12 years later. At this stage Schumann merely noted that Clara's nose was too long and her eyes too large!

After entering Leipzig as a law student in March 1828, Schumann seems to have had a first taste, real or imaginary, of the other kind of woman. During his first vacation trip in the spring and early summer of 1828 with his friend Gisbert Rosen taking in Bayreuth (where they paid homage to Jean Paul), Nuremberg, Augsberg and Munich (where they were cordially received by the sensationally popular poet Heine) his diary details various sexual encounters: "wild excitements", "pretty girls", "finger games under skirts" and "smiling whores". Who knows? Hints that his virginity was definitely under threat come with the mention back in Leipzig of a visit to the infamous Hotel de Pologne: "The whores — embraces — voluptuous pleasure — my innocence rescued by a most clever move."

Safer and cheaper than whores were the hand jobs or wet dreams in the privacy of his bedroom, where he seems to have worked himself up into an insomniac lather over Agnes, for whom he continued to yearn as his fantasised mistress-mother-sister figure: "Only one kiss from her and I would be happy to die ... She at the window — terribly sweaty night ... Excited night and beautiful magnificent dreams of her, of her."

With his good looks and playing talents, particularly his gift for improvisation, Schumann was naturally not short of female admirers. While playing at a ball during his second year of so-called law studies (which he pursued at Heidelberg University instead of Leipzig), he received an offer from a young French lady named Charlotte, which he actually turned down because he was more interested in a certain Lina. "O Monsieur Schumann," said Charlotte, "if you play like that you can lead me anywhere you wish."

However, his first full-blown steady affair began in 1831 after he had begun lodging with his teacher Wieck in 1830, and lasted on and off for several years. Christel, whom he also called Charitas, seems to have been another member of the Wieck household, perhaps as a servant or another student. She visited Schumann's room nearly every day, bringing him presents and agreeing with him that there were things in life needing even more urgent attention than writing articles or composing symphonies, *Caprices* and *Intermezzi*. As you might expect there was no pleasure for Schumann without even more pain, and this came in the shape of a very sore penis (he referred to it as a "wound" on the tip), the treatment for which his cellist-doctor friend Christian Glock prescribed bathing in "Narcissus Water", a distillate of daffodil bulbs.

The brief phrases in his diary give a vivid picture of their fraught but fervent liaison before and after the injury: "Charitas came completely and was bleeding ... full of fire and flames ... biting and devouring pain ... only guilt gives birth to nemesis ... [intercourse attempted] with fear and little enjoyment... "

His "wound" not withstanding, the effect of this introduction to regular love-making was probably profound, giving him the confidence to start producing compositions of lasting value. He had already composed part one of his exuberant piano pieces *Papillons* (Butterflies) in 1829, inspired by the ballroom scene in Jean Paul's novel, *Flegeljahre* (Adolescent Years), and by the end of this year he had completed part two. On the literary front, he had contributed his still famous and important article on Chopin to the prestigious *Allgemeine musikalische Zeitung* (German Musical Times). This piece featured the two imaginary characters he had invented, Eusebius and Florestan, to represent his alter egos: the reflective and introspective against the assertive and exuberant sides of himself. Eusebius and Florestan were to recur repeatedly in his writing and were another inspiration deriving from Jean Paul — the characters Walt and Vult in *Flegeljahre*.

*

There were, of course, men in Schumann's life as well — as friends and probably also as lovers. "That he had one and possibly several homosexual encounters seems clear" says Dr. Ostwald. There are several explicit homosexual references in his diary. After visiting a tavern in March 1829 in Leipzig with a friend Johann Renz he noted "pederasty" in his diary; after a second visit he wrote down "a voluptuous night with Greek dreams".

Schumann's first homoerotic crush, so it would seem, was on his older school friend Emil Fleschig. Frau Schumann, now widowed, selected Fleschig "to be a fitting companion for her precious darling", as he later put it. Fleschig was to Schumann "an Adonis, smiling gracefully" on whose "sympathetic bosom I must pour out my heart".

Schumann did just that in many letters, though Fleschig himself was an altogether more flat-footed fellow who recorded his friend's dreamy indecisiveness and excitable behaviour with clinical detachment. He noted, for example, that Schumann sobbed all night when

Schubert died and that "he never set foot in a lecture hall" the whole time he was ostensibly studying law at Leipzig. (This may have been untrue, but when not studying law Schumann seems to have spent his time improvising, composing songs and piano pieces, playing chamber music — especially Schubert — with a cigar in his mouth, dabbling with novels and short stories, fencing, riding, philosophising, boozing, wenching and dipping his toes into in the gay scene.) They shared rooms there, but Fleschig was soon out of favour, being "nothing but a fussy little pedant, but that in the highest degree, and there's nothing I loathe more. Therefore I just can't love him any more". By the spring of 1829 Fleschig was a "drunk son-of-a-bitch good-for-nothing".

Schumann's attachment to Gisbert Rosen was perhaps even more intense. Besides their vacation trips, they also spent many paralytic hours together in Heidelberg, whither Schumann had transferred for his studies for some 17 months in May 1829 — partly for the academic reason that he wanted to study law under the great Professor Thibaut, who was also a keen musician and writer on musical aesthetics, but really to be with Rosen, who was studying there.

Rosen, although not an anchor man for Schumann like Fleschig, was another recipient of the composer's epistolary fantasies and was as equally demotable as Fleschig when another nice young man came along. A certain Carl Semmel, he wrote to his mother, managed to "splinter" his "faith" in Rosen. Schumann kept his mother closely informed of his male bondings in his ardent letters to her.

Schumann's two most powerful male attachments in his student days were to Wilhelm Götte and "his enthusiastically beloved" Ludwig Schunke. After falling out of love with Fleschig he clung to Götte — "so noble, so lean, so dignified, so superhuman" — for at least eight weeks in an orgy of endless boozing and communing on inner fantasies and eternal truths.

Schunke, a very precocious and talented pianist whom he met in 1833, was undoubtedly his closest and most intensely loved male companion, and while they lived together in Leipzig Schumann dreamed up the idea of the *Davidsbund* — the band of David — a fraternity for spearheading the cause of musical progressives against reactionary, Philistinic fuddy-duddies. "In a short time they became indispensable to each other" says Gustav Jansen, a devoted Schumann scholar.

By 1834 Schumann's mother was 70 years old and Schunke seems to have become his new emotional lifeline. They met in a bar, in Leipzig and it seems to have been love at first sight:

> A young man approached us in Krause's cellar. All eyes turned in his direction. Some wanted to find in him a resemblance to Johannes [John the Baptist]. Others thought that if such a statuesque head were dug up in Pompeii one would declare him to be a Roman Emperor... Before he even whispered his name, "Ludwig Schunke from Stuttgart," I heard an inner voice saying: "that's the one we are looking for" — and his eyes expressed just about the same thing.

They dedicated piano pieces to each other and Schumann told his mother that he "would give up all other friends for just this one". Schunke died of tuberculosis on December 7th, 1834. Their deep mutual love was vital to both their creative endeavours and explains why at that stage Schumann was in no hurry to marry. "Living together with Schunke — thereby often a dissolute life", he wrote in his diary. They probably regarded themselves as a couple. In honour of his dead friend Schumann later christened his second son Ludwig.

Schumann also seems to have had a crush on the English composer William Sterndale Bennett, whom he met in 1836 and who inspired the march ending in his *Symphonic Etudes*. For a while Clara Wieck, who by now was in love with Schumann, seems to have regarded Bennett as a kind of rival.

Schumann's "almost dandified, if not effeminate" appearance must, in fact, have made him very fanciable by either sex:

> a powerfully built but slender young man, with a blooming, not exactly red-cheeked but colourful face, very well framed by his rather long, brunette hair, combed in a heavy curl from one ear to the temple. His eyes were deep set, dark, and glowing with passionate enthusiasm. His whole appearance was thoroughly noble, his bearing elegant, and, above all [he exhibited] a great kind-heartedness. [Violinist and fellow student Johann Täglichsbeck]

Clara (1819-1896)

An uneasy romance from beginning to end. [Ostwald]

It is fascinating to see how, from the time of their first real acquaintance in 1828 when Schumann began piano lessons with Friedrich Wieck, Schumann and Clara Wieck gradually turned from being brotherly sisterly pals into sweethearts.

When he arrived in Leipzig Schumann had lost no time in seeking out Friedrich Wieck for piano lessons while then a law student. Wieck, who had divorced his first wife after she walked out on him for another man, leaving him to cope with their five children, had trained his second daughter Clara to a peak of musicianship and pianistic virtuosity. When she started touring at the age of 12 Clara was living testimony to the world of his truly remarkable powers as a teacher who had devised his own painstakingly thought-out pedagogic methods.

But however good a teacher he was, and however tough he had been in overcoming the deprivations of his early "charity soup" background, there was a very nasty side to Wieck: mean, intolerant, violent-tempered, spiteful, sadistic even, and anti-Semitic. "One recognises a Jew-boy in every measure he plays" he said of the young talented pianist-composer Ferdinand Hiller. Wieck's obsessive control over Clara verged on the perverted, travelling with her constantly, censoring her mail, keeping her away from other men, writing in her diary ("Today my father divorced my mother."), sharing her hotel room on tour — and supervising her dressing and undressing.

Wieck much preferred travelling with Clara to staying at home with his second wife Clementine, a young clergyman's daughter whom he married in 1828. The film *Frühlings Sinfonie* (Spring Symphony), released in 1983 starring Nastassja Kinski as Clara, may not be too far fetched in portraying Wieck as murkily incestuous.

Wieck had minced no words in telling Schumann's mother exactly what was needed to become a fine pianist and in how Robert fell short: "for Robert the greatest difficulty lies in the quiet, cold, well-considered, restrained conquest of technique, as the foundation of piano playing." Nevertheless, as we have seen, Wieck took on responsibility for Schumann's musical education from October 1830. Schumann, however, proved to be an intractable and wayward pupil, reluctant to toe the line, and neither Wieck nor other teachers whom Schumann briefly consulted had much time for him. In any case, there were long gaps in tuition while Wieck was on tour with Clara.

When he actually went to live with Wieck in his spacious house, the 22-year-old Robert Schumann had already entertained Clara, then 13, and her younger brother Alwin with ghost stories and improvisations at the piano. But already there was a special patina colouring the friendship. "I often think of you, dear Clara," he wrote in his diary in January 1832, "not the way a brother thinks of his sister or a friend, but rather like a pilgrim thinks of a distant altar-piece."

The relationship changed rapidly as Clara approached puberty. She and her "brotherly" friend were now producing various musical "offspring" during their flirtatious sessions at the piano. In particular Schumann started incorporating into his compositions a melodic sequence of specific notes that Clara had suggested to him: C F G C. (It first appears in his playful and sometimes infinitely gentle *Impromptus* op. 5.)

In June 1833 Schumann was writing home enthusiastically about Clara's developing "gifts of mind and heart" and her solicitous attentions on country walks, tugging at his coat to stop him falling over bits of stone when his head was in the clouds. In July 1833 while recovering from a bout of malaria, he was writing to her that "a chain of sparks now attracts us or reminds us of one another". He suggested a favourite ploy for sweethearts who are parted. "Tomorrow morning at 11 o'clock on the dot I will play the Adagio from Chopn's variations and at the same time think about you very strongly, yes only you. Now please do the same, so that we can see and meet each together spiritually." The "fairy-tale romance" was under way.

By April 1834 Wieck was beginning to feel uneasy about Clara's devotion to Schumann and arranged for her to spend six months in Dresden. Then a year later, after returning from a six-month concert tour, Clara had the shock of discovering that Schumann had fallen head over heels for another pupil of Wieck, Fraulein Ernestine von Fricken, with even marriage in the offing.

Their secret engagement, however, soon fizzled out, not least because Schumann discovered that Ernestine was illegitimate and adopted. Schumann formally jilted her on New Year's day 1836. Ernestine was very angry and hurt: "Heaven is forever banned to me. I loved Schumann unspeakably and would have given him my life". This short and strange, but undoubtedly intense relationship had actually inspired *Carnaval* (op. 9) a musical picture gallery "of the many different mental states" Ernestine had stimulated in Schumann. (*Carnaval,* in fact contains a vast and complicated range of extra-musical symbols so typical of his literary and allegorical approach to composition.)

It was perhaps all rather a pity, because Ernestine might have been a more suitable, less competitive and threatening partner than Clara.

"Clara grows more charming every day, yes every hour, internally as well as externally" Schumann wrote in August 1835. Then in November they did it. On Wieck's front steps the 25-year-old Schumann gave 16-year-old Clara a kiss from which she nearly fainted. From their point of view, that really settled their future together. There were more snatched kisses shortly afterwards in Zwickau, where Clara was giving a concert — with Wieck in tow.

"I shall never forget that kiss," wrote Robert. "You were so sweet. And at the concert, Clara, sitting there in your blue dress, you could not even look at me." Frau Schumann, however, made it clear to Robert that she certainly would approve of the match, much preferring Clara to Ernestine.

The trouble, as everybody knows, was that Wieck would have none of it, envisaging his daughter's career in tatters through associating with a neurotic, unstable, alcoholic spendthrift, whatever his dubious potential as a composer. Wieck proved to be as intractable as Edward Barrett of Wimpole Street with another Robert. Clara was progressively cornering the female soloist market over such players as Anna Caroline de Belleville, Marie Pleyel, Marie Blahetka and others whose careers were being sacrificed to their marriages. There are many who have, of course, always sympathised with Wieck's line, and not merely because his fears of marital problems proved to be justified. Wieck may also have suspected that Schumann had syphilis.

Once again, in January 1836, Wieck took Clara to Dresden with the intention of cutting off all contact in person or by letter between the sweethearts. However, Clara soon wrote to Robert to say the coast was clear for a few days in February and he went to visit her for some more kissing, and no doubt cuddling also. He was also able to pour out his grief to Clara over the very recent death of his mother, whose funeral he was been unable to face. Without yet getting engaged they seem to have pledged undying loyalty to each other. "Fate always intended us for one another", he wrote soon afterwards. Wieck, of course, was enraged when he learned of this meeting, threatening Clara that he would shoot Schumann if she saw him again and writing to Schumann severing all relations with him.

*

Not a word was spoken between the lovers for some 18 months between February 1836 and August 1837, even though they were both living in the same city when Clara wasn't touring. Perhaps inevitably, they even turned on each other for a while. Schumann gave only very scant publicity to Clara's new piano concerto in his new journal (the *Neue Leipziger Zeitschrift für Musik*). He also attempted to console himself by reverting to the ever-welcoming arms of Christel, contemplating marriage to another Clara whose surname is unknown, and cultivating the company of the beautiful 18-year-old Scottish pianist Robena Laidlaw, dedicating his *Phantasiestücke* op. 12 (Fantasy Pieces) to her. This was also the time when he enjoyed the intimate company of Sterndale Bennett for many months.

For her part, Clara returned Schumann's love letters and asked for hers back. She and her father also toyed with and then rejected the approaches of her new singing teacher, Carl Banck.

*

All these manoeuvres and contretemps were, of course, nothing more than surface ripples on the mighty ocean of their love. As was so often to be the case, intense and unfulfilled longing for his beloved drew some heavenly music from Schumann. No less than four major works grew out of all his pain and anguish. Each of them contains references to Clara, direct quotations from her own compositions or note patterns suggesting her name (descending patterns starting on C and ending on A). His Piano Sonata in F sharp minor (op. 11) was "a solitary outcry for you from my heart". He also worked on, but didn't complete until later, his G minor Piano Sonata (op. 22) which Clara adored: "I love it, as I love you," she wrote later. "It so clearly expresses your essential self and is not too incomprehensible."

Then immediately after finishing the F sharp minor sonata he began his masterly sonata entitled *Fantasie* in C, dedicated to Liszt (whose first run-through of it brought tears to Schumann's eyes) but with Clara in mind. "The first movement may well be the most passionate I have ever composed — a deep lament for you," he wrote later. The *Fantasie* ranks alongside Liszt's B minor sonata and Chopin's B flat minor sonata as one of the greatest piano works of the Romantic period. A year later Schumann said to Clara: "You can only understand the *Fantasie* if you go back to the unhappy summer of 1836 when we were separated." To emphasise the point, the Adagio at the end of the first movement contains several references to Beethoven's song-cycle for the distant beloved, *An die ferne Geliebte.* The middle movement, Clara wrote to him from Paris, "makes me hot and cold all over ... Many images are stirred up ... The march strikes me as a victory march of warriors following a battle, and the A flat major theme makes me think of young maidens in a village, all dressed in white, each with a wreath in her hand to crown the warriors kneeling before them."

The fourth work to emerge from the enforced separation was the *Grand* Sonata in F minor (op. 14), also called the *Concerto Without Orchestra,* conceived at the height of his ordeal with Clara. Once again a descending Clara theme permeates the work.

*

Having been encouraged by a conciliatory request from Clara through an intermediary for the return of the letters she had sent back to him, Robert wrote to Clara on August 13th asking for a definite "Yes". At the time she was locked away on a country estate at Maxen near Dresden with Wieck's friends, who were fortunately very well disposed towards Schumann. Clara accepted Robert on the 14th:

A simple "yes" is all you ask? Such a tiny little word — yet so important! Couldn't a heart as full of inexpressible love as mine say this little word with its entire soul? I'll do it ... Perhaps fate wants us soon again to talk together.

They finally met on September 9th,1837, both a little uptight. On Clara's birthday, September 13th,1837, Schumann took the bull by the horns and sent a humbly worded, supplicatory, proposal to Wieck. "With all the profound emotion which an anxious, loving heart can command," Schumann ended, "I beseech you to grant us your blessing, to be a friend to one of your oldest friends, and the best of fathers to the best of daughters." All to no avail of course, the granitic Wieck replying in an interview that marriage would interfere with Clara's career, that Schumann could not keep her in the style to which she had become accustomed, and that anyway she was too young. "He has found a new way of destroying me," Schumann wrote to Clara, "by plunging the whole dagger into my heart, hilt as well as blade."

*

Their marriage would have be fought out through the courts. In the meantime Clara, accompanied by Wieck, was touring during much of the winter of 1837-38, creating a sensation in Vienna with her performance of Beethoven's *Appassionata* and gaining the Emperor's accolade of Imperial Chamber Virtuoso. Back in Leipzig, Schumann was busy with his journal and once again, "found out [that] nothing sharpens the imagination as much as expecting and longing for something".

He started composing like mad. First came the *Davidsbündlertänze* — composed, unusually, without bringing in earlier material or even any revision. "There are many wedding thoughts in the dances," he wrote to her, "which were suggested by the most delicious excitement I can remember." And later "...my Clara will understand everything in the dances. For they are dedicated to her, and more emphatically than any of my other pieces." Then in 1838 came the *Novelletten* op. 21: "I have been waiting for your letter, and as a result have written books-ful of pieces — amazing, crazy, sober stuff. You'll stretch your eyes when you open it up ... You appear in the *Novelletten* in every possible circumstance, in every irresistible form ... They could only be written by one who knows such eyes as yours and has touched such lips as yours."

These novelties were followed by yet more piano pieces: *Kinderszenen* op. 15 (Scenes from Childhood) which includes perhaps his most popular tune of all, *Träumerei* (Dreaming), and *Kreisleriana* (op. 16). "A positively wild love is in some of the movements," he wrote of *Kreisleriana,* "and your life, and mine, and the way you look. The *Kinderszenen* are the opposite, peaceful, tender and happy, like our future." Alas, it wasn't to be quite like that.

Inevitably with all the strains of conflict and separation there were tiffs and upsets. When Schumann wound Clara up by mentioning that he had received a lock of hair from Robena Laidlaw, "just so you know it", the response was hardly enthusiastic. "How could you make me sick in this way and draw such bitter tears out of me? ... I know you have many beautiful girls at your disposal who are as beautiful and maybe also as good as I am, and who would make better housewives than could be expected from an artist."

Clara was utterly torn between her father, a massive and inescapable emotional burden, and her betrothed, trying to please both. "I feel obligated to him," she wrote, "yet I've got to love you endlessly. It pains me when you throw stones at my father ... He loves me more than anything ... so forgive him, out of love for me..." The ups and downs in their letters and meetings can be imagined, especially with Clara suggesting more than once postponing their marriage in the interests of career and cash, and Schumann reacting with thoughts of suicide! "It crossed my mind to throw in [your] ring — I have an interminable yearning to plunge in after it."

Schumann had all too predictable crises of self-confidence, especially after his fruitless trip to Vienna in 1838 in search of career openings. While there he did, however, compose some more piano compositions (including *Faschingsschwank aus Wien* and the *Corpse Fantasy)* and he also unearthed some of Schubert's compositions from his brother Ferdinand, including the "Great" C major Symphony.

In May 1839 Clara wrote a desperate and passionate final plea to her father from Paris making it clear that "I can never leave him, nor will he ever leave me. I could never love another man". It was a waste of paper and emotion and in an act of amazing courage she signed a defiant Affidavit in September 1839 applying for her father's consent to their marriage to be set aside. "The moment I signed was the most important of my whole life. I set my name down with resolution, and was inexpressibly happy."

Not so Wieck, whose enraged responses included laying down

brutal conditions for his consent, banning Clara from his house (she went to live with her mother in Berlin), breaking into her private letter box, slagging both of them off to all and sundry, and spitting in Schumann's face in the street. Not for nothing did Schumann call him a *rappelkopf,* a crackpot. The ludicrous conditions included Clara losing her last seven year's earnings, some 7,000 thalers, apart from the interest; paying 1,000 thalers to repossess her piano and personal belongings; losing her rights to an inheritance from Wieck; and Schumann having to deposit 8,000 thalers to provide for Clara in the likely event of the breakdown of the marriage.

Efforts at legal conciliation were useless and in December 1839 the two parties met in court. The wrangling dragged on until August 1840, during which Wieck relentlessly denigrated Schumann as a man and musician. After the dismissal of Wieck's one remaining charge — that Schumann was an alcoholic — the court gave the couple permission to marry and even allowed Schumann to countersue for slander. The banns were published on August 16th, 1840.

Unbelievably, while all this was going on, and under the pain of continued separation, Schumann began bursting forth in a new genre — song. Although he drew a creative blank in the second half of 1839, crisis and creativity now combined to produce "so much that it really seems quite uncanny at times. I can't help it, and should like to sing myself to death. So utterly at the mercy of the ebb and flow of melody am I that I feel almost swamped, oblivious to all the disgraceful goings on around me. I fear I shall not be able to bear this exhilaration for long." The results in a matter of months were over 120 songs including a setting of the Fool's Song from *Twelfth Night*, a cycle of songs to poems of Heine (*Liederkreis* op. 24), then two breathtaking song cycles.

The first of these came immediately after the couple had spent a blissful fortnight together in Berlin in April: settings of poems of Eichendorff (*Liederkreis* op. 39). The second miracle was 16 settings of poems from Heine's *Dichterliebe* (op. 48). "I was completely inside you while composing them", wrote Schumann to his beloved. Indeed there is a strong autobiographical element in both sets, particularly *Dichterliebe*, whose themes encompass sorrow, separation, longing, jealousy, and loss in love.

For many, the 16 *Dichterliebe* rank equally with Schubert's

Winterreise in the hierarchy of song cycles, the piano once again being an exquisitely integrated and equal partner in the total conception. Schumann managed to hear Mendelssohn sing the first set of *Liederkreis* during his visit to Berlin, Clara accompanying.

The wedding took place on September 12th — symbolically one day before Clara's 21st birthday, a final rude gesture to the deplorable Wieck. There was a reconciliation of sorts two years later.

*

The Marriage

Nothing occurred to spoil the day, which shall be recorded in this diary as the fairest and most momentous day of my life ... A new life is opening up, a wonderful life ... [Clara, 1840]

And what will become of my own work? I do not know whether things can always go on like this ... [Clara, 1846]

It was certainly a loving, sexually satisfying marriage, but definitely not the fairy-tale one of popular imagination.

In view of Clara's ten pregnancies it seems unlikely that the Schumanns used any form of birth control other than abstinence, or perhaps occasionally coitus interruptus, which was then the most common method. Condoms and pessaries were, so Dr. Ostwald tells us, available in mid-19th-century Germany, but were unreliable and quite expensive. However, for whatever reason, from April 1846 Schumann started recording in his household diary every occasion they had sexual intercourse. The frequency then was every two to five days.

In his severest depressions Schumann's libido was depleted, but never went defunct. The earlier births inspired him into flourishes of composition; news of the first baby, for instance, resulted in four days and sleepless nights of sketches for his *Spring* Symphony. The later pregnancies, however, caused them both anxiety, with more mouths to feed and work opportunities for Clara missed.

It was also a marriage of true minds — up to a point. They kept a joint diary, studied Bach, Beethoven, Haydn and Mozart scores together; he encouraged her to compose, read Shakespeare and Jean

Paul; she encouraged and inspired him to write the music he wanted to write in new genres: symphonies, chamber music and other substantial works. "Even Robert cannot be more blissfully happy at his work than I am when he finally shows me what he has composed," she wrote as she heard him working on his earlier version of the D minor Symphony on Whit Sunday 1841. Is there any one woman ever who has inspired or played midwife to so much music from one man? Cosima Wagner perhaps?

"Every day," wrote Clara during their first year together, "I give thanks to God for the happiness of being able to call such a wonderful man my own." "My wife," wrote Robert, "is the very incarnation of modesty, generosity and love. Everyone can see it."

But there were problems that common interests, love and good sex could not overcome. Basically, Schumann, at the age of 30, wanted a quiet home life in which to compose. Clara, barely 21, wanted to be treading the boards, enjoying the glam and the glory of playing before enraptured audiences.

Then there was also the domestic routine. Perhaps the nittiest, grittiest issue was the noise factor. "Every time Robert composes," Clara wrote, "my piano playing must be set aside completely. Not a single tiny hour can be found for me all day! If only I don't regress too much." *Rast ich, so rost ich.* If I rest, I rust.

So much for the daringly new Romantic concept, which Schumann subscribed to in theory, that men and women should be encouraged to relate to each other as equals! Men and women were equal — as long as men's needs came first. Schumann observed in their joint diary that she studied Beethoven and read Goethe "but still chops beans when needed". The one certainty in their life together is that Schumann never chopped the beans nor peeled the potatoes, nor ever changed a diaper.

*

Clara did travel and give concerts, of course, and it caused huge problems. If Robert didn't go with her he felt neglected and couldn't compose. If he did, he felt very much a second fiddle — "Clara Schumann's husband". There was the legendary occasion when they were in Holland in 1853 and a member of the Royal family turned to

Schumann after one of Clara's stunning concerts and gave Schumann's ego a blow by asking him "Are you musical too?"

The tensions mounted. In the early months of 1842 they were both invited to Bremen and Hamburg and Schumann, to avoid being alone, tagged along. However, when his *Spring* Symphony was politely received in comparison to the rapturous response to Clara's playing he got twitchy. He returned to Leipzig and left her to continue with a female companion to Denmark, where she made a cool 1,000 thalers. The seven-week separation was more than Schumann could cope with and he hit the beer and champagne with characteristic desperation. He pinpointed the problem in a letter to her:

> The separation has again made my strange and difficult situation more palpable. Ought I to neglect my talent so that I can be your travel escort? Have you or should you let your talent go to waste because I am tied to the newspaper and my piano? We have found the solution; you've taken a companion, I've returned to our child and my work. But what will the world say? That's how I torture myself mentally. Yes, it is absolutely necessary for us to find a way to use and develop our two talents side by side.

Clara's return in late April produced a happier mood, and also the three amazing string quartets in just over six weeks. They teem with lovely tunes though their fabric is often very pianistic.

By November of that year Clara was also expressing her misgivings:

> For some days I have been in a state of depression — I do not think you love me as you used to, and I often have the feeling that I do not satisfy you ... The thought that you would have to work in order to earn money I find terrible, for you could never be happy that way. Yet I can see no alternative as long as you prevent me from pursuing any possibility I might have to earn some money. Forgive these impulsive words, dear Robert, but my feelings for you go even deeper than this. Kiss me — do not be angry. And if you can, go on loving me, at least a little. For your love is my life.

During a later four-month tour they made together in 1844 to Russia, Schumann's bouts of depression and unsociable behaviour made him an additional liability rather than a support, even though the remarkable sum of 4,796 thalers that Clara earned provided essential income. After that tour ended in May 1844, Schumann stopped making entries into their joint diary — a pointer, perhaps, to the rockier ground they were entering.

One of Schumann's severest depressions before his suicide attempt built up from the summer of that same year when even listening to music "cut into my nerves like knives". He was shivering, could barely walk, couldn't sleep, was hallucinating aurally and visually, and Clara generally found him "swimming in tears" each morning. The homeopathic physician Dr. Helbig prescribed cold plunge baths. They had some beneficial effect but Schumann never recovered completely during his remaining active life.

In an attempt to start a new life with a beneficial change of climate the Schumanns severed their connections with Leipzig (including the *Neue Zeitschrift*) for good in December 1844 and went to live in Dresden.

Schumann would work himself up into such a state of illness before one of Clara's tours that it had to be cancelled. In 1845, for instance, she was all set to go to the Beethoven Festival in Bonn and Schumann agreed to tag along. No sooner said than entries appeared in the household book that speak for themselves: "exhausted condition" (July 22nd); "bad anxiety at noon" (July 24th); "crisis of decisions" (July 26th); then "sick", "sick", and "very sick — preparing for the trip" (July 28th, 29th, 30th). They didn't get as far as Bonn. On the way Schumann complained of such "anxiety and dizziness" that they did some sightseeing in Weimar instead and then spent a few days in Zwickau. Too bad about Clara's concerts!

Being much the tougher animal, Clara sometimes had to protect him almost like a baby long before he was voluntarily institutionalised. In 1849, during the revolutionary turmoil in Dresden when Wagner and all his cronies were ripping up pavements and sewers to form barricades, guards called at the Schumann's house in *Waisenhausstrasse*. Robert fled through the back garden, followed by Clara and Marie, leaving the younger children in the care of the housekeeper. After a train journey and a walk they finally ended up with their friends Major and Frau Serre in Maxen, where Robert sat down and wrote that very evening the *Frühlingslied* (No. 18 op. 79)! Then heavily pregnant, Clara set off back for Dresden with two other women at three o'clock in the morning, walking well over two miles "across the fields under continuous cannonading", encountering scythe-armed rebels along the way. She managed to collect the children and return with them to the safety of Maxen.

Robert all the while had made good use of all this panic by letting Clara get on with it and writing songs. For the next month they stayed at the village of Kreischa where Robert, totally shielded from the outside world, worked on his *Song Album for the Young* (op. 79), *Five Hunting Songs* (op. 137) for double male chorus and four horns, and also a motet. The contrast between the outer and inner worlds of Schumann could not be more stark. Clara noted that he was able to "cast an air of supreme peacefulness over all these songs, they all remind me of spring, joyful as the blossoms ... The external terror awakens his inner poetic feelings in such an entirely opposite way". In 1849 he wrote more music than in any previous year of his composing life.

Clara's devotion to her husband was sometimes detrimental to him. Schumann most definitely wasn't cut out for professional conducting, yet such a job was precisely what financial straits compelled him to accept in 1850 following an offer, made on Hiller's recommendation, from Düsseldorf. Stroppy orchestral musicians — there were 160 in the Düsseldorf band — complaining about conductors was par for the course, but Schumann's pathetic ineffectiveness as Municipal Music Director was such that even a good many of the 490 amateur chorus members complained. That really takes some doing. When various tactful and inevitable moves were made to reduce Schumann's participation in favour of his competent deputy Julius Tausch, Clara, instead of encouraging her husband to withdraw with minimum loss of face, forced the issue by protesting at the "infamous intrigue and insult" and threatening her husband's resignation.

Knowing as she must have done her husband's limitations, this was very misplaced pride. Things had, after all, reached the stage where on one occasion or another her husband couldn't get a piece started, couldn't beat time, gave no cues, got slower and slower with his tempi, didn't notice when a piece had finished nor when individual players were playing, and even tied his baton to his hand so that he couldn't drop it.

*

It would be wrong to paint a dark picture of burdens without also focusing on their happiness, bliss even. Clara's devotion was unstinting and deeply valued. "Today we began to study counterpoint, which in spite of the labour, gave me great pleasure," she wrote early in 1845 after they had moved to Dresden. "Robert himself has been taken with a complete passion for fugues, and beautiful themes pour out of him." Indeed, as we've already noted, many more "beautiful themes" were, seemingly against all odds, still to emerge again before his death, including the Piano Concerto, the *Album für Jugend* (Album or the Young), the *Rhenish* Symphony and the Cello Concerto.

In the summer of the following year they enjoyed "their best vacation ever", and on Clara's birthday in 1849 Robert's very tangible demonstrations of his love and gratitude were a magnificent present of a grand piano, costing 204 thalers, embellished with flowers — and on top of it a new Concert Allegro for Piano and Orchestra for her together with other piano arrangements of new orchestral works. "I felt my heart begin to ache, for my joy was so great. It was the result of all his ceaseless work ... It may sound boastful, but am I not the happiest wife on earth?" she asked.

Enter Brahms, Exit Schumann

I think ... I am in love with her. Often I have to hold myself back forcibly from just simply putting my arm round her: I don't know, it seems so natural to me, as though she wouldn't mind at all.
[Brahms writing to Joachim in 1854]

You have no idea how indispensable your presence is to me, you have not the remotest conception.
[Brahms to Clara, February 1855]

If things go on much longer as they are at present I shall have some time to put you under glass or have you set in gold. [Brahms to Clara, May 1856]

As the going got ever tougher for the Schumanns, a young and idolising man entered their lives in late September 1853, the 20-year-old Johannes Brahms. Although still composing frenetically, Schumann was hitting the rocks, having the previous year suffered a paralytic attack with sleeplessness, depressions and an alarming new speech impediment; also giddy attacks, "remarkable aural symptoms", a slight stroke and goodness knows what else. He was also into table rapping and other mysteries of the occult. Even the young Brahms was aware on this first visit of a "slight nervous disorder".

Robert and Clara were both enchanted with Brahms — "beautiful as the day, with long fair hair", as their daughter Marie later reminisced — and his music. Schumann successfully put in a good word for him with the publishers Breitkopf and Härtel, and even took up his professional pen again on his behalf in the *New Music Journal,* helping "the young eagle in his first flight through the world". As for Clara, "God sent him into the world complete".

But by early February 1854 Schumann had "gone". Here he is writing to Joachim after he and Clara had returned from a successful concert in his honour in Hanover:

> It is a week since we sent you and your friends a sign, but I have often written to you spiritually, and will later reveal the invisible writing behind this letter. I will close now. It is growing darker.

Ironically, the programme had included Schumann's beautiful and extraordinary early oratorio *Paradise and the Peri* about the longings of a demi-spirit for the gates of heaven.

The crunch came on the cold rainy day of February 27th, 1854 in Düsseldorf after two weeks of psychotic hallucinations recorded by Clara or himself. On February 10th he had reported "a very strong and painful aural affection". On the 14th he became unable to read because he kept hearing the note A. Then followed "magnificent music, with instruments of splendid resonance, the like of which has never been heard on earth before"; and then "great symphonic pieces played right through with the last note held on until another piece [came] into his imagination".

On the night of the 17th Schumann took down a tune in E flat major that he said the angels were dictating to him, and on the next night the angels were transformed into devils appearing as tigers and hyenas. On the 19th he was persecuted all day by evil spirits — "those superterrestrial and subterranean men" — and auditory and visual hallucinations then continued for over a week. He was convinced he was a criminal and must read the bible. On the 26th he asked to be taken to a lunatic asylum, fearing otherwise he would do his family an injury. He ate his meal in great haste and gathered all his things for the journey, but was persuaded by Clara and the doctor to go to bed instead.

On the 27th he wouldn't let Clara even touch him because he felt unworthy of her love. Then while momentarily left under the surveillance of his 12-year-old daughter Marie, the sobbing composer gave her the slip and left the house in a thin robe and slippers. A few minutes later he threw himself headlong into the freezing cold river. Rescued by nearby fishermen, he tried to jump in again and had to be restrained and brought ashore by force.

Doctors decided to separate him completely from Clara and on the 4th March he made the eight-hour coach journey to the asylum at Endenich, a suburb of Bonn.

One wonders why Clara didn't visit Robert for two-and-a-half years. He had periods of lucidity, corresponded with her until the May 5th, 1855, and received visits from Brahms, Joachim, his young composer friend Albert Dietrich and others. Dr. Ostwald believes that the usual explanation that Dr. Richarz, the asylum director, forbade her to visit Schumann for both their sakes is unconvincing. Richarz allowed Clara to see her husband in 1856 when self-starvation had reduced him to a living skeleton, and in any case Clara could have asserted her will if she wanted to see him. She had, after all, stood up against her own father.

Dr. Ostwald's theory is that Clara "probably felt guilty and shameful because what had been a private problem was now out in the open ... The realisation that he had become dangerously psychotic was more difficult for her to integrate into the concept of a loving husband". Even more convincing is the point that Clara had to face realities worse than her father's dire predictions: although Wieck correctly predicted that Schumann would not be able to support her, he had not foreseen the composer's psychotic disintegration. Clara even had to swallow her pride and accept a cheque of 400 thalers from Paul Mendelssohn, the composer's brother, to cover some of the costs of Schumann's hospitalisation until she went back on the road concertising. This she began in the spring of 1856 with a tour to England.

Clara didn't finally face her skeletonic husband until her second visit to the asylum with Brahms on July 27th, 1856, having been cabled that her husband's death was imminent:

> He smiled at me and embraced me with great effort, because he could no longer control his limbs. Never will I forget it. For all the world's treasures I wouldn't exchange this embrace. My Robert, that's how we have to meet again. With what effort I had to search for your beloved expressions. What a picture of pain.

The next day Schumann eagerly accepted wine and jellied consommé from her fingers; "ah — he knew that it was me," she wrote. Such sudden impulsive eating after prolonged self-starving may have hastened his end, which came at 4 P.M. on July 29th.

*

Whether Brahms had an affair with Clara after her husband had entered Endenich, as is so often mooted, is intriguing but unanswerable. Without binding commitments of his own, he certainly became her main prop when she was expecting her eighth child (to be named Felix, after Mendelssohn) and was without an income. He ran errands for her, acted as a surrogate father, taught her pupils when she was unwell, and played to her Schumann's and his own compositions. For her part, Clara, still only 35, showed towards the young man who had "such a soothingly tender feeling for me" more love and understanding than anyone except his mother. She made his musical cause her own in her concert tours, which she resumed as soon as she had recovered from the birth of Felix.

The gossip actually went as far as suggesting that Brahms "the young demon" had fathered Felix Schumann. One of Schumann's grandsons Alfred, under the pseudonym of Titus Frazeni, issued a booklet entitled *Johannes Brahms, The Father of Felix Schumann*, most copies of which were destroyed by the Nazis, who considered it to be "sufficiently damaging to German honour to warrant being burned". However, since Schumann's household book shows that he and Clara had sexual intercourse seven times in the month before his committal, Alfred Schumann's accusation carries little conviction.

It seems on balance highly unlikely that a person so emotionally and sexually screwed up as Brahms would have been so positive as to lead, or attempt to lead Clara to the bedroom. He spoke characteristically, in December 1855, of the "self-denial" that Clara had taught him to endure. If anything happened, it would surely have been she who would have taken the initiative. In such charged circumstances even this seems very unlikely. Perhaps one day the American scholar Maynard Solomon, who has revealed so much about the love lives of Schubert and Beethoven, will turn his attention to this teaser!

What is certain is that Brahms backed off when the chance to develop the relationship came. After Schumann's death they went on a boat trip together down the Rhine and then to Lakes Constance and Lucerne. Nothing came of it. Perhaps the man steeped in medieval romances preferred to remain a knight yearning for an unattainable lady. Or perhaps the prospect of marrying someone 14 years older than himself and becoming the stepfather to her seven surviving children shed everything in a new light. Equally, perhaps Clara felt the obligation as the widow of the one and only man she had loved since she was 12 to mourn him for the rest of her life.

Brahms and Clara Schumann remained very close to each other nevertheless, and as late as 1876 his feelings for her were still intense enough for him to write: "I love you better than myself or than anyone or anything in the world."

*

After Robert's death Clara continued to perform in what were repeated memorial rituals, appearing always in black, bent over the piano as if in prayer. In her last years she was plagued by headaches and increasing deafness, which forced her to retire in 1892. She left 20 or so works of her own, including a piano trio and a concerto.

***

CHAPTER 12

FRANZ LISZT

ORGASMATRON, PIANO-CENTAUR AND ABBÉ

BORN: RAIDING, NEAR SOPRON (AND ESTERHÁZA)
HUNGARY, 22ND OCTOBER 1811
DIED: BAYREUTH, 31ST JULY 1886

I am at your tiny feet, beloved — I kiss them, I roll them, I roll myself under the soles of them and place them in the nape of my neck — I sweep with my hair the places where you are to walk and prostrate myself under your footprints ... You know how I adore you — O how I long to see you again!. O dear masterpiece of God ... so beautiful, so good, so perfect, so made to be cherished, adored and loved to death and madness. [July 12th, 1853, from Princess Carolyne Sayn-Wittgenstein, Liszt's mistress 1847-61]

... a smasher of pianos. [Clara Schumann]

*

Franz Liszt, the orgasmatron of the concert platform, with his mane of fair hair spreading over his shoulders, his small and pale face, high forehead, white cravat, velvet gloves, kid gloves, frock coats, Hungarian sword and decorations! Where does one start?

His frenzies of cascading octaves, rippling arpeggios, racing chromatics and pounding chords thrilled as no other music could. It's just as well that at the height of Lisztomania in the early to mid 1840s, the besotted females in his Continental audiences wore inaccessible and unwieldy knickers and bloomers rather than today's doddle-of-a-job flimsies; otherwise flying frillies would have been yet another of this showbiz magician's occupational hazards. As it was, his frenzied and swooning admirers had to make do with showering gifts on him, and fondling his relics from the predictable to the weird and fetishist. These gaga ladies, whom he would eyeball one by one during his shows, carried his portrait on their brooches and cameos, ripped his silk handkerchiefs and nonchalantly discarded velvet gloves to ribbons, and went for his long hair with their scissors. After every loud twang during a recital the concert hall became a bear garden as they surged forward to snatch the broken piano strings for turning into bracelets.

No wonder the American critic James Huneker, who heard Liszt playing towards the end of his life, said that by looking at the chairs after a concert he could always tell where the women had been sitting.

Outside the concert hall, they whipped away his nail-parings, poured his coffee dregs into glass phials which they carried around, and even fought over his cigar butts to hide in their cleavages. On one occasion in Weimar, a besotted lady-in-waiting from the royal court pounced on his cigar dimp in the gutter and had it encased in a locket surrounded with the monogram "F.L." in diamonds. Its whiff made her none too popular.

For all his phenomenal sex appeal, Liszt was not a Don Juan or predatory rake bent on scores of conquests to boost his ego, like so many conductors and orchestral leaders of today, especially the second-raters. "He is not by nature a libertine," wrote his second grande amour, Princess Carolyne Sayn-Wittgenstein, in 1875, "he is merely weak, and when a woman *wants* to take possession of him, he cannot resist her." (So it proved to be even in his late 50s when a dotty 18-year-old pupil made a beeline for him.) It was his rapport with their emotional and sexual needs that women found so rare and irresistible — as well, of course, as his stupendous stature and showmanship as an artist. By the age of 28 he had the world at his feet.

Liszt was ever an arch-romantic, in real life as well as on manuscript paper and the ivories; as when, for instance, after a brief reunion with his first-ever sweetheart some 17 years after her father had busted their romance, he sent her a talisman bracelet containing a valuable turquoise, and also penned her a beautiful song of farewell.

It is also surely significant that unlike Gluck, Myslivecek, Paganini, Rossini, Donizetti, Schubert, Glinka, Schumann (probably), Smetena, Wolf, Delius and, very probably, Beethoven — to name just a handful — Liszt did not contract any kind of venereal infection. His ladies were overwhelmingly top drawer, and he seems to have had no need or inclination to search the parks and back streets for what Beethoven called "decaying fortresses". Undoubtedly, during his exhausting touring schedules between 1839 and 1847 when he notched up well over a thousand concerts in cities as far afield as Glasgow, Cork,

Gibraltar, Constantinople, Odessa, Kiev, Moscow and St Petersburg, he will have enjoyed casual encounters with moon-struck fans or even serving wenches. But sometimes, surely, after long and tedious journeys followed by draining concerts and fixed-smile receptions, even Liszt may have wanted only to get his head down.

In our cosseted, shock-absorbed, fan-heated saloon-car world, it is all to easy to forget that Liszt travelled in bone-shaking post-chaises in all weathers, often through the night, over rough pitted roads; or sometimes even on sleighs with dog teams over the steppes in searing winds. Some of his earlier tours had not a shred of glamour. One in particular was not only backbreaking, but also ramshackle and loss-making: in 1840- 41, Liszt and four other artists covered 3,389 miles in Britain and Ireland in four months, enduring blizzards, rickety pianos, poor audiences, and even a forgotten booking. (No phones, faxes and all the rest for last-minute confirmations.) The hapless Louis Henry Lavenu, former cellist turned fixer and impresario, was over a £1,000 down on the venture, and Liszt generously let "the poor devil" off the hook by writing off all his fees! Fortunately he made a fortune during many other trips. In Russia, for instance, in one week in May 1842 he made more than 40,000 francs. In Madrid in 1844, during an Iberian tour, he received 2,000 francs for each of four concerts in the Teatro del Circo, as well as a diamond pin from Queen Isabella I when he played before her at the Royal Palace. What's more, he had the same piano in tow right across the peninsula. What he did with a pair of performing bears he received from Tsar Nicholas I in 1843 is anybody's guess. Think of the punters he would have drawn in if he took them on stage!

*

1828 — Caroline de Saint Cricq
One of the purest earthly manifestations of
God's blessing [Liszt]

His father Adam was both Intendant of the Sheepfolds, responsible for over 50,000 sheep for Prince Nikolaus Esterházy II (Haydn's last patron), and also a cellist in the court band. Franz started learning the piano with his father when he was seven and a year later began composing. Dad then began priming his precocious but sickly lad for the big time, pushing him on to local platforms when he was nine, and coaxing money out of local grandees for lessons.

When Franz was ten the family moved to Vienna, where he had free lessons and much encouragement from Salieri and Czerny. Whatever you may have read about Beethoven's famous "kiss of consecration" around this time, the truth, as methodically unearthed by Alan Walker, is as follows. Beethoven, who had an admirably healthy suspicion of infant prodigies, finally agreed under protest to admit "the young Turk" Franz Liszt for a free consultation. Beethoven was so impressed by the boy's technical ability (which included a transposition at sight of a Bach fugue) that he kissed him on the forehead with a very gracious compliment ending "there is nothing better or finer". Throughout his life Liszt regarded this hallowed occasion as "the palladium of my whole career as an artist".

In 1823, when he was 12, the family travelled through Germany, Liszt concertising en route, to Paris — the pot of gold at the end of every artistic rainbow. Too bad that the crabby Cherubini (himself a foreigner) wouldn't bend the rules to accept the young virtuoso into the Conservatoire; Liszt managed very well thank you with theory lessons from the adventurous and still undervalued composer Antonin Reicha, and composition from Ferdinando Paer, then in charge of music at the *Théâtre-Italien.*

Liszt created a sensation at his first Paris concert on March 7th, 1824 when he was 13. His diary was crammed with bookings: in the next three years or so with only his father for company he took in three tours to England (earning some colossal fees), two to the French provinces, and one to Switzerland. In 1826 he also wrote his first important composition, the *Etude en douze exercises.* In fact he worked to the point of mental breakdown, to a crisis of melancholia made worse by his lack of contact with young men and women of his own age. His father talked him out of a fervent desire to become a priest — for the time being — and after the third English tour, they went in the summer of 1827 to take the waters in Boulogne, where Adam Liszt died from typhoid fever. Nearly 50 years later Liszt had occasion to recall his father's last words "that women would trouble my existence and dominate me". Clairvoyant or no, dad was on the ball, though Liszt reports that at that point (at the age of 16) he "had no idea of what a woman could be — I naively asked my confessor to explain to me the sixth and ninth commandments, fearing that I might have unwittingly transgressed them".

Liszt returned to Paris and set up home in Montmartre with his mother, whom he had very much missed during his travels and who was to prove indispensable during the later crises in his love life. Much in demand as a piano teacher by nice young ladies, he was soon working his socks off, travelling all over the city giving lessons, keeping himself going on nicotine and alcohol rather than his mother's cooking.

Like hundreds of thousands of other private music teachers before and after him, Liszt fell deeply in love with one of his pupils, so much so that he never forgot her. What is rather less usual in this case is that he was 17, she 16.

She was the very beautiful Caroline de Saint-Cricq, slim, black-haired, dark-eyed and delicate, daughter of Count Pierre de Saint-Cricq, minister of commerce under Charles X. Teacher and pupil fell for each other hook, line, and sinker, and Caroline's mother encouraged thoughts of marriage. All too soon, however, the countess died and her death-bed plea to her husband "If she loves him, let her be happy" fell on deaf ears. The old stuffed-shirt was apoplectic at the prospect of having a wretched piano player for a son-in-law. While the crabby cat was away, the loving mice played fervently, if comparatively chastely, but the count immediately stopped these blissful trysts when he got wind of them.

Liszt had a severe nervous breakdown, which once again unleashed his intensely religious impulses. The idea of taking the cloth as a retreat from life's agonies took hold of him with a vengeance; so much so that he spent many hours kneeling on cold flagstones and begging admittance to a seminary. In the end, his mother and his confessor talked him out of it, his mother doubtless realising that her passionate son would never be able to keep a vow of celibacy!

As an exercise in damage control, poor Caroline was married off to the son of one of her father's fellow ministers and resigned herself to a loveless life of penitential misery.

Liszt met Caroline once again about 17 years later while passing through Pau on a concert tour. They reminisced over their thwarted marriage and he later sent her the beautiful turquoise already mentioned. His strength of feeling for her never weakened and he included a ring for her in his will of 1860. Sadly, she died too young to know this, but she was able to treasure the beautiful, Tristan-like farewell song he composed for her, *Ich möchte hingehn wie das Abendroth.*

"I love you with all the power of my soul" she wrote to him in 1853, 25 years after their first meeting, "and wish for you the happiness that I myself shall no longer know ... Allow me ever to see in you the single shining star of my life."

I know men aren't supposed to shed tears, but would you happen to have a spare handkerchief, please?

*

1832 — Countess Adèle and company

Liszt took a long time to recover from the Caroline crisis; indeed, his withdrawal from society even led to the publication of his obituary on October 23rd, 1828. However, he was very much alive, even if not well, and one of his pupils and life-long friends Wilhelm von Lenz penned a revealing vignette of the 17-year-old composer in his work room. Lenz found him "pale and haggard ... with unspeakably attractive features" and a smile "like the glitter of a dagger in the sunlight", meditating on a sofa, smoking a Turkish pipe. There were three pianos in the room, one with a specially reinforced action to withstand the young maestro's pounding — "four or five hours [a day] at exercises — thirds, sixths, octaves, tremolos, repeated notes, cadenzas etc".

Around this impressionable time of his life Liszt made contacts of lasting influence and drank in vast amounts of Romantic art, opera and literature: Delacroix, Devéria, Ary Scheffer, Rossini (*Guillaume Tell*), Auber (*La Fiancée*), Sainte-Beuve, Ballanche, Rousseau, Hugo, Lamartine, Heine, and, especially, Chateaubriand and his tragic love stories.

In 1830 the July Revolution brought the French monarchy to its knees and roused Liszt from his lethargy and depression into composing the *Revolutionary* Symphony, a project that fizzled out but much later became the symphonic poem *Heroïde Funèbre.* Liszt also met Berlioz for the first time on December 4th, 1830 and was so bowled over by the first performance of his *Symphonie Fantastique* the following day that he transcribed the whole work for piano. The *Symphonie Fantastique* is, of course, one of the most startlingly "new" works in the entire history of music, and it inspired Liszt to similarly adventurous if not quite so enduringly successful efforts. The two men soon became close friends.

In March 1831 he first heard the demonic Paganini, whose technical wizardry provided him with a goal to aim for. Paganini also inspired *La Campanella* (1833), a piano fantasia comparable in difficulty to the Italian virtuoso's own dazzling showpieces.

Liszt was now gaining access to the sparkling and newly fashionable salons, hosted by wealthy countesses, in the Faubourg St-Honoré and St-Germain, where all the leading artistic figures, including such exiled émigrés as Chopin, converged. Given the plethora of arranged marriages, young married women were promising quarry for randy young bachelors, and it is not at all surprising that Liszt's next lover was a countess whom he met at one of these salons in the Faubourg St-Honoré.

She was Countess Adèle de Laprunarède and was worth cultivating for her wonderful name alone. As it was she was vivacious and stunningly beautiful and lumbered with an ageing and uninterested husband. The Countess easily persuaded him to invite Liszt to join them for a winter holiday at their castle in the Swiss Alps. The snow then fell deeply and marooned the *ménage à trois* for the whole of the winter of 1832-33, thus providing Liszt with his first real dose of prolonged passion — and also his first "exercises in the lofty French style". They kept the affair well under wraps even after their return to Paris, though Adèle's ensuing love letters were later to cause a rumpus in Liszt's first *grand amour*.

After Adèle there were other flings in quick succession, which overlapped with the beginnings of the first "big one". In 1832 he took a Mlle de Barré for a trip to the Savoie, and also extended his bedroom technique with a certain Hortense, and a Madame G — . He was now without doubt, in his 21st year, the heartthrob of the salons, and young women scrapped jealously to get on to his pupil list, with only Chopin, perhaps, being a more fashionable piano teacher for the very rich families who could afford his colossal fees. Liszt's love-life was alarming his mother, who tried to fix him up with a wife. However, at this "time of struggle, of anguish, and of solitary torment" he strenuously resisted matrimony.

*

1833 — The Galley Slaves of Love: Liszt and Countess Marie d'Agoult

Sometimes I love you foolishly, and in these moments I comprehend only that I could never be so absorbing a thought for you as you are for me. [Marie d'Agoult to Liszt]

Postures and lies. [Liszt on Countess Marie d'Agoult's *Mémoires*]

When the Marquise de la Vayer's niece Charlotte Talleyrand raved to her aunt about her phenomenal new piano teacher Franz Liszt, he was very soon invited to attend one of the Marquise's afternoon salons as guest of honour in her elegant apartment in the Rue Bac, just off the fashionable Boulevard St Germain. He was to play in a choral piece by Weber for ladies' voices, among whom would be the slim, beautiful and refined 27-year-old Countess Marie d'Agoult, who invariably stole the show in high society with her "profusion of blond hair that fell over her shoulders like a shower of gold". Her golden locks, alas, also covered a Gordian knot of hangups underneath. Likewise, her doubtless perfect bosom harboured much inner turmoil. Not for nothing did she herself accept the tag of her friend George Sand, "six inches of snow on twenty feet of lava".

The story of Countess Marie d'Agoult's beleaguered life up to this point is a litany of crises and traumas that would seem far fetched even in a penny dreadful. In the wake of a childhood both emotionally deprived and over-petted, and of a frustrated love-match, she was now locked into an arranged and strained five-year-old marriage, and saddled with a suicidal half-sister. According to her tolerant and infinitely forbearing husband Count Charles d'Agoult, 15 years her senior, Marie had also, perhaps understandably, been flirting with transvestism. It is hardly surprising that she had a highly neurotic temperament given to bouts of melancholia and depression. An

was neither space, time, nor words ... only Infinity ... Love ... Forgetfulness ... Voluptuousness ... Charity!! God, in a word!!

But even so soon in their affair Marie intuitively sensed the imbalance in their relationship:

Sometimes I love you foolishly, and in these moments I comprehend only that I could never be so absorbing a thought for you as you are for me.

She proved to be spot on there, but plunged in regardless, believing perhaps only what she wanted to believe: that she could change her man once she had him in thraldom.

There were other bad omens, worse even than the weirdly accurate predictions of a society clairvoyant Marie consulted. She was dementedly jealous of Liszt's past, gnawing away at a pile of his love letters which she found from Adèle Laprunarède and others. Liszt could see nothing to regret.

A crisis came when, soon after Liszt had returned from a visit to Brittany to see his guru, the near-anarchist and dissident cleric Abbé Lamennais, Marie lost her elder six-year-old daughter Louise after a harrowing two-month illness. While in deep shock, Marie was unable to face starting up again with Liszt. However, in March 1835, what was meant to have been one of those all too familiar "final farewell" meetings between lovers turned into a steamy and abandoned reunion in the rat hole, during which they conceived their first child.

Conventions of the day prevented them from setting up a new home in Paris and they planned their elopement. After penning a genuinely regretful letter to the husband she respected but couldn't love, Marie set out with her mother (as yet none the wiser) for Basle. Liszt, deaf to the warnings of Abbé Lamennais, followed on, checking in at a different hotel and communicating with his lover in coded messages.

*

People took us for brother and sister — which delighted both of us. [Marie d'Agoult]

The countess and her (more-or-less) kept lover eventually settled "without blushing" in a hotel in Geneva on July 19th, 1835. Marie managed to placate her brother and mother regarding the arrangement, likewise Liszt his mother. They were on "honeymoon", with Marie nursing dreams of transforming her man from a mere piano player into a towering composer-genius. Her life's mission was defined and launched. She was in the grip of a "mystical delirium". It was God's will that she minister to this semi-divine being, whose appeal was a rare and irresistible fusion of the sacerdotal and the sexy. Her memoirs show that at this point she believed her mission was succeeding:

> He started to compose, and while he was working, my presence was far from unwelcome to him. On the contrary, when I tried discreetly to withdraw, he held me back, saying he found it more difficult to collect his thoughts, and that his ideas were much less coherent, when he did not feel me close to him. For me, pretending to read, but actually not missing a single movement of his pen or lips, it was a source of profound joy to watch him thus totally committed to his art, to the radiant spirit which shone in his eyes and which I worshipped in silence.

The intimate idyll, sanctified by their readings of Dante, Goethe, and Shakespeare, was soon disturbed when one of Liszt's most loved and loving pupils from Paris, 15-year-old Hermann Cohen, "Puzzi", came bounding up the stairs followed by his mother. Liszt had invited Puzzi to come for daily piano lessons, and although they rented a nearby apartment, he and his mother spent most of their time en famille with Liszt and Marie. Other frequent visitors included the cream of Geneva's men of science and letters.

Blandine Liszt, "a sweet and extraordinarily beautiful baby girl" according to her father, was born on December 18th and handed to a wet nurse, with Liszt admitting paternity on the birth certificate whilst Marie assumed a false identity out of consideration for her husband. With typical generosity, Liszt took on some teaching gratis at the newly opened Conservatory in Geneva, penning some pithy and revealing assessment reports in his class book, including "Jemmy Gambini: Beautiful eyes". As well as giving several *soirées musicales* and fitting in a trip to Paris, Liszt also found time to write some of his most beautiful music, including evocations of the sights, sounds and legends of the Swiss countryside in his *Album d'un voyageur,* prefaced with quotations from Byron, Schiller (the greatest German literary figure after Goethe) and others, and later to be recast in his *Années de Pélerinage.* (Many of his compositions were later reborn under new titles.)

Undoubtedly one of the wackiest interludes in Liszt's entire life began during this extended "honeymoon" (summer 1836) with the arrival of George Sand with her two children and her maid Ursule for a walking holiday. Sand, with whom Liszt shared a passion for liberal reformist politics, also had an eccentric travelling companion conscripted for her by Liszt, the philologist Major Adolphe Pictet, and the plan was for the party of loveable loonies to saunter along the Chamonix valley.

Picture the party: Sand — who had just successfully obtained a divorce involving assault, lesbianism and adultery — with her exotic cigars, Turkish pipe and masculine clothes; the polemical major — "who reminded George Sand of Mephistopheles dressed as a customs official" — with his fierce beard and military cap; and "that band of gypsies upstairs with long hair and smocks", as the distraught hotelier in Chamonix had so graphically dubbed Liszt's ménage.

We can pause over only one vignette in Marie d'Agoult's hilarious chronicle of the night before the trip when all the other adults were spaced out on Sand's opium joints ("poetic cigars"): Liszt was conducting the chairs with a candle snuffer, angrily shushing those who were out of tune; the major was in deep philosophical conversation with the ceiling; and George Sand was dancing around the room in hoots of laughter.

Imagine the arty (but most definitely not farty) crew as they hit the road: Liszt with his long hair blowing in the wind; the major in military cloak alongside him, fluent in Sanskrit and rabbiting on incessantly about the Upanishads, The Four Noble Truths or something like that; Sand in her male attire puffing away as usual; Marie behind on a donkey; then Sand's two children and a very girlish-looking Puzzi with hair aping his master's; and finally Sand's maid Ursule taking up the rear.

Imagine also the impact they made on the yodelling yokels when stopping at small mountain inns! The whole story you must read in the first volume of Alan Walker's wonderful *Franz Liszt*. After kisses, embraces, darlings and luvvies all round the party dispersed at the end of September.

*

Liszt and Marie returned to Paris in October, anxious to be accepted as a couple. They need have had no fears. Having set themselves up in a posh hotel on the rue Lafitte, not far from the Opéra, they were soon inundated with visitors and holding salons and soirées. All the top notchers in the arts beat a path to their door: Rossini, Meyerbeer, Berlioz, Chopin, the critics Sainte-Beuve and Heinriche Heine, Balzac, Victor Hugo... (Balzac later wrote a fictionalised and cruel account of Liszt and Marie in his novel *Béatrix*.)

It was here that Chopin met George Sand for the first time (she was renting the floor below Liszt and Marie), and their grande passion a couple of years later was quite a turnabout for Chopin. After their first meeting Chopin had wondered to his pianist friend Ferdinand Hiller, "Is it really a woman? I am ready to doubt it!" and had told his family that she repelled him. To get noticed, George Sand arrived at Chopin's next big soirée (Marie had persuaded him to invite her) in outlandish white pantaloons and a scarlet sash. Marie d'Agoult seems to have been intent on pairing them off, perhaps to help deflect gossip about herself!

This round of salons, mercilessly wagged in the satirical press, came to an end in January 1837. George Sand returned to her country pad in Nohant and Marie soon joined her. Liszt stayed behind for his famous and successful contest with his only rival in the virtuosity stakes, Sigismond "Three Hands" Thalberg. The contest, hyped up as "the indecisive balance between Rome and Carthage", was organised as a fundraising event for Italian refugees by Liszt's exotic friend, patron and later short-term *amourette* Princess Cristina Belgiojoso.

After spending about two months in the early summer with George Sand at Nohant, where Liszt practised furiously while Marie frenziedly penned her still-ecstatic memoirs, the couple made their way to Italy. On the way Liszt, ever magnanimous, gave a fundraising concert in Lyon with the tenor Adolphe Nourrit in aid of the destitute silk workers. Liszt and Marie then even found time to look in on their "very beautiful" two-year-old daughter Blandine in Etrambière! However, changing nappies was never on Liszt's nor Marie's agenda and they moved on to Italy, settling for some while at Bellagio on Lake Como in September 1837.

*

Disenchantment and Disintegration in Italy

The lovers' Italian idyll proved to be short lived. At first they read together (especially Dante's *Divine Comedy,* Liszt's lifelong favourite work of literature) and enjoyed blissful donkey rides among the olive groves, or evenings on the lake in a gondola with their gondolier spearing fish by the light of a resin torch. Marie fondly believed that Franz had kicked his craving for the limelight, that he was happy in almost hermetic isolation with her, composing his *Grandes Etudes*:

> A bad piano, a few books, the conversation of a serious-minded woman suffice for him. He renounces all the pleasures of pride, the excitement of the battle, the amusements of social life, even the joy of being useful to others, and of doing good; he has given them all up without even realising, apparently, that he has done so.

Alas, she was soon to be disabused! Liszt was ever a complex amalgam of the reclusive contemplative and the hyperactive showman, and the concerts he gave over the next months in Milan and elsewhere were nowhere near enough to satisfy his itch for bravura, cries of *bis,* and bellowing bravos.

Cosima Liszt was born in Como on December 24th, 1837 after a difficult labour and, just for a change, handed to a wet-nurse. Once again Marie's name did not appear on the certificate and Liszt's certified paternity gave him incontestable custody of the children later on when sweet love had turned rancid.

The relationship now slowly disintegrated as Marie was forced to shed her illusions and realise that her idol was as much a "mere piano player" — her term for the all-time colossus of the instrument! — as a retiring, creative genius. Liszt began to champ at the bit, unable and unwilling to settle down to the life Marie had dreamed for them. The watershed was Venice in the spring of 1838 where she wrote that

My heart and spirit are dry. It is an ailment I must have been born with. For an instant passion elevated me, but I feel that the principle of life is not within me ... I feel myself an obstacle to his life, I'm no good to him. I cast sadness and discouragement over his days.

As for Liszt, he was ever more restless ("Will the hour of virile action never come?" he wrote to Lamennais) and found his lover's depressions hard work:

Love me always, and most of all try to be a little satisfied, a little gay, a little happy, if possible.

Eventually the first chance, or excuse, came for him to get up and go. He read of the horrendous flood disasters in March 1838 in his beloved Hungary, the country of his birth that he had not seen since he was a boy of ten, and immediately decided to act. Leaving Marie behind in Venice, he set out for Vienna, arriving in mid-April 1838, and gave a series of eight charity concerts to rapturous audiences, raising no less than 24,000 gulden for the disaster fund. This was the largest single donation from a private source. His programmes were adventurous and included many transcriptions of Schubert's most famous songs, of which the *Erlkönig* was easily the favourite.

His incredible success and glamorous social life in Vienna ("I am the man of the moment," he wrote to Marie) can hardly have induced him to hurry back to his jealous, impatient and ever more depressed mistress. He wanted to move on to his native homeland but Marie had fallen ill and demanded his return: "I am waiting for you, I am still unable to leave my room. In the name of heaven, delay no more."

The near certainty that while in Vienna Liszt had succumbed to the advances of at least one female admirer also did nothing for Marie's black moods.

One day a letter came for me sealed with a female coat of arms. The thought crossed my mind that this letter must have been written at a lady's house. I tore it up.

"Franz had abandoned me," she wrote on in an unpublished novella entitled *Episode de Venise,* "for such small motives ... for salon successes, for newspaper glory, for invitations from princesses". During one violent quarrel on his return she called him a

"Don Juan *parvenu*" (a Don Juan upstart).

The nosedive of this sad love affair must be more imagined than related. The rest of 1838 saw them in various parts of northern Italy including Genoa and Lake Lugano, and in Florence, with Liszt doing an odd concert here and there "so as not to forget my trade entirely". Blandine, now three years old, was delivered to them in Milan in January 1839 when Marie was five months pregnant with her third child in less than four years — and suffering from attacks of spleen and prone to thoughts of suicide. Daniel Liszt was born in Rome on May 9th, 1839 and handed to a wet nurse, who took care of him for the next two years.

In one of his rare entries in their joint diaries Liszt gave vent to his mounting frustration with his life of semi-seclusion:

There is thunder in the air, my nerves are irritable, horribly irritable. I need a prey. I feel the talons of the eagle tearing at me. Two opposing forces are fighting within me: one thrusts me towards the immensity of space, higher ever higher, beyond all suns, up to the heavens; the other pulls me down towards the lowest, the darkest regions of calm, of death, of nothingness. And I stay nailed to my chair, equally miserable in my strength and my weakness, not knowing what is to become of me.

The boil finally burst when they were idling their time in San Rossore in the late summer of 1839, Liszt spending much of his time sitting under a juniper tree and puffing his pipe. He read of the need for funds for a memorial statue of Beethoven in Bonn and decided to pledge the shortfall. To raise the necessary 10,000 francs he would need to return to the concert platform.

And so, by mid-October 1839, Liszt had laid his plans to go to Vienna while Marie arranged to return to Paris with Blandine and her maids, collecting Cosima en route in Genoa. Their final break was still four years away in 1844, but the relationship was now irretrievable.

Incredibly, during all these traumas Liszt managed to write "400 to 500 pages of piano music" including the first versions of the *Grandes Études de Paganini,* and the *Etudes d' Execution Transcendente,* intended to be a pianistic complement to Paganini's work. With the inspiration of Italian painting (especially Raphael) poetry (Petrarch) and sculpture (Michelangelo) he also completed most of the "Italian" volume of *Années de Pélerinage*. The unique achievement of this phase was the *Dante* piano sonata.

*

Between October 1839, when they had made their emotional farewells in Florence, and May 1844 when they split up for good, Liszt and Marie saw less and less of each other, with gaps as long as eight months. The gigs and miles that Liszt gobbled up during this so-called *glanzeit,* or "glitter" period as a wandering and sensationally success-ful virtuoso both before and after their split would be a relentless grind in a royal train or a private jet, never mind in post chaises and on sledges. Between 1839 and 1844 he took in Vienna, Hungary (where they went wild and presented him with his priceless, jewelled-en-crusted sword), England twice, Ireland, Russia twice, Turkey, the Danube principalities, Poland and Denmark; and then, before falling into the arms of his last Grande Amour and fairy godmother early in 1847, he covered Spain, Portugal, Germany, Switzerland, France, Hungary, Rumania, and Russia again.

The last time Marie actually went on tour with Liszt was to Eng-land in 1840, where she had to hang around in Richmond whilst he played to and hob-nobbed with Queen Victoria, Lady Blessington, Count d'Orsay and similar blue-blooded benefactors who would have most certainly snubbed a French mistress, however well connected. Marie understandably felt left out of it and gave him a hard time: "Yesterday, all the way from Ascot to Richmond, we drove along with-out you saying a single word to me that was not a wound or an insult" wrote Liszt. Once again she became ill with phlebitis.

Their only extended, ever more gloomy spells together, with the three children, were during the summer vacations of 1841, 1842, and 1843 at Nonnenwerth, an islet with a half-ruined convent, a chapel and a few fishermen's huts that Liszt discovered on the Rhine be-tween Cologne and Coblenz. For Marie, Nonnenwerth was "the tomb of my dreams, of my ideals, the remains of my hopes". George Sand's famous soundbite "the galley slaves of love" was now painfully apt. For Liszt the days were at least productive, since it was here that he so skilfully transcribed many of Schubert's songs into gems for solo piano.

Liszt's many letters to Marie from far-flung places, as well as the newspaper reports notching up his concert triumphs, must have blistered her hands, her heart, her entire frame, notwithstanding the presents he sent her — furs, jewels, curios, rugs, china, glass... Marie doubtless pictured him all too vividly charming all the women he mentioned in his letters as old or new-found "friends": Charlotte Hagn, a gorgeous 20-year-old blonde actress; Bettina von Arnim, the not-so-young lady who had known Beethoven; Balzac's Polish mistress Eva Hanska; the young contralto Caroline Unger (who had, incidentally, sung in the first performance of Beethoven's Ninth); the virtuoso pianist Marie Pleyel, dedicatee of his *Norma* fantasy published with an accompanying letter to "my dear and ravishing colleague".

Bruised and battered, Marie was nevertheless strong enough to carve out a life for herself, reading voraciously and furiously penning her "revenge" novel *Nélida.* She also formed a new salon circle of her own which included the painters Delacroix and Ingres, the romantic writer Alfred de Vigny, the great literary critic Sainte-Beuve, and the popular English historical novelist Edward Bulwer-Lytton.

One of her last ploys with Liszt was to try to wind him up by asking him for "une petite permission d'infidelité" with Bulwer-Lytton. Liszt's reply is surely one of the clearest pointers anywhere to his ideas and feelings about possession and freedom in relationships:

> ... the facts, the deed are nothing. The feelings, the ideas, the shades of meaning, especially the shades of meaning, are everything. I want and I wish you always to have complete freedom, because I am convinced that you would always use it nobly, tactfully... If you feel the need to, or if it gives you pleasure, or even distracts you to talk to me about Bulwer, do so. I shall be satisfied and flattered; otherwise I will never mention the matter.

This, of course, did nothing to ease Marie's recurring complaints of neurasthenia, erysipelas, and phlebitis. Nor, alas, did her brief affair with the editor of *La Presse,* Emile de Girardin, or her apparent one-night stand with one of George Sand's cast-offs Charles Didier, whose diary entry for January 30th, 1842 finishes "souper chez elle. La nuit. Le Mystère".

The final straw for Marie seems to have been Liszt's tacky affair with the trollopsy but very loveable "Spanish" dancer and adventuress Lola Montez, whose bottle and bravado deserve a short section to herself. It was Marie who, "in the deepest sadness of my soul", actually steeled herself to end the affair knowing that she had become "a cause of sorrow and useless strife in his life".

*

Although Marie's claws had been scratching Liszt for some time with snide references to him as a "Hungarian peasant ... a mere piano player ... a charming good-for-nothing ... half-mountebank, half-juggler", the teeth dug in as well with the publication of her *roman à clef, Nélida,* in 1846, first in serial form, then in a bestselling book under the pseudonym of Daniel Stern. It was Marie's way of coming to terms with the rift. As Alan Walker says, "No more logical argument existed for her than to assume that the reason she did not inspire him was because there was nothing in him to inspire." The plot is an attempted put-down of Liszt, showing him as a creatively barren artist, Guermann, for whom the heroine, Nélida, gives up everything before being dumped. Guermann realises the error of his ways on his deathbed and the two are reunited.

Liszt was not seriously put out by *Nélida*. Why should he be? By 1846 he had created the *Transcendentals,* the *Paganini Studies,* the *Hungarian Rhapsodies,* two volumes of *Années Pélerinages* and basketfuls of other pieces.

Their long and bitter quarrel over custody of the children Blandine, Cosima (32 years hence to become Wagner's mistress, later his wife) and Daniel was the saddest aspect of the entire affair. Liszt's concept of fatherhood was hardly exemplary and was later to become even more warped. He didn't see them for eight years after his departure, with heavy heart, for Spain and Portugal in 1845.

Liszt and Marie didn't meet again until 1861 in Paris when she recorded their brief final, tearful encounter in her journal:

Come Marie, let me speak to you in the language of the peasants: "God bless you, and may you wish me no harm."

The Liszt magic was undiminished. She was still hooked:

Inexpressible charm! It is still him and him alone who makes me feel the divine mystery of life. With him gone, I sense the emptiness around me and weep.

Marie d'Agoult's *Histoire de la Révolution* is, incidentally, even now regarded as a prime authority on the events of 1848.

*

Princess Cristina Belgiojoso

Not surprisingly, Liszt didn't have to sleep alone on his short visits to Paris after his bust up with Marie. It would seem that his longtime friend and patron Princess Cristina Belgiojoso, who had organised the famous contest with Thalberg, was only too willing to act as a stand-in until he found another grande passion. Three years younger than Liszt, Princess Belgioso, a slim Italian beauty with "black protruding eyes ... as big as saucers, very slender hands, [and] grand and gracious manners", was also a formidably intelligent feminist and social reformer. She had the misfortune not only to be epileptic, but also to marry at the age of 16 the famous singer Prince Emilio Belgiojoso, who paid her the compliment of infecting her with his syphilis. Having escaped from her husband, Cristina, known as the Romantic Muse, formed yet another of those glittering Paris salons, stunning her distinguished male entourage with her large turbans and diaphanous "excessively low necked dresses". Those who, like the poet Heine and the famous General Lafayette had seen and enjoyed far more than her low neckline, were stunned by her bedroom, with its silk hangings, silver candelabra, and awesome raised, altar-like, ebony bed, inlaid with ebony tusk.

In 1844 Liszt spent most of June at her home near Versailles, making Balzac very jealous because he was "absolutely like the master in Cristina's house". "He goes back there at 11.30 p.m.", noted Balzac peevishly. "Cristina is no longer worthy of respect." She would surely have taken that as a compliment.

*

Lola Montez, who bared her bosom before
King Ludwig I and got what she wanted

The only thing Andalusian about Mlle Lola Montez is a pair of magnificent black eyes. [She] has small feet and shapely legs. Her use of these is quite another matter ... We suspect, after the recital of her equestrian exploits, that Mlle Lola is more at home in the saddle than on the boards. [Théophile Gautier, Paris, April 1844].

The adventuress Lola Montez has surely had an undeservedly bad press for her strumpetry and second-rate histrionic talents. In view of her humble and chequered background, she gets my admiration for her exuberant and outrageous sauciness, for her guts and get-up-and-go in making it from the back-of-beyond to a royal Bavarian boudoir. By manipulating a succession of theatre Johns, she treaded the boards all over Europe for three years and then landed what she considered to be the first prize in the kept-woman stakes: "to hook a prince". After baring her capacious and irresistible bosom in front of the eccentric artist-king King Ludwig I of Bavaria, she became his mistress in 1846, and then wielded considerable political influence on the pillow. She did far more than many to earn her ennoblement (as Countess of Landsfeld), though after the revolution of 1848 and the King's abdication she sadly faded into obscurity, dying as an impoverished penitent at Astoria, Long Island in 1861.

Like so many of the other ladies in this chapter, Lola Montez also did her bit for the insatiable memoirs market, penning nine volumes of secret revelations. Yet nowhere does she flaunt Liszt in them as one of her up-market boudoir conquests — yet another sign of her acumen.

Lola Montez was no Spaniard, having been born in 1818 as Eliza Gilbert at the Limerick Army barracks after an 11th-hour shotgun wedding between her 14-year-old mother "Miss Oliver" and her father Ensign Gilbert. Skipping on a bit, at the age of 18 she pinched her widowed mother's boyfriend, a Lieutenant Thomas James, marrying him hastily in Dublin and then repenting at leisure — living first of all with the in-laws in the peat bogs, and then in the Punjab. The couple soon began to row furiously, not least because he "slept like a boa constrictor" (whatever that means). Relieved when he ran off with his adjutant's wife, the resourceful Lola sailed back to England, whiling away the hours on the briny swell with one Captain Lennox, whom she caused no end of embarrassment on their return in a court case, *James v. Lennox.*

Lola now understandably felt she had all the credentials for a theatrical career, but Fanny Kemble (one of the many stars from the renowned extended stage family of Roger Kemble) suggested she try dancing instead. Appearing at the Haymarket as Donna Lola Montez in purple and red petticoats with castanets, she was booed off. Undeterred, she toured successfully round Europe — as far away as Warsaw and St Petersburg — with the same act, impudently flaunting her body and doing backstage encores on the casting couch when need be.

No wonder Liszt was swept off his feet before he could say *Liebestraume Number Three.* And no wonder really that Marie d'Agoult called time after this brief trollopsy escapade.

Liszt met Lola in early March 1844 in Dresden when she was 26. Talented and wealthy, Liszt was just the ticket for her, particularly as she was resting and short of readies. No doubt she lost no time in revealing more than her famed bosom to our susceptible hero. Her tarty appearance repelled Wagner when she was on Liszt's arm backstage after a performance of *Rienzi,* though Wagner, of course, had no room to talk in such matters, and he may well even have been jealous. Contrary to all manner of wild and way-out scuttlebutt, Liszt's liaison with Lola lasted no longer than three weeks in various German towns. Her show in Paris at the Opéra (see Théophile Gautier's review captioned above) coincided with Liszt's return in April 1844, and Marie d'Agoult would not be persuaded that Liszt had not set her up there as a second mistress.

*

Marie Duplessis

This briefest of encounters began in 1845 when Marie's physician Dr. Koreff introduced this fallen but beloved soubrette of the *demi-monde* to Liszt. At the age of 21, with a string of lovers to her name, she was dying of consumption and clung to Liszt as her final life-line on earth, treasuring his unfulfillable promise to take her with him to Constantinople. "I won't bother you," she told him. "I sleep all day. In the evening you can let me go to a show, and at night you can do what you like with me."

"And now she is dead ... I do not know what strange chord of ancient elegy vibrates in my heart in memory of her," wrote Liszt to Marie. To Marie, of course, Duplessis was just another nail in the coffin.

After her death two years later she was immortalised by Alexandre Dumas in *La Dame aux Camélias,* and later, of course by Verdi and his librettist Piave in *La Traviata.*

*

Countess Valentine de Cessiat, May 1845
"Sorry Franz, I want to marry my uncle when his wife dies."

On his way through France in 1845 after the Iberian tour, Liszt gave a recital in Mâcon in May and stumbled into a very weird *ménage à trois* without immediately realising it. Staying as the guest of the Romantic poet, novelist and statesman Lamartine and his English wife at his château at Monceau, Liszt set his cap at the poet's niece Countess Valentine de Cessiat. No beauty, apparently, with a "remarkably large nose and mouth", she was a horsy type, 24-years-old, and 31 years younger than her uncle. For Liszt, worn out from his endless travels, Valentine seemed nevertheless at the time a comforting prospect and he actually proposed to her.

Alas, Countess Valentine was far too attached to her middle-aged uncle to contemplate any other relationship, and was undoubtedly keeping him warm in bed. In the final tableaux of this strange tale we find Lamartine, widowed in 1863, successfully applying for permission from Pope Pius IX to marry his niece, and then dying in 1869. The Countess lived on for another 25 years. After Blandine met her years after Liszt's visit, she wrote to assure her father that Valentine was "certainly not worth the tip of your little finger nail".

This bizarre episode got back to Marie, whose acid comments are only too imaginable.

*

Princess Carolyne Sayn-Wittgenstein, "Child of the Steppes", and her "Great One"

Oh, my radiant morning star ... my adorable darling ... This poor heart hasn't a single beat which isn't for you! ... I thank and bless you for having inspired me with good thoughts and for having helped me to work for God! Be blessed 1,000 and 1,000 times! [Liszt in various letters to Carolyne]

All my joys come from her, and all my sufferings go to her to be appeased. [Liszt of Carolyne]

In 1845, after the unveiling of the Beethoven monument in Bonn, Liszt made his way through Transylvania and crossed into Russia in January 1847.

A charity donation of 100 roubles left anonymously after a concert he gave in Kiev in January 1847 set Liszt on the trail of the most important woman in his life, Princess Carolyne Sayn-Wittgenstein. She it was who persuaded him to abandon his ceaseless roaming and spend more time on composing; who intoxicated him with her ever-wafting incense of adoration, and who conjured from him so many monumental works: the macabre, melodramatic, Faustian B minor piano sonata (perhaps his greatest and certainly his most technically demanding work, and one of the corner stones of the entire Romantic movement in music); other magnificent solo works for piano and organ; the two Piano Concertos; the *Faust* and *Dante* symphonies, the unique if not equally great 13 symphonic tone poems, the first of their kind ever to be written; the Grand Mass, his first great piece of church music — and much else besides.

With Carolyne's vital support Liszt also displayed unrivalled zest, energy and courage in spearheading the New German School of Weimar, promoting especially the work of Wagner and Berlioz, even if those two fanatics were sometimes hard to satisfy. Caroline also exerted considerable influence over his later prose writings as collaborator and co-author of two full-length books and many essays and articles.

On the negative side, so their detractors say, she also made him smugger and more bigoted, pumped him with her reactionary politics and exercised a near-evil influence over the way he treated his daughters in the tug of war with Marie d'Agoult.

Princess Carolyne Sayn-Wittgenstein, 28, was filthy rich and separated from her husband. With some 30 thousand serfs living in miserable huts at her beck and call, she ruled with a rod of iron over her unimaginably vast estates of grain fields at Woronice, some 150 miles southwest of Kiev in the Polish Ukraine. During Liszt's ten-day stay at Woronice in February, he once again became a woman's *raison d'être*. It was probably on this occasion that "the blue-stocking of Woronice" as the princess was often monickered, took possession body and soul of her Great One.

It was all too tempting to turn down. Liszt was whacked with the endless round of concerts, speeches, banquets and presentations. ("Always concerts! always to be a valet of the public, what a trade!" he had said seven years earlier.) True, Carolyne was plain and not madly fanciable with her dumpy figure and foul-strength cigars: no less a consummate master of the pen than Marian Evans (later known as George Eliot) described her seven years later as "short and unbecomingly endowed with embonpoint" with an unpleasing face, "blackish teeth", a "harsh and barbarian" profile, but with eyes conveying "vivacity and strength". No matter; female adoration of the kind she gave Liszt can be an overpowering aphrodisiac and Carolyne was also highly cultured and a very discerning music lover. Like Marie d'Agoult she also shared her lover's passion for Dante and Goethe.

After their few days in February, Liszt finished his scheduled engagements through Russia, Turkey and the Ukraine, spending a few weeks in July with Carolyne in Odessa. After giving his last ever paid recital in Elisavetgrad (now Kirovograd) in September, he made his way for the second time to Woronice, where Carolyne and her "poem in action" spent the autumn and winter of 1847-48 on "honeymoon". They made a decision to settle in Weimar, where Liszt had already, in 1842, been appointed Court Kapellmeister Extraordinary and where he could concentrate on composing, conducting and producing operas.

Marie d'Agoult, after hearing from Liszt about the new woman in his life, replied that Carolyne "will not want to be one of your mistresses". Carolyne's reply was that if necessary she would indeed tolerate just such a situation "because there are devotions without limits". She proved to be as good as her word when her vow was put to the test!

*

Weimar 1848-1861

In February 1848 Liszt arrived in Weimar and got stuck into work straight away, also penning many letters of love and devotion to his "radiant morning star". In April, Carolyne and her daughter Marie met up with Liszt in Grätz where he had travelled to meet her, doubtless pleased to learn that she had 1,000,000 roubles in her pocket (from the sale of an estate) to keep the wolf from the door. The Grand Duchess of Weimar, Maria Pavlovna, was the sister of the Tsar Nicholas I and Liszt and Marie were therefore confident that her divorce could be fixed to enable them to marry.

Liszt's Weimar years proved to be artistically momentous, though far from idyllic on the personal level. Many of the greatest pianistic talents of the day beat a path to his door, most notably Anton Rubinstein, Carl Tausig and Hans von Bülow, soon to become his son-in-law. He introduced Weimar to Wagner's *Tannhaüser, Lohengrin* (a world première) and the *Flying Dutchman,* to Berlioz's *Benvenuto Cellini,* and to many other Berlioz works during festivals dedicated to him in 1852 and 1855. Many other operas were also produced, including four by Gluck, two by Mozart, three by Rossini and others by Schubert, Schumann, Meyerbeer, Cherubini, Spontini, Donizetti, Verdi, and many others. There were also many adventurous orchestral concerts in which Liszt, like Wagner, extended the expressive aspects of the conductor's role. That probably means that the poor players couldn't follow his beat very well and had to rehearse pieces to death.

In spite of personal setbacks, Liszt and Princess Carolyne enjoyed the pleasures of a spacious 32-room mansion placed rent-free at their disposal by the Grand Duchess — the Altenburg, set in six acres of woodland on the "new" side of the town. Carolyne predictably turned it into a shrine for her Great One, adding to the aura of sanctity by installing a prie-dieu for him and a large wooden crucifix over her own bed in her separate wing of the house. A selective glimpse at some of the literally priceless contents (fascinatingly detailed by Alan Walker) takes the breath away: Beethoven's Broadwood piano and death mask, a Haydn writing case, a spinet that had belonged to Mozart, an Erard concert grand, two Viennese grands, and a massive, earthquaking, specially commissioned "piano-organ" with three key-boards and a pedal board, which was effectively a one-piece band for trying out orchestral works. There were jewels and gold medallions presented to Liszt on his travels by half the crowned heads of Europe, and touring souvenirs including Oriental rugs, mother-of-pearl ta-bles, Turkish pipes, Russian jade, a silver breakfast service ... There were vast quantities of books and music, including autographed scores by Chopin, Schumann, Beethoven, Wagner, Mozart and many more; and paintings too numerous to mention apart from Dürer's *Melancholia* and two life-sized portraits of the maestro himself. Live assets comprised a staff of five including Liszt's colourful man-servant Becker, who like his master was a conjurer only reportedly better. Pinching the best chair, no doubt, was Madame Esmeralda the cat, while Rappo the dog lolloped all over the house and barked under the window of Liszt's Blue Room, where he composed at his Boisellot grand.

Their soirées included leading artists from all over Europe whose names would fill up the rest of the chapter, but the great German dramatist Friedrich Hebbel has left a vivid thumbnail sketch of Liszt in action at the piano with Marie turning the pages (a job never to be underrated!):

> At the piano he is a demi-god; and behind him, in Russo-Polish national costume with a tiara and golden tassels, stood the young princess turning the pages, a task which compelled her at times to pass her hand right through his long hair, sent fluttering all around him in the heat of his playing. It was as fantastical as a dream!

His effect at the piano on George Eliot was similarly over-whelming:

> [He] is the first really inspired man I ever saw. His face might serve as a model for St John in its sweetness when he is in repose; but seated at the piano he is as grand as one of Michelangelo's prophets.

Loving any excuse for a celebration, Liszt would also organise elaborate *tableaux vivants,* refreshing everybody with such goodies as oysters, champagne, truffles and ices. His wine bill for one soirée might cost more than half the year's salary of a rank-and-file violinist in the court orchestra! And no doubt his brandy bills were pretty horrendous also, since on his own admission music and "intensity of emotion" too often drove him to "intemperance in the use of spirituous liquor".

But the sumptuousness of the surroundings was no real anodyne for pains of the heart. In a small petty-minded town where adultery was still punishable by imprisonment, the chain-smoking Carolyne, living over the brush, was virtually blackballed by the court and exalted town circles. She spent almost a third of her time during the Weimar years away from the town to escape from the hostile atmosphere and to take the waters at Bad Eilsen, where Liszt often visited her, in an effort to cure her frequent boils, abscesses, rheumatic complaints, and even typhoid fever. To rub salt into all her wounds, the Tsar, hypocrite beyond compare, not only refused to sanction her divorce but also confiscated her fortune and deprived her of her Russian nationality.

Chief of the many crosses Liszt had to bear was the sometimes savage hostility shown towards his New Music ideas, policies and performances. Yet even here he was incapable of retaliatory malice. He never bore any ill will, for instance, against the young virtuoso violinist Joseph Joachim, who had led the Weimar band for him and whose career he had wholeheartedly promoted, when the younger man turned viciously against his progressive music. "We must oust the name of Liszt," became Joachim's motto. When Joachim went to seek Liszt's forgiveness 20 years later, it was freely given.

*

Agnès Street Klindworth

Between 1854 and 1856, Princess Carolyne also had to contend with her lover's infidelity as well as her own severe illnesses. Like a weak-kneed drooly teenager or love-lorn dotard, Liszt fell hook, line and sinker for one of his pupils, Agnès Street Klindworth, who was the daughter of a Metternich spy, the highly colourful and mercurial Georg Klindworth.

Agnès lived in an apartment on the Carlsplatz, a stone's throw from the Weimar theatre. Georg Klindworth's professional zeal stopped at nothing and included having his daughter using her charms to lure secrets from left-wing revolutionaries on their pillows, especially those of Karl Marx's friend Ferdinand Lassalle, founder of the Workers' Party of Germany. Indeed, her real reason for being in Weimar was not to have piano lessons, but to gather intelligence in a town known as a haven for exiles and fugitives.

The lovers' correspondence, like Wagner's with Judith Gautier, was conducted through faithful intermediaries, including Liszt's trombonist and orchestral librarian. They arranged trysts not only at Agnès's place in Weimar (dangerous) but also in other cities — Berlin, Cologne and Düsseldorf — where Liszt was working. Fragments from Liszt's letters reveal the strength of his guilty enchantment:

> I still cannot pass by those windows [of her apartment] without an ineffable thrill ...

> They have just brought me your letter (no 7). I embrace and bless you ... No more light at your windows, but I will bring our candlestick to Cologne. [Agnes used to leave a candle burning to signal her availability.]

> Burn all my letters before you leave, like a faithful slave ... [She treasured and filed them all lovingly but was otherwise a model of discretion.]

> Keep the memory of our cabin. Tell me it remains sweet and radiant in your heart.

> Here [Berlin] even the snow and ice are burning with memories for me, and since I no longer see you at the Brandenburg Hotel, I am in a hurry to leave, with a goad in my side and a burning coal in my breast! My thoughts and my desire swell up and boil over. Agnes, I cannot write to you, and I cannot manage to go on living like this.

He clearly had it bad, yet once again, as with Marie, he was incapable of possessiveness. Although dementedly in love, his response to the possibility of her marrying Lassalle (to whom she had borne a child who died in infancy) was characteristically mature and unselfish:

> If ever this change in your life were to happen, I would not misunderstand you, believe me, and would certainly not cause you either embarrassment or bother of any kind.

Carolyne found out about the affair from gossip spread by Lassalle in Berlin, and there is no way of knowing precisely how she reacted with Liszt at the time. But it is safe to assume that he came completely clean about it all and that Carolyne forgave what she considered to be a temporary aberration. It didn't seriously rock the boat, possibly because the strong bonds between them were not primarily physical.

*

In December 1858 Liszt resigned his Weimar post, following a fiasco of orchestrated booing and hissing during the première of *The Barber of Bagdad* by Peter Cornelius, one of his assistants and acolytes in the New German School. After further delays in Weimar, Liszt arrived in Rome in October 1861, Carolyne having preceded him by some 17 months to arrange for her divorce and their marriage.

Carolyne actually obtained an annulment and from January 1861, had they been swift off the mark, they could have married. But her husband's relations, hell bent on not losing any money through her remarriage, were having none of it. On the eve of their wedding, arranged for Liszt's 50th birthday, the pope was persuaded to revoke his sanction of the wedding.

It is a moot point whether, in spite of his repeatedly expressed hopes in letters that they would soon be reunited "for ever", "for all eternity", Liszt had gone off the boil as far as marriage was concerned. Carolyne's sharp-eyed friend Adelheid von Schorn was in no doubt that "a legal tie with her was no longer a necessity for him ... her fine feminine feeling recognised that it would have been merely in fulfilment of duty. And so she, too, never spoke of it again — and thus sacrificed the principal object of her life".

From then on Liszt continued to occupy his rooms at 113 Via Felice and went every evening to see his princess, who immersed herself in her magnum opus of 24 volumes: *Causes intérieures de la faiblesse extérieure de l'Eglise* (Internal Causes for the external weakness of the church). The third volume alone, which Liszt on one occasion had to rescue from the customs, runs to 1,149 pages!

Carolyne's husband died in 1864 but her former lover had now turned his heart heavenwards — sort of!

La Vie Trifurquée
Abbé Liszt and Olga Janina, the
"Cossack Countess" (Olga Zielinska-Piasecka)

"... this troublesome parasite ..." (Alan Walker)

"Yesterday", wrote the Roman Catholic priest Ferdinand Gregorovius in his *Roman Journal*, "I saw Liszt clad as an Abbé. He was getting out of a hackney carriage, his black silk cassock fluttering ironically behind him. Mephistopheles disguised as an Abbé ... ".

Liszt, his cheeks deeply lined and hollow, his face now marred by several large warts, took minor holy orders in 1865, receiving four of the seven degrees of priesthood. Although not allowed to celebrate Mass or hear confession, he was doorkeeper, reader, acolyte, exorcist and honorary canon.

It was a kind of release from a period of great stress, not least because of the deaths of his son Daniel at the age of 21 in 1859 and of his eldest daughter Blandine at the age of 27 in 1862. Her death had inspired him to compose his great *Variations* for Piano Solo based on the bass lines of a Bach cantata and the Crucifixus of the *B minor Mass*. On the day of his entering the church Liszt took up his new apartment in the Vatican and then, after some months, moved into the Villa d'Este at Tivoli, placed at his disposal by his friend and patron Cardinal Hohenlohe.

Here he composed with renewed vigour, completing two oratorios, *Christus and The Legend of St. Elizabeth* and the *Hungarian Coronation Mass*.

In 1869 he was invited, without the princess, to return to Weimar to teach and give master classes, and given the use of the court *Hofgärtnerei*, a four-roomed house formerly occupied by the head gardener. For the next 17 years he spent April, May and June of each year in Weimar, giving free lessons to the world's most gifted young pianists. He spent from July to December in Rome composing, and then, from 1871, the first three months of the year in Budapest, teaching at the new Academy of Music, which he had helped to launch. Hence the *Vie Trifurquée,* or three-pronged life.

As we have seen so often, no celebrity approaching the age of 60 is free from the romantic attentions and transferences of impressionable young females. Liszt's final known adventure, with Olga Janina, began when he was 58 and almost literally ended with a bang two years later!

A lot more pathological and loopy than Lola Montez or any of the others, Olga Janina took her name from her husband, whom she had married at the age of 15 and viciously horse-whipped after their wedding night. Neither Cossack nor countess, her real married name was Karel Janina Piasecki, and her social pretensions were based on her father Ludwik Zielinski, a boot-polish maker.

She was a very thin, young and boyish looking 18 or 19-year-old with large black eyes when she began lessons with Liszt in Weimar — dressed, so she tells us in her memoirs, in white *crêpe de chine* laméd with silver. Smitten with his "shaft of sunlight" smiles, Janina leapt at the possibility of completing her piano lessons in the bedroom after having been offered a cigar in the music room. But her extreme neuroticism made even Liszt wary of getting involved, and he re-treated to the Villa d'Este in Rome to escape her attentions.

Not one to be deprived of her ambition, Janina gained access to the villa by disguising herself as the gardener. Maybe it was her boyish outfit that unhinged our ever-endearing Abbé, because he was then wrapping her in his cassock before she'd wiped her gardening boots. Janina joined him in his *vie trifurquée* and the dotty pair naturally outraged the Abbé's clerical fraternity and set tongues wagging 19 to the dozen over cappuccinos and kaffee-klatch.

There are infinite variations in print on the later stages of this affair and we must wait for volume three of Alan Walker's biography for the truth or its nearest approximation. The story I like best is that what brought Liszt to his senses was hearing Janina play at one of his recitals. Her pathetic passagework and muddy pedalling drove him mad and sent his libido into such a nosedive that he called time. After recovering from a massive overdose of opium, Janina reacted to Liszt's continued rejection by bursting into his room at Budapest with a revolver and threatening, unsuccessfully, to murder him and then kill herself.

She was finally deported from Budapest by the Hungarian po-lice and lost no time in signing up with the Liszt's Ex-Lovers' Appre-ciation Society. Her memoir-novels, *Souvenirs d'une cossack* and its sequel *Mémoires d'une pianiste* by "Robert Franz", and *Les Amours d'une cosaque par un ami de l'Abbé X, ou le roman du pianiste et de la cosaque* by "Sylvia Zorelli" all predictably did nothing for the reputation of the hapless Abbé. Olga made sure that even the Pope received copies.

If the Supreme Pontiff read the *Mémoires,* as I'll bet he did, he will have been intrigued to learn how, after repeated attempts at self denial, Abbé "X" finally confessed his love for his Cossack pupil, "covered me with passionate kisses" and gradually allowed his embraces to "last a little longer than the one before". The crunch soon followed when "X ... looked like a man who had come to some violent decision ... Coming in the [Villa d'Este] after me, he turned the key in the lock, advanced with open arms and dilated eyes and said: 'I can resist you no longer!' We did not dine that evening ... ". Naturally, la cosaque contemplated killing her Abbé with a little dagger she just happened to be carrying, in order to preserve their ecstasy for all eternity and prevent him from returning to the all-forgiving Father.

"That one was not wicked" said Liszt referring to Janina a few days before his death, "just exalted." As for Princess Carolyne, deeply involved in her "stupendo libro", as Liszt called it, she was as usual philosophical. She wrote to Liszt's younger step-uncle Eduard, explaining that she objected more to her former lover's *flaunting* of his liaisons than the infidelities themselves, which he was utterly incapable of resisting.

Princess Caroline actually completed her 24th volume of her *Causes Intérieures* a few days before her death in 1887.

After Janina, we know of no more women in Liszt's bed, though that doesn't mean there weren't any. His close attachment in his 60s to the 33-year-old widow Baroness Olga Meyendorff was far more than a mere *amitié amoureuse* in the eyes of Caroline, but there is no proof of consummated passion. Liszt and the Baroness certainly spent a great deal of time together, and she was only too pleased to act as his hostess. With her dominant personality and intellectual and musical gifts, (she was a decent amateur pianist) she was just his type, especially as she had opened their account by sending him a declaration that "your words penetrate the depths of my soul". They exchanged animated letters with each other when he was away from Rome.

And there, alas, we must leave the most loveable musician in this saga — though perhaps Haydn has an equal claim. Liszt wrote many more very fine works before his death, some perhaps reflecting the essential loneliness of his old age: *Nuages Gris, Czárdás Macabre,* the very strange and haunting *La Lugubre Gondola, Unstern, Am Grabe Richard Wagner* (By Richard Wagner's Tomb) ...

In January 1886 he bade farewell to Princess Carolyne for the last time and set off in his top hat and soutane for his final tour of unpaid recitals and appearances in celebration of his 75th birthday. He spent a triumphant two weeks in London then made his way via Antwerp, Paris and Weimar to Bayreuth for the wedding of his grand-daughter Daniela. After another journey to Luxembourg he returned to Weimar and went again to Bayreuth for a performance of *Tristan.* After developing pneumonia he died on July 31st.

Let us tear ourselves away from him with a most beautiful account of his magnetism as a teacher in his 60s in Weimar by Amy Fay, one of his young American pupils from Chicago. Her book of reminiscences, *Music Study in Germany,* is, as one would expect, far more evocative than anything spoken or written by his finest male pupils — Hans von Bülow, Carl Tausig, Emil Sauer, Eugène d'Albert, Frédéric Lamond or Moriz Rosenthal:

> The more I see and hear Liszt, the more I am lost in amazement! I can neither eat nor sleep on the days that I go to him ... Anything so perfectly beautiful as he looks when he sits at the piano I never saw, and yet he is almost an old man now. His personal magnetism is immense, and I can scarcely bear it when he plays. He can make me cry all he chooses... Liszt knows well the influence he has on people, for he always fixes his eye on some one of us when he plays, and I believe he tries to wring our hearts.

***

CHAPTER *13*

RICHARD WAGNER

"ALL MY WENCHES NOW PASS BEFORE MY EYES"
(Wagner describing his dreams to his
second wife Cosima, shortly before his death)

BORN: LEIPZIG, 22ND MAY 1813
DIED: VENICE, 13TH FEBRUARY 1883

... when you have heated the stove, open the door so that the room warms up. *And plenty of perfume: buy the best bottles, so that it smells really sweet.* Heavens! how I'm looking forward to relaxing with you again at last. *(I hope the pink drawers are ready too???)* — Yes, indeed! Just be nice and gentle. *I deserve to be well looked after for a change* ... Love and kisses to my darling! Until we meet again! [Letter to his maid Fraulein Marie Völkl ["Mariechen"] December 6th, 1863]

*

Wagner the silk-and-satin freak would undoubtedly have taken his time peeling off the clothes of his many female admirers — sometimes leaving something on them for added kicks during the sampling and application of all those exotic scents and oils to which he was addicted. But there were times when, as a pressing alternative, he made do with conjuring money from the purses of his female devotees, particularly if their inner garments no longer concealed nubile delights or were guarded by vigilant husbands.

The donations from his female groupies are perhaps even more impressive than his conquests. Some of the more notable Lady Bountifuls included Frau Julie Ritter, the wealthy widow of a Russian merchant, who settled an annuity on him of 800 thalers from 1851 to 1859; Julie Salis-Schwabe, the Jewish widow of a Manchester industrialist who lent him 5,000 francs (with no question when it might be repaid) towards offsetting the losses from his Paris concerts in January and February 1860; and Countess Marie Muchanoff, a gifted pianist and one-time lover of Liszt, who forked out over 10,000 francs to cover heavy losses on Wagner's Brussels concerts in March 1860 and who often proved be an effective impresario. Then there was Countess Pourtalès, wife of the Prussian ambassador in Paris, who showered 1,200 thalers on him, so delighted was she with the libretto of *Die Meistersinger* and an *Albumblatt* for piano dedicated to her. The Grand Duchess Helena Pavlovna, having sat through four readings by the composer of his *Ring* poems in St Petersburg in the winter of 1863, parted with 1,000 roubles. (Other rich, more earth-bound grand duchesses, not to mention grand dukes, would have paid that much to be spared the experience, opting instead for a session of roulette or *The Barber of Seville*.)

As to Wagner's amorous adventures, on the recurring evidence of his roving eye right up to his death at the age of 69, it is safe to assume that even his most assiduous biographers have not unearthed all of them from his extensive travels, particularly when his beady-eyed first wife, Minna, wasn't around. Although the current official count of Wagner's serious and casual affairs comes to about a dozen, there must have been many undocumented short flings, or even one-night stands, with adoring rich men's wives, divas, chorus ladies, actresses, other musicians' wives and fiancées, landladies or their daughters, hotel chambermaids, and even *filles de joie* who took the maestro's fancy when he was temporarily alone working the theatres and concert halls from St Petersburg to Paris and Prague. Moreover, it has now been seriously suggested that Wagner's final fatal heart attack was brought on by a furious row with his second wife, Cosima, when the aging and incurable Lothario announced that he had invited his favourite young Flower Maiden in *Parsifal,* the pretty soprano Carrie Pringle, to join the family party for another "audition" in their apartment overlooking the Grand Canal in Venice.

Ah well, at least he died in Cosima's arms rather than *in flagrante delicto* in the attic.

The Viennese conductor Heinrich Esser neatly summed up the situation to the publisher Schott in 1863:

> If he starts a new love affair in every town he happens to visit, that's his business, and nothing to do with me. Perhaps his tender heart is incapable of resisting the eccentric, enthusiastic ladies who throw themselves at him, and with all my heart I wish him joy in the soft embraces of so many gentle arms.

Wagner's almost gnomic proportions — "about as high as a stein of beer with an enormous head" — prove yet again that women go for the magnetic man in spite of his physical imperfections (he was actually five feet six-and-a-half inches):

... he had a narrow escape of deformity: he was not in the least deformed, yet the immense head was poised on the shoulders at an angle peculiar to hunchbacks; it caused him to fall an easy prey to caricaturists. [Mary Burrell]

Besides his charisma, Wagner's noted acrobatic skills will, of course, have enhanced his appeal in the bedroom. And *if* film-maker Ken Russell could be believed in Steven Ruggi's recent Channel 4 production of *Wagner's Women,* the legendary size of the composer's member also played a part in his success. However, as Russell, ever camp and tongue-in-cheek, laconically points out, "we can't dig him up and measure the size of his dick".

If money is as much the food of love as music, one woman had much cause to love Wagner: the Viennese milliner and seamstress Bertha Goldwag, who supplied the master with his legendary wardrobe and furnishings. When Wagner had prised money out of anyone, luxuries took precedence over necessities. "Mine is a highly susceptible, intense, voracious yet uncommonly sensitive and fastidious sensuality," he wrote to Liszt in January 1854, "which must somehow or other be flattered if my mind is to accomplish the agonising labour of calling a non-existent world into being."

Although Wagner was sometimes tardy in settling his bills, Frau Goldwag's eyes must have gleamed every time an envelope with his distinctive handwriting arrived at the shop containing orders for velvet drapes, portières, silks, satins and other indulgences. Let one tiny fragment, an order for a satin house-coat, epitomise the multitude she received from the arch hedonist:

February 1ˢᵗ, 1867 ... And so — how much would it cost to make the house-coat described herewith?
Best wishes, your devoted servant, RW.

Pockets with puffed ruche and bows of same material Pink satin. Quilted with eiderdown and *sewn in squares,* like the grey and red cover which I have of yours; exactly the same thickness, light, not heavy; and of course the outer and inner material must be quilted together. Lined with a light-weight white satin. Width of coat at lower hem *six* lengths, i.e. very wide. Also, sewn on extra, *not* stitched to the quilting! — a puffed ruche of the same fabric, all the way round; from the waist down the ruche should issue in a puffed inset (or trimming) wider towards the bottom and closing off the front. Examine the drawing closely ...

Clearly such self-gratification in a man who was as vain as a peacock had its artistic justification in the "really voluptuous sensual pleasure" that Baudelaire for one expressly found in his music.

It was not only women who fell under Wagner's spell, of course. The 19-year-old homosexual King of Bavaria, Ludwig II, was perhaps the most adoring, if in some respects unhinged, royal groupie in the history of music. He proved it over a period of nearly 20 years by giving Wagner in stipend, cash, presents and rent a total of 562,914 marks — a very generous sum, though not in comparative terms as profligate as has often been claimed. Suffice it to say that from childhood, in the seclusion of the castle of Hohenschwangau (High Swan Land), Ludwig the crown prince, introverted and melancholic, had been enthralled by the Wagnerian opera legends. The castle walls were painted with stories from *Lohengrin* (where the Knight of the Grail appears on a boat drawn by a swan) and *Tannhäuser*. When proclaimed king in 1864 he sent for Wagner, installed him in a fine villa near the royal castle and, just for starters, gave him 4,000 gulden to cover his most pressing financial needs and obligations. "He loves me," wrote Wagner to his friend Eliza Willes,

> with the intensity and fire of first love; he knows everything about me and all my works, and understands me like my own soul. He wants me to stay near him always, to work, to rest, to have my own works performed; he wants to give me everything I shall need for that purpose; I must finish the 'Nibelungen' and he will have it performed as I want.

Here we certainly find a king in love, though exactly with whom or what is difficult to pinpoint — possibly as much with himself as the 51-year-old composer:

> My Only One! My godlike Friend ... each day that passes my love
> glows more ardently for the only one I love in this world, the one
> who is my sublime joy, my comfort, my trust, my all! O Parcival,
> when will you be born? I worship this highest love ...

Ludwig also at one point even seriously contemplated abdication so that he could "be united with [Wagner] and living at his side". Hungry for his cash and artistic patronage, Wagner very understandably talked him out of that one.

Although their relationship was strained from time to time because of Wagner's adultery with Cosima, his clumsy political manoeuvrings and various clashes between them concerning the production of three of his operas, it was Ludwig who rescued the Bayreuth Festival from financial collapse by clearing the massive debt in 1878 with a new loan on generous repayment terms.

Poor Ludwig was declared insane in 1886 and deposed on June 10th. On June 20th he was found drowned in Lake Starnberg with his doctor — a sad end to an unfulfilled love life with a string of equerries, actors and hangers-on.

*

It seems that Richard Wagner was a chip off the old block, both in his passionate and insatiable addiction to the theatre and in his flexible interpretation of marriage and monogamy. The giant multinational, Wagner JCB Incorporated, have still not dug up proof that the composer's parents ever married, and his putative father, a police official in Leipzig named Carl Friedrich Wilhelm Wagner, spent all his spare time in amateur theatricals. Herr Friedrich was apparently often detained late at the office with important police documents on account of an actress named Friederike Wilhemine Hartwig. The composer's mother, formerly the teenage mistress of Prince Constantin of Saxe-Weimar-Eisenach (*not* his illegitimate daughter), seems to have made the most of her husband's absences by enjoying the attentions of his friend and occasional lodger Ludwig Heinrich Christian Geyer. Geyer was a portrait painter and competent itinerant actor and may well have been Wagner's real father. (On the other hand, some biographers have pointed out our composer's striking physical resemblance to his uncle Joseph.) At any rate, nine months after Carl

Friedrich's death in November 1813, and when Richard was still only in swaddling clothes, Johanna married the hard-working Geyer, who proved to be a humane and diligent stepfather. Sadly, he died when Richard was still only eight.

Wagner's loss of two fathers, and all the uncertainties surrounding his parentage (later fuelled by the composer himself on many occasions) have lead to much informed — and also very fanciful — speculation about their traumatic effects on his emotional life: his mother fixation, his repeated pursuit of attached women, his view of marriage as joyless and destructive, his unconscious yearning for the unattainable in love, his elevation of incestuous relationships in the *Ring,* his childhood passion for stroking his sisters' theatrical dresses, his fetish for silk, velvet and fur, his inordinate love of dogs and parrots, his erysipelas (nervous skin disease), his gastric problems, his wayward vegetarianism... Be all that as it may, Wagner's burning conviction that blindness and debility (the lot of his friend-turned-enemy the philosopher Nietzsche) could be caused by excessive masturbation was then very much the received medical opinion.

*

Wagner married for love both times, though by the second time, when he was 57, he had retrieved his brain from his trousers.

After his appointment as Music Director of the Magdeburg Theatre in July 1834, our 21-year-old hero soon developed a consuming passion for a very laid-back stunner named Minna Planer, one of the leading actresses with the same company. She was nearly four years older than Wagner and already hardened in the school of life.

Minna was to become his own thumping heartbeat. His judgement was to be wrecked by tidal waves of passion, by her wide blue eyes, rich dark wavy hair, dainty nose, sweet scents, and by dreams of her soft musky nakedness — the threshold to timeless ecstasy. But she most definitely had a history and, both before and after she became seriously interested in Wagner, she made all the running and led him a bit of a dance.

She was seduced at the age of 16 by a guards captain and struggled to survive as a single mother with her daughter Natalie, whom she passed off as her sister. In the ensuing fight for survival she had had little alternative but to exploit her attractiveness on the casting couch and elsewhere, notching up in the line of duty quite a string of theatre managers and important patrons. Sleeping for work was standard then in the theatre world, talent or no; and much better to work as an actress, confining loveless but necessary encounters to non-theatre hours, than sit at home all day as a kept woman à la Zola waiting to pleasure some pompous overfed John at his beck and call.

By comparison, Wagner was a novice in the school of love, having in his previous season as chorus master at Würzburg had his "first love affair" (so he says) with Therese Ringelmann, a flighty chorus girl who wanted to have her cake and eat it (that is, both a proposal from Richard Wagner and freedom to play the field). His second affair was with the dark-eyed Friederike Galvani, also a singer, whom he enticed away from her fiancé during a wedding with those soulful gazes that were to become his sure-fire winner for nearly 50 years. The hapless fiancé was the orchestra's principal oboist, who could have had his revenge fouling up the orchestra's intonation when blowing the opening A. Alas, he probably decided that nobody would have noticed and so meekly accepted the situation. Wagner was becoming confident of his pulling power.

For some while Minna did not reciprocate Wagner's growing if not yet besotted ardour but, to his surprise, she accepted his advances. "How can I help it if you're stronger than I am and kiss me half to death?" was her explanation as reported verbatim by her suitor in a letter to Theodore Apel, a close friend from their university days. Date rape was clearly an alien concept to her. "You can have the Planer girl too," Wagner wrote generously to the same friend; "she has transfigured me quite sensually a couple of times — it made me feel quite splendid." Minna might well have agreed to her lover's chauvinist trading of her charms if she had known of Apel's good contacts in the theatre.

It seems that before Minna became keener — and perhaps to try to make her so — Wagner also guiltily bedded two other easygoing theatre girls, a certain Toni who remains a mystery and a tarty Frau Christiani. Wagner's interest in the latter may well have been strategic because Minna seized the opportunity he gave her of publicly ousting Christiani at his New Year's Eve party.

He was getting there, but to win her heart, Wagner had to resort to a tactic (besides the soulful gazing) that was serve him well with future women — playing on her protective instincts. By December she loved him enough to nurse him when his face was swollen and disfigured from his unsightly skin complaint, and, "to convince him that the unpleasant rash around his mouth did not repel her, kissed him in friendly fashion on the mouth". His winning manoeuvre, early in 1835, was to arrive very late one day for tea, blind drunk. Minna decided to let him sleep it off in her own bed while she slept on the settee. That's what he swears by at great length. The next day they went for a walk and became acknowledged lovers. In Wagner's own words, "we gave ourselves up freely and without embarrassment to our tender interest in each other." They became engaged in February 1835.

Little did Wagner imagine, then highly sexed and in hot pursuit, that 23 years later he would be persuading the family doctor to forbid further sexual intercourse between them!

Wagner was caught up in the theatre whirlwind as well as the Minna magic, of course: page calls, spotlights, overtures, arias (Mozart, Beethoven, Bellini, Rossini, Weber, Auber, Cherubini, Marschner et al), costumes, coifs, makeup, encores, curtain calls, body odour, grease-paint; a world he had craved from inside the womb, and which — even when he met with all the backstage tattiness, back-biting, in-fighting, wife pinching and endemic insecurity — was the only life he wanted. Indeed, his whole life was to be essentially "theatre", especially his extra-marital love life and his later penchant for dressing up in quirky outfits: say, a pair of pastel-shade pink pantaloons with a bathrobe of yellow quilted silk, ermine-lined at the neck and wrists, and embellished with a sprinkling of pearls — and, of course, the inevitable black velvet beret à la Rembrandt or Dürer.

Wagner returned to Magdeburg for the 1835-36 season in spite of the company's very dodgy balance sheet; fees, half-fees or no fees, the company director Bethmann knew that wherever Minna was, Wagner would follow.

But lover or no lover, the placid and practical Minna felt compelled, especially with Wagner being in no position to get married, to leave the Magdeburg company for a better offer in Berlin. The heartbroken Wagner bombarded her with passionate love letters and they succeeded in getting her back. Minna returned to Magdeburg within a fortnight of leaving, turning down further offers in Berlin.

At the end of that season in March 1836, Minna had to take a job in Königsberg, hoping to secure for her debt-ridden fiancé the job there as music director. He first went to Berlin to try to have his *Das Liebesverbot* accepted following its chronically under-rehearsed première at Magdeburg, when the tenor ad-libbed and the orchestra drowned everybody. (The second night, with an audience of three, was perhaps the most noteworthy fiasco in the history of the theatre. It was aborted after a backstage punch-up, started by the cuckolded husband of the heroine, led to an all round fracas.)

It was no go in Berlin nor, to Wagner's agony, was there any chance of a job in Königsberg, and the couple were again separated. A further set of even more desperate letters ensued imploring marriage, of which the following is typical (not least in the number of dashes):

> June 22-26th, 1836
> I have become a serious melancholy fool, — ah, Minna, life, happiness! — Have pity on me, have pity, my angel, you will make me well again, then my heart will break into a thousand pieces, or else — happiness, — happiness — Minna! Ah, I despair of ever finding happiness on earth; — love me, — keep on loving me, but do not insult me, have pity on a miserable wretch, for he is, after all,
> Your
> Richard

Besotted and desperate for his woman, Wagner managed to borrow money from another good friend and in July followed Minna to Königsberg, where he was given a very small retainer as assistant conductor and promised the job of music director the following season. He was also promised a benefit performance before their wedding.

The first of many recurring tableaux in a lurid tapestry of betrothal and marriage now unfolded: jealous tantrums, violent quarrels, recriminations, and unstable reconciliations. During the Königsberg period Wagner's sexual addiction — and jealousy — were at their peak. Reminders of Minna's former love life, as well as her still rather easy way with other men useful to her, would provoke him into tirades of abuse. Her inevitable response was to wind him up even more.

The next-door neighbours' ears were glued to the walls (must have been) after Wagner found some love letters. They were from a Jewish businessman who had pursued Minna — with what degree of success we can only guess, but I bet she did — while she had been separated from Wagner a few months before in Berlin. After the screaming and fighting stopped the poor neighbours would have no choice but to put the kettle on and wait for the surefire sequel in such charged relationships: the pounding of the bed springs, and the banging of the headboard against the wall.

Their tempestuous engagement and early married life must have been the hottest theatre gossip in the changing rooms and band room throughout the season.

Wagner's constant debt exacerbated the situation. The marriage omens were all bad, but were obliterated by his libido, and by his need for her motherliness. The couple even quarrelled about his extravagance on the day before their wedding, which took place, attended by the theatrical demi-monde, on November 24th, 1836.

It is pointless to say they should not have married; they did, and like so many other mentally ill-matched pairs, they were to become bound for a long time by the marital superglue that holds so many couples together in inert disgruntlement or misery.

All the same problems continued immediately after their marriage for exactly the same reasons: poverty, jealousy, Wagner's uncompromising and swelling ego, and their fundamental incompatibility. By the end of the following May, Minna had had more than enough and made off with a businessman named Dietrich, one of the theatre's patrons with whom Wagner had already quarrelled. Dementedly jealous, Wagner pursued her to Dresden where, after a "painful, and anxious week" there was an apparent reconciliation, but the adulterers disappeared again. "Whips, pistols, D. already gone," he noted in his diary after searching in vain for the seducer.

*

In June 1837 the abandoned Wagner, with a mind for divorce, was appointed music director at the theatre in Riga in Latvia. However, following some tactful intermediary moves by Minna's sister Amalie (newly chosen by Wagner as his prima donna), and after

receiving from Minna "a really moving letter" admitting her wrongdo-
ing, he forgave her and accepted his own share of the blame. A very
contrite Minna arrived with Amalie in Riga in October to rejoin her
overjoyed and doubtless rampant husband. Plenty of scope here for
budding or seasoned scriptwriters to recreate the passionate
reconciliatio — and, of course, the cause of the next quarrel. It was
almost certainly over money because, having been eased out of his
job, he bade Minna pack the bags for a swift escape from creditors and
a roundabout journey to Paris.

Abandoning her career, Minna gave him her undivided attention. They were then to stick at it for 13 years before the marriage
entered its drawn-out terminal phase.

*

Despite her often decried feet of clay dragging alongside a winged
mystic soaring through eternity, Minna stood by her husband through
their many ensuing years of poverty and dashed hopes, linked in what
Wagner later described as their "thousand chains of old and mutual
suffering". The prevailing pattern of Wagner's career until 1864 and
the fairy-tale arrival of Ludwig II was to be one of rejections, disappointments, vitriolic press reviews and debts punctuated by occasional successes, and windfalls that were quickly squandered.

When the couple finally arrived in Paris in 1839, Minna could
almost certainly have walked out of the marriage for a second time.
They had already endured a perilous land and sea journey from Riga
via Norway and London, dodging armed frontier posts, with Minna
injuring herself when a rickety cart overturned in a farmyard. Many
women would have cried "Enough!", and Minna could undoubtedly
have worked (and slept) her way towards a comfortable enough lifestyle in Paris as an actress and mistress.

Instead, she proved her worth as a supportive partner with guts
as strong as her husband's. While in Paris, they plumbed their lowest
depths of poverty and disappointments, and it was Minna who eventually clinched a loan from Theodore Apel, which just managed to
keep Wagner out of the debtors' prison in November 1840. In spite of
these dire straits Wagner managed to complete *Rienzi*.

*

The Wagners enjoyed the only period of comparative serenity and contentment in their married life for a year or two after he took a proper job, something he shied away from because of the distractions from composing. He was appointed as second Kapellmeister (but doing most of the work!) to the Court of the King of Saxony in Dresden in 1843. The offer came following the spectacular success of *Rienzi* there, a level of acclaim he was not often to enjoy again for many years.

If he had been more content, like Bach and Haydn before him, to live within the constraints of his servant role at the court, and to continue to write more readily accessible music, Minna would have been well pleased; but neither husband nor wife ever successfully bends to the image either would prefer of the other. Wagner the uncompromising idealist and innovator was intent on moving mountains, and confronting dragons and giants with his invincible sword, while Minna the bourgeois housewife was content with bobbin and Bellini in their large well-appointed villa overlooking the Zwinger. In Liszt's words, he was "like Vesuvius in eruption, blazing up sheaves of bouquets, pink and lilac".

His writings over the next decade on politics, aesthetics, and philosophy were meaningless to her, and his operatic development shot out of her limited orbit. Instead of his leitmotivs (sort of "signature tunes" each associated with a character, theme or object), "free singing lines" and "endless melody", why on earth couldn't he write stirring set-piece choruses and arias like the highly successful Meyerbeer, who had given Wagner so many lifts up the professional ladder? Why not have Meyerbeerian *grand spectacle* (however vacuous) — five acts, a ballet, full-scale choruses, elaborate scenery and effects, magnificent costumes — instead of those drawn-out, morbid and confusing German and Nordic myths and legends? Who on Earth wanted operas about Elemental Forces and Eternal Truths, about Greed, Power, Love and Death? "It looks as though he won't be writing anything enjoyable in future," she wrote later. "He left whole crates whose contents the world still does not know." She could identify with nothing after *Tannhäuser* in 1845.

Well, that was her side of the story, and there are many

anti-Wagnerians who did or do agree with her. Schumann, for instance, was none too keen, considering Wagner's music when not staged to be "shallow, often downright dilettantish, worthless and disgusting".

Six years after arriving in Dresden, Wagner was fleeing the country. More serious than the trouble he stirred up in his job by generally needling the management (including demands for radical orchestral reform), was his involvement in subversive political activity with the Russian anarchist Bakunin and others. Although Wagner's prime motives were artistic rather than political, his part in the Dresden rising of 5th May, 1849 led to the issue of a warrant for his arrest.

Minna despaired of her reckless husband, who may well have ordered hand grenades from a brass founder. If he had not escaped he would, according to King Johann of Saxony, have been tried and probably sentenced to death. No *Tristan,* no *Meistersinger,* no *Ring,* no *Parsifal,* no *Siegfried Idyll* nor *Wesendonck Lieder.* He was not to re-enter Saxony until 1862.

With Liszt's help he fled the country, and, after a fruitless visit to Paris in search of work he eventually took up residence in Zurich.

*

"Oh False, Treacherous Creature!"

Ironically, it was Minna who then set in motion Wagner's first known love affair since their marriage. She had joined him very reluctantly in September 1849 in Zurich, where he had eventually settled as an exile after a fruitless short stay in Paris.

> I hope you will understand, my dear Richard, that in coming to you I make *no slight sacrifice.* What sort of future do I face? What have you to offer me? Almost two years may elapse before you, by a stroke of luck, may count on some income, and depending on the good will of one's friends only is a dreary existence for a wife ...

Minna saw Wagner's only chances of work as being in Paris, despite his recent return from there, and would have none of his protests. "Go back and try again!" she screamed (I guarantee she did!), "we won't possibly be able to live on the 3,000 francs a year that

Frau Ritter and that Mme. Jessie Laussot have promised you. The debts from your publishing fiasco with Meser are piling up, and thanks to your mad politics we've lost your steady income from Dresden. Since *Rienzi,* you've made hardly any money from *Hollander* and *Tannhäuser.*"

Wagner duly obeyed, if only to escape from the wife, and set out in January 1850, but Minna got more than she bargained for. The attractive and talented 21-year-old Mme Jessie Laussot mentioned above was an English lady living in Bordeaux with her French husband Eugène, a wine merchant, and her rich widowed mother. The couple invited Wagner to stay, travelling expenses paid, at their Bordeaux residence. Wagner was still "resting" so he eagerly accepted, arriving on March 16th.

He was soon in seventh heaven. Not only was Jessie beautiful, in the pale and interesting English way, she was also a talented pianist. She was most definitely an adoring Wagner groupie, having not only persuaded her husband and mother to join in with Frau Ritter to provide her idol with the 3,000 francs a year, but having also commissioned his portrait. Most important of all, it soon became clear that she was unhappily married. So would you be if your wet and unchosen husband was your mother's cast-off and still living substantially off her money, as was the case here.

Richard and Jessie poured out their woes to each other and spent some enchanted evenings while he read to her his own works, including *Wieland der Schmied,* (Wieland the Smith) and she played Beethoven. These trysts do not appear to have ended forever with a soulful gaze, and the frustrated, love-starved Jessie probably threw herself into Richard's arms and led him to the bedroom — an experience undoubtedly already familiar to him, and definitely to be repeated.

Wieland undoubtedly put ideas into their heads. It is the tale of a smith who, united with his swan bride Schwanhilde, soars on self-made wings above the world that has held him in bondage. The lovers planned a new life together in Greece, Turkey... why not India, China?... anywhere far, far away at last from their unbearable matrimonial manacles. Wagner could live out his own storyline. Such an escape would also enact his burning contempt, expressed in another concurrent (and aborted) work, *Jesus von Nazareth,* for conventional bourgeois values: respectability, loveless marriage, propriety.

A haranguing, fishwife's letter from Minna deploring their continued and demeaning dependence on charity strengthened Wagner's resolve: nothing would prevent the flight of Wieland with his Schwanhilde.

He returned to Paris on April 5th, determined to go ahead but not yet quite sure what to do. Perhaps naively, Jessie sent Minna a letter avowing the family's continued support for the master. Smelling a rat, Minna was scornfulness itself: "Oh false, treacherous creature", she scrawled over the letter.

We must cut swiftly to the dénouement. Wagner's plan was for them both to set sail for Malta from Marseilles on May 7th, and thence via Greece to Asia Minor. Jessie was to pretend that she was going to visit Frau Ritter in Dresden.

On April 16th Wagner penned an emotional parting letter to Minna, making no mention of his elopement plans. However well meaning, he must surely have known that his attempts at consolation and self-justification would cut no ice. The very long letter ends:

> ... Farewell! Farewell! My wife! My old, dear companion in misfortune! Oh, if you could only have shared the joys which I draw from *my great faith*, how happy you would have been with me despite all privation! ... Farewell! Farewell! ... Think only of the happiest hours we spent together ...

Minna sped to Paris in pursuit of her husband, but he hid from her and then retreated to Villeneuve at the eastern end of Lake Geneva. Wagner wrote her another letter telling her of the impending voyage, but still not coming clean about Jessie. Minna replied, full of reproaches and self-pity, and protesting that they had been happy before his revolutionary activities. However, she didn't insist on a reunion; she would go back to the theatre or into service.

The lovers did not sail into the distance. Pistols or no, the final act is definitely bad box office. For some reason, young Jessie confided their plans to her mother, who promptly informed Eugène — who, said Jessie in her letter about all this to Wagner, was very anxious to put a bullet through him. After writing to Eugène lecturing him on the folly of holding his wife in a loveless marriage, Wagner hurried to Bordeaux intent on reasoning with him. Instead he was intercepted by the police and later found the Laussot house empty. Wagner left

Jessie a letter, which she may never have seen, urging her to extricate herself from her "shameful relationship" and then returned to Villeneuve. Shortly afterwards Jessie, her swan's wings now cruelly clipped, sent Wagner a message that any further letters from him would be burned unread.

It is difficult to treat this episode seriously 140 years on, but the 37-year-old Wagner definitely did so, as is clear from this letter to that very loyal friend of his Frau Julie Ritter (who paid his allowance even though he had caused her some embarrassment as a friend of the Laussot ménage):

> I am placing in your hands the testament of a love of which I shall never be ashamed and which, although physically dead, may perhaps be a source of joyful memory and consoling recollection until my dying day ... it was nothing but *love:* we dedicated ourselves to the *God of love* ... [June 26-27th, 1850]

Interestingly, this affair was the only serious one that inspired no music, possibly because it was more "physical" than the later ones.

Jessie subsequently left her husband, incidentally, and went to live in Florence with the historian Karl Hillebrand, pursuing an active career as conductor and administrator. Good for her. Wagner would undoubtedly have been gratified by her bid for fulfilment. He met her again at the première of *Meistersinger* 18 years later.

*

Blessed be Mathilde!

(Inscription on Prelude to *Die Walküre*)

... The angel who has raised me so high ...

That dirty bitch!
[Minna Wagner 1862]

Sept 1858
Dear Madam,
Before I leave, I must tell you, with bleeding heart, that you have succeeded in estranging my husband from me of almost twenty two

years. I trust that this noble act will help to bring you happiness and peace of mind.
Minna Wagner

After Jessie Laussot had stood him up, Wagner eventually returned to the conjugal bliss of rows and ructions in Zurich; bliss that led to repeated attacks of erysipelas, severe bouts of depression and thoughts of suicide for him, and a steady deterioration in Minna's health, with whey milk cures and, later, opium being necessary for her heart condition. The main marital props were undoubtedly the succession of dogs and parrots to which they were both devoted. Then one of Wagner's periodic windfalls, and also one of his major crises, came in the shape of the Wesendoncks, whom he first met in 1852.

The windfall was money and sponsorship from Otto Wesendonck a rich, refined and neurotic silk merchant who in 1854 cleared part of Wagner's accumulated debts of 10,000 francs and settled a regular allowance on him in exchange for receipts from future performances of certain works — a ploy Wagner was to repeat more than once, sometimes re-advancing an advance when really pressed for cash.

The crisis was his next love affair, with Otto Wesendonck's wife, Mathilde. Next, that is, discounting two very passing fancies of little consequence to anyone but poor Minna: the singer Frau Emilie Heim who, being lumbered with the local choral conductor for a husband, was inevitably prone to casting Wagner languishing looks, and a Frau Johanna Spyri, who, being newly married, was on her guard against his gallantry.

Can one call an intense but almost certainly unconsummated relationship of missives, embraces and kisses between a 44-year-old married man and a 29-year-old married mother a love affair? Yes, yes, I hear many say, especially women readers. They might point to the poet Robert Graves, who lived with his wife on Majorca and imported a succession of live-in muse goddesses — Cindy Laraçuen, Judith Bledsoe, Margot Callas, Julia Simonne — with whom he had minimal sex or none at all. In any event, Wagner's affair went on right under poor Minna's nose.

Although all the crosscurrents between the principal parties were definitely high voltage, the entire sequence of events has, at one level, the feel of a playlet with clouds of dry ice and just an occasional faint touch of farce. The wholly serious aspect is the stimulus it gave to Wagner in creating, in *Tristan and Isolde,* the world's supreme music drama of a yearning, tragic passion between two lovers that can only be fulfilled in death. Saturated with Schopenhauer, Buddha and Feuerbach — a mix of renunciation, the abnegation of the "will to live" and nirvana, tempered somewhat conveniently by "the glorious necessity of love" — Wagner wooed and absorbed Mathilde into his quasar worlds.

When she first met Wagner at the age of 23, Mathilde was already another swooning groupie, having first caught the bug after hearing the *Tannhäuser* Overture. Wagner was soon lapping up the adoration of this Aryan blonde, Titian virgin lookalike, with her soft features, small round chin, rosebud mouth, wide eyes, and impressionable nature. He wrote her a piano sonata in 1853.

The pair started to spend whole evenings together in the same year while he played her passages from *Walküre.* The enraptured Mathilde, now 26, gave her "Twilight Man" an "indestructible" gold pen with which to work, and during his absences fond letters were exchanged that included Wagner's accounts of his reading of Indian Sagas.

The affair reached a peak in late 1857. Adjacent to his own new villa, Otto had, at his wife's pressing insistence, built the Wagners a home — *Asyl* (Place of Refuge) — which they started occupying at a favourable rent in April 1857. In August he began the prose sketch of *Tristan and Isolde,* and both he and Mathilde became lost in each other as the tragic lovers in the eternal triangle, Tristan, Isolde and King Mark.

Wagner's storylines and music could undoubtedly dissolve women (apart from Minna, of course) into puddles. That summer, during soirées at the Asyl, the music of *Die Walküre* was played through at the piano by Hans von Bülow, one of Wagner's most valued acolytes, who was on a honeymoon visit with his wife Cosima. Wagner also read his prose version of *Tristan*. Both Mathilde and Cosima were jellified, and when Cosima was asked for an opinion, she could sometimes only respond with tears. Perhaps even then she dimly imagined herself in the role of Wagner's saviour.

Not so Minna, who clearly felt redundant in these evenings dripping with emotion, and who always hated *Tristan*, finding it "disgusting, immoral, almost indecently passionate". Her weak heart would certainly have conked out if she had ever divined the truly erotic nature — the "orgiastic ecstasy" — of the music: "In Act II the lovers ejaculate simultaneously seven times," so the critic Virgil Thomson tells us, at points that are "clearly marked in the music".

The Richard and Mathilde affair entered its headiest phase in September when Wagner had finished his poem of *Tristan*, as he tells in a diary entry of September 18th:

> I finished the poem of Tristan and brought you the last act. You led me to the chair by the sofa, threw your arms around my neck and cried: "Now I wish for nothing more!" This day, this hour marked my rebirth. A sweet creature, demure and coy, plunged into a whirlpool of pain and suffering to make this wonderful moment possible and to say to me: "I love you". Since that time there has been no more conflict in me. ...

Mathilde expressed her readiness to die: *Then, for the first time, her strength failed her, and she told me she would die,* wrote Wagner later, though with a new baby on her hands this may have been another of those attacks of the luvvies in the heat of the moment.

By the end of the year things had become too much even for Otto, what with lovers' trysts almost daily at the back of the Wesendonck villa or in Wagner's first-floor room at the Asyl. Each morning Mathilde would sail blithely past the seething Minna to faint over the latest bars of *Tristan* or whatever. Wagner had begun composing the music for Tristan on October 1st and in November he also began setting some of his lover's rather tame poems to music — music he himself considered to be his very best and which became known as the Wesendonck Lieder. This must have turned the young lady's head more than anything else. He orchestrated one of these songs and performed it at the villa on his lover's birthday, December 23rd.

The vibrations during social gatherings, with Wagner monopolising Mathilde, finally goaded Otto, "consumed by jealousy" (according to Wagner) but hitherto suffering in silence for his wife's sake, into crying "Enough!". In the new year Wagner had to clear off to Paris for a while so that "the suffering of the good-natured Otto could be relieved to some degree". Wagner the egotist of course really believed that it was Otto's privilege to donate his wife as lover and muse. In any case, Wagner's suffering as an artist and lover far exceeded that of the neglected husband, whose extreme wealth entitled him to nothing but misery!

Wagner returned in February and continued to monopolise Mathilde in like fashion, but his possessiveness soon got out of hand. Mathilde had the audacity to take lessons in Italian — nothing else — from a handsome 40-year-old teacher named Francesco de Sanctis. Wagner the megalomaniac could not handle this at all and on the evening of April 6th he spoiled for a quarrel over nothing. The next morning, a contrite Wagner sent a gardener with a letter addressed to Mme Mathilde Wesendonck containing a "Morning Confession". The ever watchful Minna intercepted the letter and read it:

> Ah, no, no, no. It is not de Sanctis I hate but myself, for catching my poor heart unawares in such frailty again and again! ... when I look into your eyes, then I simply cannot speak any more; then everything I might have to say simply seems as nothing! When this marvellous, holy glance rests upon me then everything becomes so indisputably true to me, I am so sure of myself, and I submerge myself within it. ... Be good to me, and forgive my childishness of yesterday: you were quite right to call it that! ... The weather appears to be mild. Today I will come to the garden, as soon as I see you; I hope I may be with you for a moment, undisturbed! — Take my whole soul as a morning greeting!

"Not any more," screamed Minna, and stormed up to Wagner's room. He was unable to convince her of the innocence of the relationship but persuaded her temporarily not to jeopardise their position at the Asyl. Soon afterwards, though, Minna was provoked by a family friend Emma Herwegh into tackling the scarlet woman. Mathilde was deeply offended when confronted with Minna's veiled threat that "any ordinary woman" might show Otto the letter, and immediately went and told her husband everything that had happened.

Minna had blown it. Mathilde would have nothing more to do with her and both she and Otto were offended that Wagner had concealed from his wife what he always insisted was the "purity of these relations". Wagner persuaded Minna to take a health cure and attempted a reconciliation, while the Wesendoncks took off to Italy.

There is no space for the minute ramifications of the dénouement. Wagner did actually suggest a "union" with Mathilde, which she rejected as "sacrilege". In the end Wagner accepted — in a spirit of Tristanesque renunciation, naturally — that the affair must finish. Mathilde returned to bourgeois life with child and husband, though just how happily it is hard to say.

Wagner left Asyl for good on August 17th for Italy, to work on *Tristan*. Minna left in September for Dresden, after doing the packing and firing her parting shot in the "Dear Madam" letter quoted above. Wagner continued to send intimate letters to Mathilde from Venice on the theme of renunciation, replacing Tristan and Isolde by the Buddhist pair Ananda and Savitri and foreshadowing the indispensability of human suffering in *Parsifal*. The letters fell off as *Tristan* was completed. Some of Mathilde's few surviving replies support Wagner's frequent claims that she still loved him, and hint at dissatisfaction and unhappiness in her life, maybe even in her marriage:

> The weft of the mysterious weaver who intertwined the threads of our mutual fate is not to be unravelled, but only to be torn asunder.

Wagner subsequently visited the Wesendoncks in Venice in November 1861, where a newly pregnant Mathilde rubbed it in that his Isolde had never really betrayed King Mark. They continued to correspond, however, and Mathilde managed once more, in 1862, to incense Minna by sending him some expensive presents — tea, Eau de Cologne, an embroidered cushion and pressed violets.

In a letter of 1863 Mathilde gave Wagner some very sound advice of enduring value to the entire human race:

> You seize on each new illusion in haste, apparently to blot out the dissatisfaction engendered by past illusions, and no one knows better than yourself that it cannot be, nor ever will be. How will it end, my friend? Are not fifty years experience enough, and should not the moment come at last for you to be completely honest with yourself?

Five years after the end of the affair Wagner was still describing Mathilde as "my first and only love", though in later years he belittled Mathilde's role in his life, and in particular her contribution to *Tristan*.

*

Separation, Flirtations, Proposals, Takeover

The pattern of Wagner's love life from the Asyl débâcle in 1858 to the firm bedroom takeover by Cosima in June 1864 is very patchwork: further estrangement from Minna, sundry flings and flirtations including two rather desperate proposals, and a growing bond with Cosima.

After Asyl Wagner spent only two more periods with Minna. In a fit of goodwill and in a last bid to save the marriage, he invited her to join him with dog and parrot — and the no-sex proviso already mentioned — in Paris in November 1859. Minna soon found herself sacking the valet and chambermaid, whom she suspected of providing supplementary services, and keeping a watchful eye on the charming and lively Blandine Ollivier, Cosima's elder sister. Wagner was smitten, but reigned in.

Alas, the effort to retrieve the marriage was a failure, with tantrums and quarrels very soon irrupting — shades of Königsberg 23 years earlier. Baroness Malwida von Meysenbug, a political activist of remarkable independence for her time, was an admirer and friend of Wagner and provides us in her memoirs of this Paris phase with a sympathetic summing up of this sad and depressing marriage:

> Because of [Minna's] total inability to understand the nature of his genius and its effect on his relationship to the world, there now arose almost daily conflict and torment in their life together which, as they were childless, lacked any possible tenderness and reconciliation. Even so, Frau Wagner was a good wife, and in the eyes of the world it was she who was the better and long-suffering member of the pair. I judged the situation differently and felt boundless sympathy for Wagner, for whom love should have built a bridge across which he could have reached other men, instead of which it merely embittered the already bitter cup of life.

After the notorious and humiliating sabotage of *Tannhäuser* by the Jockey Club in March 1861 at the Paris Opéra, Wagner set off on his own for various destinations (including Venice where, if you remember, he met the newly pregnant Mathilde) before settling in Biebrich, across the Rhine from Mainz, in February 1862. It was a grim time for him both artistically and emotionally. Prospects for having his operas performed were bleak, and there was no loving and lovable woman at the centre of his life; only Minna haranguing him and raking up the Wesendonck affair in their correspondence and elsewhere.

One respite from the prevailing gloom came while he stayed in the apartment of a Dr. Standhartner in Vienna. His hostess was the doctor's niece, a lovely young lady called Seraphine Mauro — "Seraphinchen" or "Dolly" — with black ringlets and an alluring bosom. She apparently fell for the master's winning ways, much to the chagrin of her lover, the composer Peter Cornelius, one of Wagner's less pliable admirers. Cornelius was naturally distraught, but fortunately Wagner soon moved on.

The doggedly persistent Minna appeared uninvited on Wagner's doorstep at Biebrich in February to give him a final "10 days of hell" — a hell exacerbated by the arrival of those presents already mentioned from "that dirty bitch" Mathilde. In deference to her poor health, Wagner still could not bring himself to suggest divorce. The arrangement he proposed, which she accepted grudgingly and bitterly, was that he would provide her with 3,000 marks a year (certainly a reasonable sum) and a home in Dresden, where a room would be set aside for his occasional visits. In November they met briefly for the very last time, though Wagner continued to write to her during 1864 and 1865. He also made a quarterly allowance to Natalie (Minna's daughter), to whom he promised there would never be a divorce by coercion.

After receiving news of Minna's death some three years later in January 1866, Wagner went into deep shock, especially as she had loyally rebutted in her own shaky hand a news item in the *Volksbote* that he had left her at the mercy of the Poor Law Authorities whilst he wallowed in luxury.

He then carried out a kind of ritualised exorcism of all their marital demons. When he discovered soon afterwards that their old dog Pohl had died at Asyl, he dug the animal up, put a collar round its neck and buried it in a specially ordered coffin in a different spot overlooking the lake. Much later he also erected a monument to Minna in Jura stone at Wahnfried, his last home in Bayreuth.

The exorcism was not wholly effective. Four years later Cosima recorded that he shouted in his sleep: "Go away! You're dead!" while dreaming that she was standing at the foot of the bed making offensive remarks!

Moving back to 1862, two other women had entered Wagner's life after his separation from Minna. One was the chaste and charming Mathilde Maier, of whom more later, and the other an actress named Friederike Mayer, certainly not chaste. Friederike appears very briefly to have strayed from the bed of her theatre manager and "master", one Herr von Guaita, to relieve Wagner of his nocturnal solitude. In the following summer (1863), his 17-year-old maid Lisbeth Völkl, whom he described as "sweet-tempered, obliging", may also have served more than breakfast in bed whilst briefly in his service.

*

Cosima had seen Wagner suffering at Asyl during her honeymoon visit in 1857, and her heart was already his by the time she left. Her own marriage to Hans von Bülow, whom Wagner held in such in high esteem, was also a disaster. Only 12 months after her wedding she actually set out in a boat to drown herself in Lake Geneva, but had to retract when her accomplice, also miserably married, suddenly decided he would jump in after her. She also made further unsuccessful suicide attempts.

According to Wagner she gave him a "timid look of enquiry" in 1861 when they parted after he had visited her with her two sisters in Bad Reichenall.

Finally, on November 28th, 1863, they made a commitment to belong to each other during a carriage ride through Berlin while poor Hans was taking a rehearsal for a concert that night:

> This time the jesting died away in silence. We gazed speechless into each other's eyes; an intense longing for an avowal of the truth overpowered us and led to a confession, which needed no words, of the boundless unhappiness that weighed upon us. With tears and sobs we sealed our confession to belong to each other alone. It came as a relief to us both ...

Despite such intense, no-going-back avowals, the master kept a sharp lookout for whatever diversion might be at hand during such an unsettled period in his life. The other half of his bed was still unoccupied. Within a week or two of his pledges with Cosima, he sent the famous naughty "pink drawers" letter already quoted to his sassy maid Marie Volkl, ("Mariechen"). During this rudderless phase Wagner also courted a widow, Henriette von Bissing, but she got cold feet on hearing of his profligacy. In the following June he asked his good friend, the homely and dependable 31-year-old Mathilde Maier, to come and be his housekeeper, at the same time guaranteeing strict propriety to her mother. He became so desperate that he made a number of further suggestions — doubtless improper, because they have been blacked out in the autographs — to his "dearest sweetheart" Mathilde. In June he even made her a proposal of marriage.

On June 29th 1864 however, Cosima arrived at his new home — Villa Pellet, recently rented for him by Ludwig II and overlooking Lake Starnberg near Munich — with her two young children and a nurserymaid. Wagner had invited the von Bülows to stay for the summer, but mother and children came in advance of Hans, who was too unwell to travel. Cosima then grasped the nettle; she threw herself into Wagner's arms and led him to the bedroom.

Wagner hastily retracted his marriage proposal to Mathilde Maier. They remained good friends, and another potentially disastrous match had been averted; however suitable in many ways she might have been as a wife — she was attractive, intelligent and sympathetic — Mathilde was going deaf.

*

Cosima

O Cosima, you're the soul of my life, utterly and completely. You are the only one who made me complete. With the others I just delivered monologues ...

Everything is yours before I write it.

Sat July 27th, 1878 R. slept well. In the morning he gives me the single hairs from his eyebrows which had grown too long above his left eye, and I am carrying them around with me...
[Cosima in her diary]

Common! ... a rather dissolute creature. [Minna of Cosima]

*

Wagner had written to Mathilde Maier in January 1863:

I lack a womanly being who might resolve — in spite of everything
& everyone — to be to me what only a wife can be in such pitiful
circumstances, and *must* be, I say, if I am to survive ... [a woman]
prepared to withdraw from all contact with those human relations
that have no useful place in the life and work of a man like me.

Clearly 1864 was the most important year in Wagner's life: he
had now found the right woman and also somebody to take care of his
heavy bills (King Ludwig). However, it was more than five years before
Cosima was able to move in with him permanently, and more than six
years before they could marry, by which time they had produced three
children: Isolde, Eva and Siegfried. In the meantime, pending Minna's
death and Hans's long-delayed agreement to a divorce, there was to
be a drawn-out, anguished and tortuous "Bach double fugue", as
Wagner so aptly called it.

Cosima was the second illegitimate daughter of Franz Liszt and
his mistress Countess Marie d'Agoult. After these highly neurotic lovers drifted apart, Cosima and her two siblings were dumped by Liszt
on to granny and governesses and suffered many cruel wounds in the
relentless cross-fire between their parents. At the age of 19 Cosima
plunged into her disastrous match with Hans von Bülow — ailing,
unstable, moody, irascible, and, however talented, totally unsuited
for marriage. We have already seen that she was very soon driven to
several suicide attempts.

Cosima was not really pretty, much less so than her elder sister
Blandine, who had earlier so captivated Wagner. "Stork", as Cosima
had been nicknamed on account of her lankiness, had an unusual
face with a conspicuous nose, lean taut cheeks, large bright eyes, and
light brown hair usually worn plaited low on her neck. Her outward
coolness and aloofness belied her burning inner determination to
sacrifice herself entirely to her master's genius, no matter what the
price in suffering, guilt and embarrassment.

Cosima had no time, incidentally, for the "pale and sickly"
Mathilde Wesendonck who, she considered, lacked the courage "to
break her existing ties and surrender herself to love and give support
to her lover". In the context of her time, Cosima's courage should not
be underestimated.

Cosima's startling takeover marks a sea change in Wagner's love life: from dream love to real love. No more Buddhist or Schopenhaurian ecstasies of deprivation! The exotic perfumes and bath oils that he craved from his sweethearts were now mingled with the earthlier whiffs of human breath and bodies together in bed, the silks and satins rumpled and stained by lovers' clinches, contortions, gyrations and all the rest, during which Cosima conceived Isolde during the eight nights before her husband's arrival. Wagner must have been beside himself with joy waking up at last beside a woman whom he wanted, both submissive and strong, and who would eventually be there for keeps. Come to think of it, they were both probably in their own beds by first light to avoid confusing the children.

Any reader who has been a "guilty" party in a triangle will be able to relive vividly the dense and charged atmosphere at the Villa Pellet after Hans's arrival eight days after Cosima. Without doubt it is the most famous, or notorious *ménage à trois* in the history of great composers' love lives. Richard and Cosima had revelled in their first nights of love. Each was discovering every nook and cranny of the other by touch and taste. In the daytime there were caresses in the corridor, sneaky cuddles in the garden — and at dinner the glow and tingle for them both in knowing that his erections under the dinner table and her desire for them would be satisfied shortly afterwards.

Then in comes Hans. How do the "sinning" couple suddenly avert glances, shun eye contact, avoid the passing caress, the protective arm, the instinctive flicking of fluff off the coat sleeve...? How do Tristan and Isolde cope with the arrival of King Mark?

How does Cosima suddenly change men under the same roof? At this time she was utterly Richardised and probably couldn't bear Hans near her after those eight days. Hans would have to make do with those motherly good-night pecks of guilty women and with the exaggerated concern for his health in lieu of the passion spent on Wagner. If Cosima was telling the truth in the ensuing paternity dispute over Isolde, that she had sexual relations only with Wagner during the time Hans was also at Villa Pellet, how could he avowedly not know for such a long time what was going on? How could he not have sensed everything? We shall never know until all letters and notes are released, but Hans appears to have blocked the truth from his mind because it was so unbearable to contemplate. It wasn't until the arrival of the lovers' third child, Siegfried, five years later, that he openly acknowledged the reality.

Wagner probably had less problem in being duplicitous than Cosima. After all, he still needed Hans to conduct his operas for King Ludwig in Munich. Hans was his most valued assistant, knowing "every last fragment by heart" of *Tristan.* Wagner even manoeuvred out of the king two new specially created jobs for Hans, first as *Vorspieler,* or court pianist, and later "Court Kapellmeister for special services". Wagner also genuinely admired Hans's own compositions.

Hans's plight is heartbreaking to contemplate, no matter how inevitable: he slowly had to face to the shattering realisation that the man whom he most admired in the world and whose music in the New German School he had so vigorously promoted and lovingly conducted was cuckolding him.

*

The trials and tribulations towards Cosima's open cohabitation and marriage with Wagner are a book in themselves. Suffice it to stress the adulterers' ridiculously prolonged protestations of moral rectitude (to avoid antagonising the king) and the suffering of all parties, Hans most of all. Cosima was wracked by guilt and even Wagner was prone to fits of weeping, but was unable to talk to his disciple about their "complex personal emotions". Hans was gashed further by a newspaper article in May 1866 referring to "Madame Hs. de Bülow and her 'friend' (or what?) in Lucerne", and also by a scurrilous bedroom cartoon in circulation showing him catching the lovers embracing in their night attire.

The cover-up was finally blown after Wagner had spurned the summons to marriage of Malvina Schnorr, one of Wagner's singers and now the widow of his favourite former tenor, Ludwig Schnorr. Malvina's summons followed an instruction sent through the spirit world from her dead husband (via a deranged intermediary) that she was to spend the rest of her life at Wagner's side. When Cosima showed Malvina the door she ratted on the adulterous couple to the king, precipitating a prolonged conflict, extending to other matters but eventually resolved, between him and Wagner. (Wagner's obsessive political meddling and massive unpopularity in court and city circles had left the king with no option but to banish him from Munich in December 1865.)

On November 16th 1868, towards the end of a year that included the triumphant royal première of *Die Meistersinger* (conducted by Hans), Cosima, Isolde and Eva moved in for good with Wagner at Tribschen, where he had lived for over two years. Cosima delayed asking Hans for a divorce out of sympathy for both him and her father, now Abbé Liszt. A week after her third child by Wagner, Siegfried, was born on June 6th, 1869, she finally pressed the matter. Two days later poor Hans finally caved in, his life wrecked.

Although his personal and professional life was in ruins (his resignation as Kapellmeister being also unavoidable) Hans's letter to Cosima must surely be one of the saddest and most magnanimous in the history of love and marriage:

> You have preferred to devote your life and your incomparable mind and affection to one who is my superior, and far from blaming you, I approve of your action from every point of view and admit that you are perfectly right ... May God protect and bless the mother of the happy children to whom she will continue to devote herself.

Hans von Bülow remained magnanimous, contributing 40,000 marks to the Bayreuth Festival in 1867 and consoling Cosima in her grief at Wagner's death.

Wagner and Cosima were married on August 5th, 1870, his life now having "finally found a meaning". Perhaps the most wonderful testament of their new-found peace and happiness is the *Siegfried Idyll*. Wagner conducted it with 15 musicians on the staircase at Tribschen as a "Symphonic Birthday Greeting" for Cosima on Christmas Day of the same year. It is surely the most moving expression of tender conjugal love in all music, a birthday present unsurpassed in any art form. No wonder that it was played three times over that morning and that the entire household was reportedly in tears! Cosima also inspired other music, most notably the final love scene in *Siegfried,* and her influence extended even to the structuring of Wagner's operas.

In September 1872, after six of the happiest years of his life at Tribschen, the Wagners moved to Bayreuth, which he settled upon as the most suitable venue for his projected productions of the *Ring* at special annual festivals.

*

Judith Gautier

Precious soul! Sweet Friend! ... Oh how I long to kiss you once more, dearest sweetheart ... the last gift of the gods ... Love! Love! Love me forever! ... Du! precious beloved soul!!! ...

I embrace you my beautiful love, my precious adored soul. My child, my Judith! [various letters]

Nowhere does reflected beauty shine with greater sadness or intensity than in the love letters of an ageing man.
[Martin Gregor-Dellin]

Here we go again!

With the possible exception of the mysterious Carrie Pringle, Wagner was seriously bewitched by only one woman during his marriage to Cosima. His final dose of love-drenched ambrosia, lasting some 18 months, was provided by Judith Gautier. In a role similar to Mathilde, she became his muse and consolatory sweetheart during his composition of *Parsifal* and the concurrent setbacks in launching and establishing the Bayreuth Festival.

Judith Gautier and her husband, Catulles Mendes, both ardent French Wagnerites, first visited Wagner at his Tribschen home in 1869. Dubbed by Baudelaire in her childhood as *la petite grecque,* she was now a volatile 24 and soon captivated Wagner when he discovered her gazing rapt and dumbfounded at his workroom door: exquisitely beautiful, with jet-black hair, dark, deep eyes, gold-tinted skin [someone else said her complexion was white, faintly tinged with pink, but no matter], ivory teeth ...

Her adulation was bound to feed his ego and his fantasies. On a boat excursion on the lake she had eyes only for his transfigured profile, while her soulful gazes in the garden induced Wagner to show off his acrobatic prowess — up the trees, up the side of the house, and on the swings. Cosima was obliged to ask Judith to go easy for fear of her husband's safety. Wagner favoured Judith very specially with try-outs of parts of *Siegfried* (shades of Mathilde and *Walküre* and *Tristan*) and they played duets together ...

Cosima was also drawn to Judith and confided in her, in particular the problems of the divorce and Abbé Liszt's opposition to it.

Wagner and Judith met again briefly in 1870 but by the time the affair flared up in 1876, the first year of the festival, Judith had separated from her husband and taken on a lover named Benedictus, an amateur composer who ought to be grateful for his unmerited posthumous publicity.

Despite Benedictus, however, during and following the inaugural year of the Bayreuth festival (1876), the 63-year-old Wagner had Judith's undivided attention. Her adoration had not diminished from the Tribschen days, and her radiant smile was the master's lifeline from all his plaguing problems. But not just her smiles. There now were stolen kisses when they were out of view — in the wings, up in the flies, behind the backdrop, among the scenery. These kisses, you will have guessed, were the sweetest he had ever known. When he visited her apartment he was all agog at her exotic perfumes and luxurious furnishings and rather took her back with the intensity of his earthly desires, when ostensibly so deeply immersed in the chaste ideals of *Parsifal*.

Judith allowed herself to be smothered in his kisses — but that was it! Although he seems to have made more headway than he did with Mathilde Wesendonck, Wagner still didn't penetrate the defences; neither her bodice nor petticoats, and certainly not her drawers — whose colours, alas, we shall never know. On one occasion she even showed him the door. She was firmly in charge.

Wagner's postal intermediary in Bayreuth for his more compromising letters to Judith was his barber Bernhard Schnapphauf. These contained familiar Wagnerian copy:

> The memory of your embraces fills me with the wildest intoxication; they were the crowning glory of my life. In my supreme moments I feel a sweet, blissful yearning to embrace you and never to escape from your love, You are mine — is it not so?

They also contained requests for all sorts of sensuous accessories from Paris: silks and satins with colours precisely specified,

Turkish slippers, bath essences, exotic perfumes, powders, cold creams and other applications to remind him of the scent of her skin — milk of iris, white rose powder, ambergris, rose de Bengale, balm of Arabia ... all food for his infatuation and for his creative inspiration while composing *Parsifal.* He christened his chaise-longue "Judith", requested a beautiful coverlet for it and reclined on it as a substitute for her embraces when she was absent. Many biographers have noted the baffling paradox of so many earthly pleasures being summoned to inspire themes of chastity and renunciation.

Wagner was thrown off balance when Judith wrote and asked him to look over her lover's mediocre scores, but continued to send her impassioned letters and arranged for her to have the libretto of *Parsifal,* which she wished to translate into French.

The Wagners never quarrelled through the course of this affair, but we now know that it was Cosima who, on catching her husband burning some letters and then prising the truth out of him, brought the affair to an abrupt conclusion. "Be kind to Cosima: send her some nice long letters," he wrote in a sudden change of tone on February 15th, 1878. The two ladies maintained a friendly, businesslike correspondence for some time afterwards, and Wagner was apparently embarrassed when she turned up at Wahnfried "in a rather revealing outfit" three years later. Of Wagner's three main affairs, this ending was the cleanest cut.

As well as the *Parsifal* translation, Judith wrote a three-volume memoir of Wagner and various essays on Wagnerian topics.

*

Carrie Pringle

Why should the Wagners have quarrelled so violently over this lady on the morning of his death in the Palazzo Vendramin in Venice? She auditioned "very tolerably" for a Flower Maiden part at Wahnfried in August 1881, for the performance in 1882. The following February, on the day before his death, he appears to have sent word to Carrie, then working in Milan, to come for *another* audition for the next *Ring.* When Cosima learned next morning of Carrie's impending visit, she obviously rumbled her husband's excessive auditioning zeal for a minor solo part. Hence the quarrel, or "mental excitements" mentioned in the death report, which precipitated the fatal heart attack.

The ambitious Carrie Pringle may well have already responded to Wagner's soulful gazes, or at least have given him distinct cause for hope!

Carrie ceased to exist, of course, when the distraught Cosima rushed to Wagner's room after he called for both her and the doctor. Wagner died in her arms in the apartment he had converted, with such typical abandon, into a blue silk replica of Capri's Blue Grotto. She clung to him for 24 hours, and wept unceasingly for several days and nights, refusing to eat. After the 34-hour train journey with the coffin from Venice to Bayreuth, she was too grief-stricken to attend the funeral, emerging only for the private burial at Wahnfried, where she herself was buried later.

*

It is very hard for husbands and wives of the 1990s to comprehend the total sacrifice that Cosima Wagner made of herself for her husband. But who knows, perhaps another Wagner would even now attract another Cosima. Her adulation stretched even to relic-worship, preserving single hairs from his eyebrow and doting on them daily. However unfair he was to her, however emotionally vicious, as when he abused her and sulked after she failed to spot immediately that he had finally completed the *Ring,* she suffered in silence, taking therapeutic relief in the diaries she started on January 1st, 1869. Cosima even had to contend with Wagner's jealousy of her affection for her own father.

Her diaries, which lay unread in the vaults of a Munich bank until 1972, are endlessly fascinating as a chronicle of a marriage and an era. A recurring theme is her guilt at leaving Hans and her attempts to redeem it. Indeed it was partly to explain her conduct to her children that she had begun the diaries:

> Nowhere can there be such a wretched creature as poor Hans. He feels miserable because I have left him, yet never was I able to give him pleasure, let alone make him happy ... Our marriage was based on a complete misunderstanding. Yet he would have lost me if Fate had not brought into my life the man whom it became my unquestionable vocation to live and die for. There is not a single

thing for which I can blame him, though the burden of these past years has been almost beyond endurance
This case [her leaving Hans] makes me so clearly aware of the tragedy of life and the unatonable guilt of existence — that is to say *my* guilt.

Her influence over Wagner was not totally beneficial, since her own virulent anti-Semitism fuelled and exacerbated his voluminous and crackpot published diatribes against the Jews.

She died in 1930, having devoted her life after Wagner's death to his music and to Bayreuth. Her devotion, alas, drove her into frenzies of letter burning: especially those from Wagner to herself and to Mathilde Wesendonck. Many others letters were censored when she prepared them for publication in 1888.

*

Postscript

One cannot resist speculating idly whether Wagner would have been turned on by his Rhine Maidens and Valkyries in their latest creations (1994) for Richard Jones's much-booed *Ring* production in London; the pneumatic Rhine Maidens were kitted out like surrealist sumo wrestlers in "nude" latex, and the Valkyries in gym slips and track suits. The chances of Wagner's approval are about even, but either way both Rhine Maidens and Valkyries would have either enjoyed or endured his renowned attention to detail in every aspect of his operas.

***

Acknowledgements

The author has used information and quotations from the followingbooks with the kind permission of the publishers or author's agents.

Bodley Head Ltd. *Tchaikovsky* by Alan Kendall, 1988.

Constable Publishers Ltd. *Nocturne: A Life of Chopin* by Ruth Jordon, 1978.

Davis-Poynter Ltd. *The Lives of the Great Composers* by Harold C. Schonberg, 1970.

Faber and Faber. *Schubert: The Final Years* by John Reed, 1972; *Franz Liszt* Volume 1 & 2 by Alan Walker 1983 & 1989 by permission of David Higham Associates.

Robert Hale Ltd. *Puccini* by Howard Greenfeld, 1981.

Hamish Hamilton Ltd. *On Wings of Song* by Wilfred Blunt, 1974; *Royal Palaces of France* by Ian Dunlop, 1985.

Harper Collins Publishers Ltd. *Richard Wagner His life, His Work, His Century* by Martin Gregor-Dellin, translated by J. Maxwell Brownjohn 1983; *Franz Liszt* by Ronald Taylor, 1986.

Macmillan Press Ltd. *The Letters of Beethoven* Emily Anderson (Ed) 1961; *The Letters of Mozart and his Family* Emily Anderson (Ed) 1966, revised 1985; *New Grove Dictionary of Music and Musicians* 1980.

Novello's Editions. *A Mozart Pilgrimage, being the Travel Diaries of Mozart and Constanze in the year 1829*; Nerina Medici di Marignano (Ed), Rosemary Hughes (Ed), 1955.

Northeastern University Press. *Schumann: Music and Madness* by Peter Ostwald, 1985

Omnibus Press. *Illustrated Lives of the Great Composers.* *Bach* by Tim Dowley 1981; *Beethoven* by Ates Orga 1978; *Liszt* by Bryce Morrison, 1989 *Mendelssohn* by Mozelle Moshansky 1982; *Rossini* by Nicholas Till 1983; *Schubert* by Peggy Woodford 1978; *Schumann* by Tim Dowley 1982; *Vivaldi* by John Booth 1989; *Wagner* by Howard Gray 1990.

Oxford University Press. *Gesualdo* by Glenn Watkins 1991; *Portrait of Liszt* compiled by Adrian Williams 1990; *Mendelssohn* by Philip Radcliffe (Dent) 1954; *Rossini: A Biography* by Herbert Weinstock, 1968; *Schubert* by John Reed 1987; *Selected Letters by Richard Wagner* by Stewart Spencer & Barry Millington (Trans/

Ed)1987; *Richard Wagner: A Biography* by Derek Watson 1979; *Beethoven: The Last Decade* by Martin Cooper, 1985; *Vivaldi* by Michael Talbot,1978.

Princetown University Press.*Thayer's life of Beethoven* by Elliot Forbes (Ed) 1967.

Putnam Berkley Group. *Puccini:* by Howard Greenfield,1975.

Thames and Hudson. *The Beethoven Compendium* Barry Cooper (Ed)1991; *Hadyn: Chronicle and Works* by H.C. Robbins Landon (London and Bloomington, Ind. 1976-80); *Handel* by Christopher Hogwood 1988; *Haydn, His Life and Music* by H.C. Robbins Landon and David Wyn Jones 1988; *Mozart - The Golden Years* by H.C. Robbins Landon 1989; *The Mozart Compendium* by H.C. Robbins Landon (Ed)1990; *Vivaldi: Voice of the Baroque* by H.C.Robbins Landon,1993; *Wagner Compendium* by Barry Millington (Ed) 1992.

University of California Press (19th Century Music, Spring issue 1989). *Franz Schubert and the Peacocks of Benvenuto Cellini* by Maynard Solomon.

Other Sources Consulted;

Beyond Desire by Pierre Lamure (novel based on life of Mendelssohn), Cedric Chivers, Portway, Bath 1976 by arrangement with The London and Home Counties Branch of the Library Association.

Donizetti by Herbert Weinstock, Methuen and Co Ltd. 1964.

La Vie Illustre et Libertine de Jean-Baptiste Lully by Henri Prunières. Paris Librairie Plon. Les Petits-Fils de Plon et Nourrit.

Mozart and Constanze by Francis Carr, John Murray, 1983.

Mozart's Death by William Stafford, Macmillan, 1991.

Mozart: A Life by Maynard Solomon, Hutchinson, 1995.

Georg Philipp Telemann by Richard Petzold, Ernest Benn, 1974

Robert Schumann - His Life and Work by Ronald Taylor, Harper Collins Publishers Ltd, 1982.

Love Lives of the Great Composers
from Gesualdo to Wagner

© Basil Howitt

All Rights Reserved

SOUND AND VISION PUBLISHING LIMITED
359 RIVERDALE AVENUE
TORONTO, CANADA M4J 1A4

Canadian Cataloguing in Publication Data

Howitt, Basil
*Love Lives of the Great Composers
from Gesualdo to Wagner*

ISBN 0-920151-18-3

1. Composers — Biography. Composers
— Sexual behavior. I. Title
ML390.H68 1995 780'.92' C95-932157-8

Typeset in Garamond on acid free paper

First printing, October 1995
Printings: 15.14.13.12.11.10.9.8.7.6.5.4.3.2.1

Other music books from Sound And Vision

by David W. Barber & Dave Donald
A Musician's Dictionary (1983)
isbn 0-920151-03-5

Bach, Beethoven And The Boys (1986)
Music History As It Ought To Be Taught
isbn 0-920151-07-8

When The Fat Lady Sings (1990)
Opera History As It Ought To Be Taught
isbn 0-920151-11-6

If It Ain't Baroque (1992)
More Music History As It Ought To Be Taught
isbn 0-920151-15-9

Getting A Handel On Messiah (1994)
isbn 0-920151-17-5

by Kathleen Kimball
The Music Lover's Quotation Book (1990)
A Lyrical Companion
isbn 0-920151-13-2

by Phil Dellio & Scott Woods
I Wanna Be Sedated (1993)
Pop Music in the Seventies
isbn 0-920151-16-7

If you have any comments on this
book, or any otther books that we publish,
please write to us at:
Sound And Vision 359 Riverdale Avenue
Toronto, Canada M4J 1A4